LA ROJA

LA ROJA

How Soccer Conquered Spain
and How Spanish Soccer
Conquered the World

JIMMY BURNS

NATION
BOOKS
New York

Published by Nation Books,
A Member of the Perseus Books Group
116 East 16th Street, 8th Floor
New York, NY 10003

Nation Books is a co-publishing venture of the
Nation Institute and the Perseus Books Group

Books published by Nation Books are available at special
discounts for bulk purchases in the United States by corporations,
institutions, and other organizations. For more information, please
contact the Special Markets Department at the Perseus Books
Group, 2300 Chestnut Street, Suite 200, Philadelphia, PA 19103,
or call (800) 810-4145, ext. 5000, or e-mail
special.markets@perseusbooks.com.

Photos for Chapters 1, 2, 3, 4, 5, 16, 21, and Epilogue, courtesy
of the author. Photos for Chapters 11, 17, 18, 19, 20, 22, 23,
24, 25, 26, 27, 28, and 29, © Getty Images.

Designed by Brent Wilcox

Library of Congress Cataloging-in-Publication Data
Burns, Jimmy, 1953
La roja : how soccer conquered Spain and how Spanish
soccer conquered the world / Jimmy Burns.—1st ed.
    p.   cm.
Includes bibliographical references and index.
ISBN 978-1-56858-717-2 (pbk.)—
ISBN 978-1-56858-718-9 (e-book)
1. Soccer—Spain—History.   2. Soccer teams—Spain—
History.   I. Title.
GV944.S65B87 2012
796.3340946—dc23
                                    2011053183

10 9 8 7 6 5 4 3 2

For Kidge, Julia, and Miriam

CONTENTS

PREFACE

The human wave started in a town in South Africa, watched by a worldwide audience of more than a billion people, and gathered force as it swept up the continent, before crossing the Mediterranean and rolling across the stark landscape of Castile–La Mancha and crashing onto the streets of Madrid. The heat and dust of a suffocating local summer were refreshed by sheer human effervescence, as more than a million Spaniards filled the center of the Spanish capital, celebrating the return of their heroes, the winners of the 2010 Soccer World Cup.

After being honored by King Juan Carlos and Queen Sofia at the royal palace, the players boarded an open-roofed double-decker bus and began a slow progress toward the banks of the Manzanares River. The route took them from the palace of the prime minister, José Luis Zapatero, and through the Plaza de España, the square that has at its center a monument to Cervantes, creator of *Don Quixote*. In that short journey, the character of a nation seemed defined.

Throughout its turbulent history, pockmarked with foreign invasions, coups, and civil wars, Spain has had its fair share of great and disastrous monarchs, political leaders, and failed missions. But whereas Zapatero was once a popular socialist leader who was on his way to being politically sunk by his administrative incompetence in the face of Europe's financial crisis, King Juan Carlos endured as a symbol of national reconciliation. It was this king who had assumed the role of head of a democratic state after the death of the dictator Franco in 1975 and resisted an attempted army coup six years later. This defiance of the army was in startling contrast to his grandfather Alfonso XIII, who in the 1920s had passively accepted the bloodless uprising of General Miguel Primo de Rivera. Perhaps the most significant aspect of the 1981 coup was not that it happened but that it failed. Spaniards woke up to the benefits of democracy and rallied around it. Spain had changed irrevocably since the dark days of Franco, and there was no turning back. Yet it was the statue of the fictitious literary figure Quixote that still served as a reminder that this was a nation personified in a "hero" whose nobility and achievement—so celebrated by Spanish philosophers seeking to place their country on a moral and political pedestal—proved delusional.

In the lead-up to Spain's bloody civil war in 1936, Manuel Azaña, the then president of the Second Republic, remarked that in the defeat and disappointment of Don Quixote was the failure of Spain itself. He might have added—with an eye to the future—that Spain's soccer had for much of its history also mirrored its politics, touched as it was with its tales of individual brilliance, occasional collective effort, but ultimate underachievement of the national squad in contrast to the international success of rival clubs. Yet in the summer of 2010, beyond Quixote's statue, thousands lined the streets and avenues before closing in as the victory bus made its slow progress, each individual citizen stretching out their hands in collective admiration—or, rather, making sure they were not dreaming.

This was no ordinary homecoming. For starters, the celebrations extended across the country, from Seville in the South to Barcelona in the North, a reflection of the rich mix of regional identity represented by the champions. In the Basque Country, where the terrorist organization ETA was still waging a bloody campaign for independence from Spain, a shopkeeper was beaten by thugs for celebrating the team's victory, while right-wing Spanish "patriots" covered a statue of a Basque nationalist politician in the red and yellow of the Spanish flag. In Catalonia a few radical Barca fans who also wanted independence from Spain refused to watch the World Cup and staged a counterdemonstration. But these were isolated incidents. The pervading image was of an explosion of Spanish flags all over the country, even in the most nationalistic anti-Spanish neighborhoods, as if the shared and successful enterprise in soccer had for a moment at least set aside the seemingly irreconcilable political, social, and cultural prejudices that had separated Spaniards from different regions and backgrounds for much of their history.

This was not only the first Spanish team to win the World Cup in the tournament's history but one that had done so with an artistry that many believed represented the best soccer ever played. *La Roja*, the Red One, was how the team had been nicknamed. The name was aired almost as a matter of fact in an early press conference given by Luis Aragonés, the national coach under whose command a new creative and winning style of soccer came to be played by Spain in the run-up to its victory in the European Championship of 2008. Red had been one of the main colors of shorts and shirts worn by the national squad as long as most Spaniards could remember; only politics had seemed to get in the way of accepting it as a brand like, say, the Azzurri in Italy or the Bleus in France. When he used the word, Aragonés felt that enough water had flowed under Spain's political bridge for Spaniards to call a spade a spade, or a team's gear by its proper color. But even in 2008, those old enough to remember the civil war and to have supported Franco found Aragonés provocative. To be a Rojo in the civil war was to be anti-Franco, and whereas Real Madrid played in white, Barca had red in its colors and the Catalan more red stripes than the Spanish flag. As for Zapatero, Real Madrid fans were not pleased to have in power the first Spanish prime minister ever to declare himself publicly a Barca fan—even if he was born in the very Castilian town of Valladolid.

The summer of 2008 was the honeymoon period of the Zapatero socialist government, prior to the global banking crisis detonated by the collapse of Lehman Brothers. That spring Spain's Socialist Party had again triumphed in elections, giving Zapatero a fresh mandate to pursue his agenda of sweeping social, political, and cultural reform. Despite a bitterly fought campaign, the election victory appeared to endorse Zapatero's boldest decisions, such as the withdrawal of Spanish troops from Iraq, the granting of more autonomy to the regions, and the legalization of homosexual marriage.

The future looked red. To that extent, Aragonés stood accused of political opportunism by certain elements of the Right. But then Aragonés was not a politician. In fact, he had a reputation for saying what he felt like when he felt like saying it, however politically incorrect, as when he incensed the English media with his racist jibes against English black players. But somehow *La Roja* caught on and grew in popularity, not because of Aragonés but despite him (before the World Cup campaign was under way, Aragonés had been replaced by Vicente del Bosque), as if the term appealed subconsciously to a national mood, of marking the point at which Spain had moved from being a failed state to being a civilized nation, which could also be good at soccer and find in this a sense of common purpose.

The incisive English traveler Richard Ford rode on horseback the length and breadth of Spain in the mid-nineteenth century before penning arguably one of the best books ever written on the country by a foreigner, *A Handbook for Travellers in Spain and Readers at Home.* Ford reached the conclusion that one of the fundamental characteristics of the Spanish people was their incapacity or unwillingness to pool their energies for the common good, what he called their "unamalgamating" tendency. "Spain is today as it always has been," Ford wrote, a "bundle of small bodies tied together by a rope of sand, and, being without union, . . . also without strength."

La Roja was the passion that ran through the nation's veins, but, in its modern context, one that was life-giving. This was the color of a sporting achievement recognized by fans across frontiers, not the red of execution squads that for centuries had set Spain apart from the rest of the world. It was soccer played by players with style and unity of spirit and purpose. One for all, and all for one.

The World Cup tournament in South Africa would be remembered for many things—the deafening *vuvuzelas*, England's abject failure, the United States' relative success, the humiliating exit of France amid a major dressing-room revolt, Maradona's eccentricities, the brutishness of the Dutch, the pervasive good cheer of the local people—but most of all for the fact that the best side won. I don't know how many soccer fans around the world remember where they were at the precise moment in overtime when in Johannesburg's Soccer City stadium Spain's Andrés Iniesta coolly controlled a bouncing ball from Cesc Fàbregas and then drove a beautifully struck half-volley into the Dutch goal. But I will never forget where I was, watching it live on television, under a starlit sky on a beach in southern Spain near where a group of Englishmen had played the first game of soccer on Spanish soil back in 1887. When Iniesta scored, we knew Spain had finally done it and broke out into a collective dance.

The Dutch had played in their traditional orange, the Spaniards in dark blue, shedding their usual red for the sake of visual clarity. But the Spanish team stuck to their nickname, La Roja—the Reds. It had brought them success, after many years of agony, making them first European and finally world champions—the Red had prevailed. *Viva La Roja!*

INTRODUCTION

I blame Mendizabal for giving me an enduring obsession with Spanish soccer. He was a Spanish boy of Basque origin (I only remember calling him by his surname) who brutally interrupted my first serious attempt, age seven, at trying to engage with the beautiful game. I had just begun to run with the ball toward the opposite goal when the venture ended as abruptly as it had begun. Mendizabal, taller than me and twice my weight, hacked me from behind and sent me tumbling onto the frozen turf of a school playground near London's Hammersmith Bridge.

Mendizabal, my classmate from Bilbao, got a cautionary warning from our English physical education teacher, Mr. Atkinson, while I was left nursing a bleeding hole where part of my knee had once been and clutching one hand in agony. Now in middle age, I wear my permanent scar on the leg and my broken finger like a badge of honor— my rites of passage into a game that was destined to remain an inseparable part of me through childhood, youth, and adulthood, although I admit only as a fan and an amateur, not a pro. My dreams of becoming a professional player evaporated that day Mendizabal's boot broke my run as easily as the windmill shattered Don Quixote's lance.

I now see that my experience of the game had been defined from birth. I was born in Madrid to a Spanish (Castilian) mother and a father with mixed Scottish, English, Basque, and South American blood. It meant that when it came to soccer, my allegiances and interest were destined to wander between continents and within Spain in its full geographical, cultural, and political diversity.

If the Argentine Alfredo Di Stéfano was my first soccer hero, it was because childhood—except the times I studied at an English prep school with Mendizabal—was spent for long periods with my mother in Madrid, during the 1950s. This was a period when Franco's Spain struggled on account of its isolation from the rest of Europe. It was days before mass tourism, when Spain, and Madrid in particular, was still regarded by most foreigners as a sinister, backward, and repressive place. Spain's national soccer squad barely resonated beyond the Spanish border, but these were golden years for Real Madrid, when the club attracted an enthusiastic following that defied political and national barriers. My mom remained a lifelong *Madridista* and to her dying day could never understand why my loyalties were never permanently anchored at the Bernabéu. The answer lay in the fact that although the hospital where I came bloodied and screaming into this world was a couple of blocks away from the Bernabéu, my mom never took me to the stadium. She took me to bullfights instead, and my visits to the Bernabéu were dependent on the occasional acts of generosity of an old friend of my grandfather Gegorio, an eminent doctor who had kicked the ball around in his youth, in the early days of Spanish soccer.

I remember on my first visit, looking up at the giant stadium, glowing in the dark like an illuminated cathedral and dwarfing all the buildings nearby, and being touched by the genuine warmth and excitement of the crowd. Of Real Madrid, I remember the dominating presence of Di Stéfano, around which not just a team but a whole game revolved. Whereas most of the players seemed to stick to their positions, Di Stéfano seemed to be all over the field, tracking back and supporting his defense or leading endless attacks on the opposite goal. He had extraordinary energy and superb skill, and the crowds loved him.

I found the atmosphere of Madrid's main bullring, Las Ventas, and the Bernabéu to be very similar, each as respectful of skill and domination as it was brutally dismissive of blunder and submission. Di Stéfano carried on his shoulders the destiny of a game as surely as a star *torero* that of a corrida. In time I would see other analogies between bullfighting and Spanish soccer—in the fury and the grace, in the perfect kill and perfect goal, in the scrappy cape movement and failed pass, in the ease with which the emotional pitch of the crowds could switch from roar of celebration to a litany of abuse, in the sense of life and death, in the precariousness of achievement. Only the use of white handkerchiefs marked a difference. Whereas in Las Ventas they were brought out to petition trophies, in the Bernabéu they symbolized disgust, with a referee's decision, with an off-form Real Madrid, with a game that was played without guts and ended in humiliation.

In adulthood my horizons broadened, and I followed Spanish soccer wherever I felt I could see it best played, and that meant continuous visits to Camp Nou, where certain Dutchmen, notably Johan Cruyff, cast their own particular magic spell on Spanish soccer. Yet to have even a drop of Spanish blood during the 1950s was to be aware that Di Stéfano was the best player there had ever been and Real Madrid the best club in the world. Real Madrid was a goal factory in those days, and its players fought like lions to score as many goals as they could—and it was Di Stéfano whose stickers I collected on the many days I was left imagining him. To watch him now on YouTube is to barely glimpse the greatness of a player who occupied space and time, dominating a game with his personality and skill. Thank God for the memory of our elders.

I might have spent those early childhood years at some London stadium or becoming, like Mendizabal, a fan of Athletic Bilbao, the best of the premodern Spanish clubs, were it not for the fact that my father, who spent much of his time in England, was never really interested in soccer; his school days had been spent playing tennis, rugby, and cricket. No tribal loyalties there. In adulthood he lost interest in sports altogether, partly because he slipped a disc, but mainly because he spent the war years as a spy rather than watching Stanley Matthews and then spent the rest of his life using up his spare time with books, painting, and chess. But school and vacations in Spain and later work as a journalist gave me plenty of experience of seeing how a variety of Spaniards of all ages played, and they seemed to play a great deal of soccer whatever the regime in power.

This is a story about how one of Europe's most impoverished nations endured political turmoil to become a creative melting pot of sporting talent. Over the years I have reported on soccer in Europe and South America, and I came to realize how the development of soccer in Spain could only really be explained within the country's political and social context and its openness to foreign influences from the Old and New Worlds. This book covers a period of history during which the geographical epicenter of the game, with its early English influences, has moved over the past century from the Basque region across the Atlantic to South America and back again to the antipode of Madrid and Catalonia, where two clubs, Real Madrid and FC Barcelona, respectively, not only share a majority of local fan clubs around Spain but also command a mass global following, live, on television, and on the Internet.

From its early beginnings when the first soccer was played in the mining towns of southern Spain and near the shipyards of Bilbao by British engineers and sailors, through the influx of South American stars and other Europeans, the engagement of foreigners with home-

grown Spanish talent overcame political adversity and produced soccer of sublime skill, passion, and huge entertainment value. But it
proved a long road.

This book takes us on a journey through some of the extraordinary characters, and games, that have defined Spanish soccer from the
early days when a few enthusiasts developed their talent for kicking a
ball on a piece of industrial wasteland to the emergence of professional
native talent, groomed, among others, by expatriate Englishmen. The
story continues with the cross-fertilization of Spanish and foreign
players and the profound impact on the success of clubs like FC
Barcelona and Real Madrid—among the most powerful and successful sporting institutions in the world—and major contributors to the
first Spanish national team ever to win the European Nations Cup
and World Cup.

This is a journey through some of the landscapes, cities, people,
myths, and real circumstances that contributed to Spanish soccer's
transformation from pupil to master. *La Roja* is about how world soccer's great underachiever became world soccer's great champion. It is
about the country I was born in and how its soccer became beautiful.

London/Madrid/Barcelona/Sitges
February 2012

Rio Tinto: Where it all began

CHAPTER 1

La Furia

During Franco's dictatorship between 1939 and 1975, soccer was a pastime that was actively encouraged by the state—that is, as long as it was not exploited by the enemy. And the enemy ranged from communists, Freemasons, and free thinkers to Catalan and Basque nationalists, most of them decent human beings whose clubs were rooted in local cultural identities. It gave Spanish soccer, when I was growing up, its political edge; it separated us soccer lovers into democrats and fascists.

Franco was brutal on and off the field. Far from magnanimous in his hour of victory, Franco emerged in 1939, at the end of the Spanish Civil War, determined to rule his country with an iron grip. Spaniards were divided between those who continued to support him and his military rebels and those who had fought against him on the side of the democratically elected Republican government. The former were rewarded with jobs, social security benefits, and new houses. The latter faced imprisonment, execution, and social exclusion, including exile.

Culturally, Spain was reduced to a playground, carefully controlled. With an increasing number of Spaniards migrating from the countryside to the big cities, in particular Madrid and Barcelona, and the spread first of radio and then television, soccer overtook bullfighting as the most popular pastime, tolerated by a regime that saw sports through the prism of self-preservation, a vehicle for defusing antagonisms of a dangerously political ilk. Of those years, one of Spanish soccer's most eminent native commentators, Alfredo Relaño, has written, "Soccer kept growing. Spain began to rebuild itself after the war. It was a time when there was little to do except work as many hours as possible . . . pick up the pieces from the ruins, and on Sundays go to the soccer match. These were hard years, of shortages, cold, and few diversions. There was a radio in each house (the invention of TV was on its way), a cinema in each neighbourhood and soccer. At times there were cycling competitions, boxing fights, and bullfights but above all soccer, and not much else."

During the 1920s, when Spain's first professional players began to make their marks, it was the direct, aggressive, spirited style of the Basque team Athletic Bilbao that set a benchmark, although the term *furia* (fury) that came to denote the style could not claim originality. Basques played the way they did because they were taller and physically stronger than other Spaniards and because they were accustomed to playing in wet conditions, whereas much of Spain was a semidesert. In the old days of emergent Spanish soccer, few fields were covered in turf.

Spaniards at the time were quite happy to recognize that the aggressive, spirited game of soccer had its roots in Britain and the English teachers that came to Spanish clubs. Under Francoism things changed, and the term *Furia Española* (Spanish Fury) became part of the regime's militarist nomenclature. *La Furia* was redefined and promoted by the state's propaganda machinery as one of the leading virtues of the New Spain. It was resurrected from the mythology of conquest and glory that belonged to the country's imperial past, such as the recovery of Muslim Granada by the Catholic kings and the creation of Spanish America by the early conquistadores—conquering warriors. It also drew on the national stereotype mythified in the literary figure of Don Quixote, the incarnation of the spirit of noncompromise, with his hopelessness and failure forgotten beside his nobility of purpose.

As the Falangist newspaper *Arriba* wrote in 1939, a few months after Franco had emerged triumphant from the Spanish Civil War: "The *furia española* is present in all aspects of Spanish life, to a greater extent than ever. . . . In sport, the *furia* best manifests itself in soccer, a game in which the virility of the Spanish race can find full expression, usually imposing itself, in international contests, over the more technical but less aggressive foreign teams." In other words, soccer was to be played as if the ground was a battlefield and the players soldiers. What mattered were courage, sacrifice, and above all the physical annihilation of the opponent. Neither skill nor creativity, let alone fair play, was part of the armory.

Franco liked the phrase *La Furia*—The Fury—because he felt it exemplified the essence of Spanish nationhood. Unsurprisingly, it was a Basque-born player sympathetic to the regime who became emblematic of the cause. The occasion was the 1950 World Cup in Brazil, when Spain faced England in the group stage. The player in question was Athletic Bilbao's Telmo Zarra. The leading scorer in six Spanish championships, Zarra had already achieved the popular iconic status previously attained by the legendary Spanish bullfighter Manolete, killed in the bullring of Linares three years earlier. It was popularly said that Zarra played with three legs, the third being his devastating head. Zarra rammed home with his foot rather than headed Spain's winning goal, having beaten defender Alf Ramsey off a cross from Agustín Gaínza. When the match was over, Spanish soccer's top official, Armando Muñoz Calero, told Franco, "Excellency: we have vanquished the perfidious Albion." Thus did Franco's Spain get its own back for the defeat of the Invincible Armada of 1588. Well, up to a point.

It proved a Pyrrhic victory. In a four-team final mini league, Spain's chances of winning the World Cup ended after being beaten 6–1 by Brazil. This perhaps explains why Franco consoled himself with the thought that the crowning moment of soccer achievement was when Spain showed a lot of *Furia* and beat the Soviet Union in the final of the 1964 European Nations Cup, the only major trophy the Spanish squad won during the three and a half decades of Franco's dictatorship.

Long after Franco died, there would be no shortage of Spanish commentators who would blame Spain's failure not on *La Furia* but on the lack of it among certain players on the national squad. Yet bad luck and a dearth of inspired coaching at the national level as much as politics lay behind Spain's record of underachievement. With the exception of its gold medal in the 1992 Olympics, democratic Spain had to wait until 2008 before it won the European Championship again, after enduring years of pain and disappointment under a succession of mainly lackluster coaches.

By then Spain's national team had caught up with the quality of its great clubs, found a decent coach, and forged a consensus around how soccer could best be played in a way that was not only effective but also wonderful to watch. I myself had become a Barca fan, a conversion that got under way in the 1970s when Johan Cruyff came to Catalonia. Like Di Stéfano, his personality and way of playing influenced a whole generation of players, although his presence proved more enduring. And to fans like me, he came to personify in soccer the best of Spain after Franco. It helped fuel my later enthusiasm for La Roja and the way it refined *La Furia* into a new aesthetic, where the nobility of purpose became entwined with creative play as a winning formula.

A very British exploitation

CHAPTER 2

British Roots

The piece of land where the first game of soccer in Spain was played lies buried underground in an abandoned mine in southern Spain. To find it, I set off one chilly winter morning from London's Victoria Station on the Gatwick Express. Four hours later I was in a rental car, driving out from the Seville airport, the local Olé radio station blaring flamenco music, a warm sun struggling to break through the Atlantic clouds. I drove toward the hills of Aracena, through olive groves and strawberry fields and pastureland where fighting bulls grazed.

Off the main highway to the Portuguese border, a secondary road took me to the giant open-pit mines of Rio Tinto, one of the oldest mining areas in the world—the site, some say, of the legendary King Solomon mines—where generations of men have carved their enduring and brutal imprint on a once beautiful landscape. It is as historian David Avery vividly described it more than thirty years ago, "a labyrinth of strangely sculptured and brilliantly coloured interlocking valleys where hands and machines long ago tore the hillsides apart into gigantic fissures and carved them into a series of deeply descending angular terraces." This is not just a multicolored cavity in a desolate landscape. It is nature consumed by man's advance. Whole mountains, valleys, and villages have disappeared, making any sense of orientation that much more difficult. While the rain pelted down, the countryside seemed to subside, and down the hillside and across the fields ran water stained, like the river, bloodred by the oxidized mineral residue.

Thankfully, it had stopped raining by the time I reached a magnificent viewing point over the Corta Atalaya. Under fading daylight, the open-pit mine presented a kaleidoscope of colors: a pinkish rock face speckled by lines of leaf green and gold, high escarpments of black and purple slag, and the leveled banks of silver-gray pyrites. My guide was José Antonio Delgado, the young bearded former mayor of Rio Tinto, the local town that owes its existence to the foundations laid by some British pioneers in the second half of the nineteenth century. Antonio was not a soccer fan. He was a socialist who knew something about the Spanish Civil War graves recently dug up in the nearby village of Nerva.

One of those buried there was Luis Ruiz, a local veterinary surgeon who had played as a goalkeeper for his local village team in the lead-up to the Spanish Civil War in 1936. A year before the outbreak of the conflict, the vet denounced the local butcher to the health authorities for selling meat from diseased cows. The butcher never forgave Ruiz for the fine he had to pay and the lost trade. When the village was taken over by Franco's forces, the butcher accused the vet of being a "red." The vet was taken away and summarily executed. I met his niece Pilar in a cramped first floor apartment near the village square. Chain-smoking and with a face that seemed already at death's door, she told me how her family got their revenge many years later when the butcher was gored to death by a fighting bull. "The bull was called Justiciero, the Just One," she said before she was gripped by a coughing fit.

José Antonio wanted to share with me his concern about more contemporary issues—the decimation of the local environment, the growing youth unemployment, and the local drug trafficking. He then pointed to the mine's slag. "Spain's first soccer field is buried in there somewhere," Jose Antonio said.

I then met Rafael Cortes, a sepulchral-looking local historian who knew something about soccer. "Soccer is part of our heritage," Cortes told me. We sat sharing a bottle of red wine and a large piece of roasted local pork with José Reyes Remesal, the president of the local soccer club, Riotinto Balompié, a genial rogue who looked like a man who spent much of his day enjoying himself. Cortes had no doubt that Rio Tinto was the true cradle of Spanish soccer, although he bemoaned the fact it had never received sufficient recognition from the state or from the world of soccer generally. Part of the problem was that since the mines stopped operating in the early 1990s, Rio Tinto had lost its way. The majority of the local bars had been turned into fan clubs of Real Madrid and FC Barcelona. The only other club in town was because the Basque Country shared a mining tradition. Usually drunk on the local firewater, the unemployed villagers watched the most popular matches on television. "People here follow Real Madrid and Barca because they can afford the best players, win the most trophies," said Cortes.

His friend Remesal later took me to the local soccer stadium. It dated from the early 1930s, when the British had built a new town for the workers after gradually destroying the old one. Of the earlier period little remained, except a few picturesque houses and an Anglican church from the exclusive British neighborhood of Bella Vista, named after the panoramic views that only the senior managers and engineers were able to enjoy. The stadium was eerily empty. With its ragged turf and stone perimeter, with standing room for about three thousand fans, it resembled a giant sheep pen. It was easy to mistake the two small changing rooms for public bathrooms. The local club played in a minor regional division. Being its president, Remesal admitted, was more of a hobby than a full-time occupation. But he proudly showed the "trophy room." It was filled with a few cups dating back to the "glory days" of the early 1930s, when Riotinto Balompié won an intervillage championship.

Precisely where that first game on Spanish soil was played and who contested it remains a subject of dispute, for it is not just a soccer field but a whole town, originally known as Minas de Rio Tinto, that today lies buried under a slag heap. However, early photographs suggest that the most likely playing field was near where the Rio Tinto English Club had its offices, at 2 Calle Sanz, near the mayor's office, along a street of whitewashed and red-tiled houses. It was there that the Rio Tinto Soccer Club gathered its players for their inaugural kick-around on the local feast day of San Roque in August 1887. San Roque, or Saint Roch as he is known in France, was a medieval saint who has a popular cult following on both sides of the Pyrenees. Legend has it that he was struck down by the plague but endured thanks to a piece of bread brought to him by his faithful dog. The saint's image, pointing to an open sore on his thigh, and the dog by his side, was once displayed in practically every Spanish church, before falling victim to the ravages of the Spanish Civil War.

Nonetheless, that first soccer game in Spain proved an innovative act in a country that had largely fallen behind the European mainstream from its heyday as the world's most powerful nation in the sixteenth century. Having squandered the immense wealth derived from its American empire, Spanish power in Europe had gone into steady decline, thanks to a series of long, costly wars and internal revolts. Although some parts of northern Spain benefited from a belated industrial revolution and overseas trade, and gathered a growing number of migrants to its major towns, a majority of the country remained a largely rural, semifeudal society steeped in mainly Catholic traditions and vulnerable to foreign predators.

It was an investor from London named Hugh Matheson who one February morning in 1873 financed the purchase of the moribund copper mines of Rio Tinto from the Spanish state. At the time Spain was immersed in one of its periodic dynastic struggles between conservatives and liberals after the overthrow of the Bourbon monarchy and its temporary replacement by a republic prior to the restoration of Alfonso XII. Matheson took advantage of the extended period of political instability and financial weakness of the Spanish state and cut a good deal. Of the £3.5 million he paid, a first installment in gold coins was transported by train and bullock-drawn carts. Railways came belatedly south of the Pyrenees, so many parts of Spain, not least the South, remained in a primitive state of underdevelopment.

Matheson then used the capital he had raised in London to secure not just mineral rights—and one of Spain's prime assets—but also powers for the compulsory acquisition of land for the building of railways linking the mines to the sea, along with the absolute freehold in perpetuity of all land and buildings owned by the Spanish state within the Rio Tinto boundaries. On March 29, 1873, the Rio Tinto Company was registered, thus beginning a process that was to transform the run-down works into one of the most profitable and ruthlessly exploitative mining enterprises in Europe.

Over the following decade, the population of Rio Tinto and its neighboring village Nerva grew from one thousand to ten thousand, with the local farming population swamped by the influx of new migrants from surrounding Andalusia and beyond, including a strong contingent from the northern region of Asturias, where there was similarly high unemployment. The enduring traditions of the nearby *pueblos* (villages) were subsumed into a working class subjected to the pressures and tensions of a cash economy driven by ruthless managers. The mining camp coalesced into a community that felt itself subject to rather than a part of the foreign presence. The new miners were nick-named by the old villagers *los mohinos*, a word that has several mean-ings in English. The most relevant are "stubborn" and "prone to violence." On the other side of the social divide, the surveyor of the north-lode open pit in those early days was a man named Douglas Gordon, who carried out his inspections astride a jet-black horse and wielding a riding crop. The miners called him Don Diablo.

In 2011 the only native English speakers I came across in Rio Tinto were a couple of wild-boar hunters from some US shooting club in Wisconsin. But then the mines—nationalized by the Spanish state during the 1950s—had long since ceased to function, and whatever sense of community that had once resided there had had the stuffing knocked out of it.

But let us return to the time of that first soccer match in 1887, a time when poverty and rootlessness contributed to the violence that was rife among the miners. Under the influence of the local firewater made from potato spirit, knife fights easily broke out among the men. The feast days of San Roque, patron saint of the sick and the disabled, was an occasion for the local population, however poor or oppressed, to indulge in some collective fun, with an extended fiesta lasting over the course of two days. Daytime entertainment, when the men were still sober enough to keep standing, included a local version of tug-of-war, donkey and mule races, and climbing a greasy pole.

When the British acquired the mines, they extended the railway line through the site of the local bullring but quickly built another one just outside the village, in the style of Seville's Maestranza. It was in-augurated in 1882 with a huge, enthusiastic crowd turning up in support of the two stars of the ring, Currito Cúchares and El Morcilla (the Black Pudding). While the newly arrived Brits looked down at the fiesta and the activity of an uncouth underclass of local natives, they had the good sense not to boycott it—at least not right away. Two years after the bullring was built, the company bought it from its Spanish owner and pulled it down, claiming it had become a gathering point for prostitutes and drunks. Within three years, a group of mining staff, including managers, chose to mark the day of San Roque with a soccer match between two teams picked exclusively among non-Spaniards.

The early kick-around of the English expatriates on Spanish soil almost mirrored the primitive folk years of soccer in England, the land where it had all first begun. As Hunter Davies records in his social history of the British game, *Postcards from the Edge of Football*, soccer in its early days in England was usually held on festive holidays, with two teams of unlimited numbers trying to get a ball from one end of a village or neighborhood to another and reaching a designated goal. "Kicking each other, fighting, settling old scores, using weapons or any sort of physical violence was allowed, and people did get badly injured and, sometimes, killed." The first soccer match recorded in Spanish history near the mines of Rio Tinto was almost as loosely played, although *Los Ingleses* aspired to bring a culture of civilization to one of the least-developed areas of Europe, with its backward feudal economy and endemic political turmoil.

When not forming the focus of a loose scrum, the hard-won leather ball was kicked as far as possible from one end of the field to the other. Heading was a widely used if awkward tactic of a game the British played in cloth caps to protect them from the harsh local sun. Spaniards watched from the sidelines. No written account or oral tradition survives that might have fleshed out the details of that particular game on the feast of San Roque. But one can imagine the local crowd being initially unimpressed by the crude physical antics of the foreigners. The game seemed to ape the violence into which their drunkenness occasionally descended. It also lacked both the creativity and the brinkmanship of the one popular local entertainment they could claim as their own but to which the company had effectively laid waste—the bullfight.

The myth would have us believe that this first game was born as a gesture of sportsmanship that reached out and engaged Englishmen with Spaniards. The reality was rather different. These early expatriate pioneers played soccer much as they might have played polo, rugby, tennis, or croquet: as a way of asserting their difference over the natives. The British who kicked a ball around locally for the first time were watched by the Spaniards like visitors from another planet, the banter of the players—cries of "Hooray!" and "Jolly good!" would no doubt have resonated around the makeshift soccer field—as foreign to them as the Anglican church, bereft of images, and the Victorian home-county villas the managers built for themselves in the privileged quarter of Bella Vista.

The faded photographs that survive from the period are evocative of the British Raj of imperial India, with the men's and women's uncompromising dress code—white flannels, large hats, voluminous silk dresses, and parasols—and tea habits contrasting with the stark surrounding landscape and roughly hewn shirts and trousers of the Spaniards. Other museum pieces that survive remind one of the relative luxury enjoyed by the British: the general manager's private train compartment, its interior resplendently carved in mahogany wood and furnished in leather, and the *casa grande* (palatial home), similarly decked out in the style of a colonial governor.

Huelva: A monument to the unknown soccer player

CHAPTER 3

Spanish Roots

The primitiveness of the poor Spaniards who first set eyes on a soccer ball is not difficult to imagine. It was made vivid by Antonio, a local taxi driver from the port of Huelva whose grandfather had been a miner. Antonio told me of an enduring ritual to which a local cuckolded man resorted in order to "cure" himself of his wife's alleged infidelity. It involved having a local witch identify the wife's lover by smelling her panties after she returned from her latest liaison and then burning them. Along with "evil spirits" and *brujeria* (witchcraft), it was bullfighting, flamenco, saintly relics, weeping Virgins, and bleeding Christs, that the locals of the villages and towns near Rio Tinto were familiar with, not the sight of uptight white-skinned Anglo-Saxons and Celts in rolled-up sleeves and variously colored shorts kicking a ball around and barging into each other on a patch of wasteland marked out with poles referred to as "doors." The game was played by the British according to their language and their rules, and when the game was over, the players returned to their clubhouse, with its portrait of Queen Victoria, billiard table, and back issues of the *Times* and the *Illustrated London News* to which no Spaniard had access.

The early history of Spanish soccer—and its legacy—would have been very different had the Rio Tinto Football Club not evolved gradually as a local Spanish club, under native management and recruiting from an increasing pool of players within the mining company. The breakdown of barriers in the region was facilitated by the increased flow of personnel between the mines and the nearby port of Huelva once the railway connection had been built and inaugurated in 1875 with fifty miles of track, ten bridges, and four tunnels. Soccer then began to attract the growing interest of much larger segments of the local population, not just as spectators but also as participants. Small ad-hoc teams began to spread among the surrounding villages. Soccer belatedly took on a Spanish identity.

The Rio Tinto Soccer Club for a while tried to maintain its self-imposed exclusivity—registered as a British sporting entity, just as the mining company had been registered as a British company. However, in Huelva the British community found itself forming an alliance—out of sheer economic self-interest—with local representatives of the landed and trading classes, several of whom had been educated in English schools and had learned to play soccer.

From the early 1870s, a small but thriving British community made this corner of the southwestern coast of Spain—a half day's sail, on a good wind, from where Nelson confronted the French in the Battle of Trafalgar—their home for much of the year. In early July, led by their women and children, they displaced to Punta Umbria, a hitherto undiscovered beach where they built their well-appointed vacation homes on a stretch of virginal sand. In the 1870s, British investments in Rio Tinto were given protection by a garrison of the English army, as Spaniards fought Spaniards over the future of their monarchy in the Carlist Wars. "Marched out of Huelva on Wednesday. Played soccer with some railwaymen for about an hour out. The only diversion we truly had," wrote a British officer, Captain W. F. Adams, in September 1874.

In Huelva, as in Rio Tinto, the British tried to monopolize the game as long as they could. A local newspaper report on a game played near the mines between Rio Tinto and a team of visitors from Huelva on May 6, 1882, shows that a majority of players on both sides were Englishmen and Scots, with names like Brady, Campbell, Stourton, Higgins, Simpson, Crump, and Alcock. A journalist from the local *La Provincia* newspaper wrote, "On a beautiful afternoon and before a large crowd the long awaited game between the teams from Huelva and Rio Tinto were played. We may have to wait for some time before we witness another match as well organised and balanced with teams of equal strength. Although Rio Tinto had some tough players, Huelva played with greater subtlety and craftiness. Huelva was on the attack right through the game, but at the last minute it was Rio Tinto that slipped in the winning goal."

The Huelva Recreation Club (later renamed the Recreativo Club de Huelva) was officially founded in December 1889 by Alexander Mackay, a Scottish doctor employed by the Rio Tinto Company. Unlike its rival based nearer the mines themselves, El Recre, as it came to be known, was quickly registered as a Spanish entity—a move that would eventually lead to its incorporation into the nascent Spanish Soccer Federation, with entitlement to participate in official competitions across the country. The club played its first game a year later in Seville against employees of the British-owned and -operated Seville Water Works at the Tablada hippodrome. El Recre passed into Spanish hands in the first decade of the twentieth century and then disappeared from the map of topflight soccer, as the focus of the sport shifted elsewhere in Spain.

To this day Huelva disputes with Rio Tinto its claim to be the *cuna del fútbol español* (birthplace of Spanish soccer). Although El Recre has foundered relegated to the Spanish second division in modern times, a large monument to an unknown soccer player stands at the entrance to the town. It is cast in a similar mold to the one that stands near the soccer stadium in Rio Tinto. Both projects display that boldness and foolhardiness that characterized a mining community while risking great hubris, much like the big statue of Maradona that stands defiantly at the entrance to the Boca Juniors stadium museum in Buenos Aires. The province of Huelva, like Argentina, hangs on to its great myths, although the reality is that the game was exported years ago.

What is beyond dispute is that by the early twentieth century, Recreativo had ceased to be foreign, with Spaniards making their presence increasingly felt in its club administration and its team. Among the most influential of the Spaniards involved with Recreativo's early development was Manuel Pérez de Guzmán, a landowner originally from Jerez who moved to Huelva and developed business ties with the British. Pérez de Guzmán became vice chairman of the club in 1906, while four of his sons joined as players. Of the siblings, the most legendary was the third born, José or "Pepe," who shared his love of soccer with an equal passion for flamenco and bullfighting.

In the interwar years Pepe achieved a reputation as a gifted musician and writer and of the local fandango, characterized in its dance form by slow arching and spiraling movements played to distinct guitar rhythms and sung verses dedicated to the beauty of the Virgin of El Rocio. Pepe also liked to bullfight on horseback and developed a close friendship with the hugely popular Ignacio Sánchez Mejías, one of the most famous and cultured bullfighters in the history of the "sport." Sánchez Mejías's fame as a bullfighter grew when most of Europe was fighting the First World War and Spain remained neutral. The bullfighter would later defy the traditional cultural norms that inspired his profession and forged strong friendships among the so-called Generation of '27, a movement of left-wing young poets who experimented with new forms of writing and living in an attempt to break out of the repressive hold the Catholic Church and the military traditionally had on Spanish society. Sánchez Mejías was badly gored on August 11, 1934, in the bullring of Manzanares and died soon afterward of gangrene, his life and death forever mythified in the moving eulogy written by his friend the poet Federico García Lorca. Local soccer fans also honor him as the onetime president of Real Betis, one of the two rival clubs based in Seville.

Before leaving Andalusia, I drove back to Seville and caught up with Sol, an old childhood girlfriend, who was one of Manuel Pérez de Guzmán's descendants. Although not a great soccer fan herself, she had agreed to introduce me to some friends who were, in the old Gypsy Quarter of Triana, on the left bank of the coiling Guadalquivir River. She took me down a narrow street lined with balconies filled with geranium pots. It was midday, and a small group of mainly middle-aged men sat propped up in a bar decorated in colorful tiles. The walls were covered with religious icons and soccer posters. Two images appeared to be the subject of particular veneration. One was the neighborhood's favorite virgin, Esperanza de Triana, whose statue is carried across the bridge every Good Friday in a moment of high emotion at the culmination of Holy Week. The other was of the Virgin of the Kings, who, legend has it, appeared in a dream to King Fernando of Castile, Saint Fernando, the Spanish monarch who began Andalusia's fight back against occupation by Arab Islamists in the thirteenth century by taking Seville first. Every local soccer fan knows the battle hymn she inspired by heart: "*A tus plantas se postra Sevilla por rendirte homenaje . . . Reina aquí, pues tu Sevilla, que Fernando conquisto*" (At your feet Seville kneels . . . our Queen, for it was this Seville that Ferdinand conquered). Near both virgins was a giant poster of the Betis team of 1935. It was the only league championship Betis had ever won, and they did it the year before Franco's military uprising sparked the

Spanish Civil War. The next trophy the club won was more than forty years later—the King's Cup—when Spain had become a democracy. "We were given the title royal by the king's grandfather Alfonso XIII in the 1920s, but we never owed our victories to Franco," said Cayetano, a gaunt-looking and somewhat intense schoolteacher.

Next to him, his elderly companion, a long-retired dockworker with the girth and ruddy face of Sancho Panza, was prompted to share a different if somewhat contrasting piece of history. He recalled following a Spanish national-squad team in Franco's time in the Cold War years to a game behind the iron curtain. "The stadium was full of Russians—all looking rather serious and severe. So I and my mates started singing some flamenco to try to humor them. The Russians thought we were crazy."

Another member of the group, a young off-duty taxi driver with Gypsy looks, called José Maria, tried to explain why he was a Betis fan: "To be a Betis fan means supporting the team even if it loses. It's a sentiment that goes beyond success or failure. Our colors are predominately green—which represents hope."

One of Lorca's most stirring refrains and one of my favorites focuses on the color green as a powerful image of nature at its most essential and prolific:

green I want you green
Green the wind and green the boughs
The ship upon the ocean seen
the horse upon the hill . . .

I often wonder what might have happened to Lorca had he not ended up being shot and buried in an unmarked grave near Granada after the outbreak of the Spanish Civil War. Perhaps this sensitive and vulnerable gay artist would have detested the whole mythology of *La Furia* and the self-conscious virility of soccer during the Franco years. On the other hand, his presence at the occasional match might have helped counter the macho image of its more radical fans, indeed helped produce one of the more lyrical rallying chants in soccer, embellishing still further the sound of rhythmic flamenco that thankfully is the more dominant sound one hears these days whenever one or the other Seville clubs play—or when La Roja plays in Seville.

Some Betis fans admitted that their fathers or sons belonged to the city's other club, Sevilla FC—mainly because it was a club that had proved more successful in Spanish and international club soccer. Sevilla FC won the first-ever Copa del Generalissimo after Franco came to power. Although the losers were Racing del Ferrol, the club from the Galician town where Franco was born, the cup was handed out by the new sports minister, General Moscardo, one of Franco's most trusted generals, and in the Montjuïc stadium in Barcelona, home to the city's other club, Espanyol, whose loyalty to the new regime was never in doubt. Sevilla FC also won the league title for the first and only time in the 1946–1947 season before securing four Copa del Rey and two UEFA Championship titles over the next sixty years (2005–2006 and 2006–2007), mainly thanks to foreign players.

Tradition has it that Betis was the club of the people, with its roots in a neighborhood once famous for its poverty and radical politics, as opposed to Sevilla FC, the club of the *señoritos*, the upper-crust rich kids. Betis was given the royal title as a way of restoring some social balance between the two rivals and defusing class conflict. Such token patronage proved unnecessary. Social distinctions between the two clubs blurred anyway over the years with shifting patterns of immigration and urban development. Today each has a separate stadium in upscale neighborhoods of the city, and class and political divisions between their soccer fans here are as deceptive as in other parts of Spain.

The Spanish can be very proprietorial over their soccer, not inclined to acknowledge outside influences. I met Juan, a middle-aged Andalusian shopkeeper who supported Sevilla FC. He was adamant that "Spanish soccer belongs to us just like our bullfighting and our flamenco music. It comes from our soul." When I mentioned the English roots, he insisted that it was the "Basques that owe their soccer to the English." He did acknowledge that it was Basque players who made up the spine of Betis's championship team. Still, I was intrigued by Juan's comments, so I flew to the Basque capital of Bilbao.

Bilbao: Athletic Fan Club

CHAPTER 4

Basques

The Basque people claim ownership of their very own ball game, *pelota*. They say it came into existence long before the English kicked their first soccer ball. Played with the hand or a basket scoop against a wall, it demands great skill as well as strength and endurance to keep hammering the hard leather ball in unexpected directions at great speed. *Pelota* figures large in local mythology. The *jentilak*, legendary Basque giants, are reputed to have played their own version of a ball game, kicking and throwing the great boulders scattered by glaciers on upland meadows in the Pyrenees and the Cantabrian mountains. Other contemporary mythmakers suggest that the first soccer players in the Basque region were Neolithic shepherds. However, the first documentary evidence of *pelota* in the Basque Country is a 1509 prohibition against the sport being played in the Cathedral of Santiago in Bilbao. But it was the coming of the English that was destined to make soccer even more popular than *pelota*, even in the Basque Country.

The UK link existed in the sixteenth and seventeenth centuries when Bilbao's old port of El Arenal was the gateway for the wool trade between Castile, London, and Flanders and for the Basque manufacturing trade. Nearby woodland provided charcoal for smeltering iron. Then, when the forests were exhausted, coal was imported from England, on ships that exported iron, and later steel on the return journey.

As in the south of Spain, the British connection in the nineteenth century asserted itself on the Cantabrian coast in the context of political instability and economic underdevelopment. During the Peninsular War in the early nineteenth century, Wellington's Eighty-Fifth Infantry regiment "liberated" the Basque city of San Sebastián from Napoleon occupation only to proceed to sack it. The pillage lasted all day and into the night, during which the darkness was dispelled, so bright was the light from the burning buildings. The population felt abused and humiliated at the destruction of the city by their "allies." It was, they suspected, a deliberate act to stifle northern Spain's commerce with France.

British troops would make some amends in 1833 when they helped defend the town during the First Carlist War, one of Spain's periodic nineteenth-century dynastic struggles. The war pitted the supporters of Don Carlos, the brother of the late autocratic pro-French king Ferdinand VII against the regime of the more "liberal" and enlightened regent Maria Christina, supported by the ill-equipped British auxiliary force.

Many of his soldiers did not survive to tell the tale. Some of the bodies of the English volunteers lie discreetly in a small cemetery above the city of San Sebastián on the slopes of Monte Urgull. The memory of Wellington's sacking was not easily eradicated from the local memory and partly explains why local club Real Sociedad has never claimed to owe anything to *Los Ingleses*. During the Carlist Wars, British troops also died in Bilbao, but this town they chose not to pillage. Those killed in liberating it from the French were buried on a piece of wasteland on the banks of the river Nervión. The area, today the site of the Guggenheim Museum, is still known as the *Campa de los Ingleses* (the Field of the English), and it was where the British kicked their first ball around in the late nineteenth century. By then, the invention of the Bessemer furnace, which converted low-phosphorous iron—Bilbao's specialty—into high-quality steel, had turned the Basque capital into an industrial dynamo.

As in Rio Tinto, the first games of soccer in Bilbao were linked to the nearby mines, and the English who exploited them. Nevertheless, whereas Rio Tinto was run like a mining camp set in a Victorian colony, with the natives effectively segregated, Bilbao's industrial development was never fully surrendered to the British, and soccer in its beginnings provided a vehicle for integration between the foreigners and the local Basque shippers and industrialists who formed the vanguard of Spain's entrepreneurial class. Several of the more prominent Basques were educated in English public schools. Bilbao also created an urban working class, which along with their employers refused to submit themselves to the rule of a British colony and whose pay and conditions, while still miserable, were generally better than those down south. To this day the ritual chant that rises from the belly of San Mames, the stadium of local soccer club Athletic Bilbao is "Aliron, Aliron, Athletic Campeon." The Royal Spanish Academy's official dictionary says that *Aliron* comes from the Hispanic-Arabic *al'ilan*, meaning "proclamation," and that is its most common usage in Spanish soccer—except in the Basque Country. At Bilbao's mining museum you will be told that the word derives from the phrase "All Iron," which an English mining technician would write in chalk if a mined rock was found to have more than 70 percent iron content. Such a discovery earned the poorly paid Basque miner a bonus and was a source of some contentment, if not jubilation. Thus did *Aliron* make its way from the mines to the soccer field.

The game's Anglo-Saxon roots in the Basque Country had to contend from an early stage with a strong sense of local culture and political identity, as I discovered when visiting this part of Spain over many years. On a return visit to Bilbao early in 2011, I was invited to lunch by the city's main soccer fan club in a building they owned in the *Casco Viejo*, or Old Quarter. The so-called *Siete Calles*, or seven (narrow) streets, is a tightly knit community of tapas bars and other hidden temples to Basque gastronomy. Ours was no ordinary soccer lunch over endless rounds of beers and cheap snacks. It began with several glasses of Rioja at the entrance to a bar and developed into a feast lasting all afternoon in the large basement of an anonymous building equipped with a large kitchen and several dining tables and chairs. This was the fans' private club or gastronomic society, known colloquially as *txoko*.

There was more Rioja to be drunk, along with several bottles of Patxaran, the local Pyrenean liquor made from anise and blueberries. But the focus of activity revolved around the dishes prepared by our host—a fanatical soccer fan turned in an instant into a master chef. For our meal he produced several plates of tapas—from cured meats and tortillas to stuffed peppers and prawns—and followed this with a large cod baked in green pepper sauce. Then came the cheeses, and the ice creams, and the cakes.

Food enough to indulge one's culinary tastes proved the perfect complement to our soccer conversation, this *txoko*'s favorite topic. I began asking my host, Juan Maria Arana, the president of Athletic's association of fan clubs, why he was a fan. He replied

I was nine years old when I went to see my first match in our stadium, San Mames, in 1946. My father was in the navy and spent most of the time at sea. But my grandfather took me along with my brothers. It was after the war—what we called the years of hunger because of the postwar food shortages. But somehow watching Athletic lifted the spirits. We beat Oviedo 4–2. The two goals were scored by a Basque player, which felt like a bit of betrayal! We weren't allowed to speak our language then, or wave our flags—but we had our red and white colors, and that was the reason of our existence. It still is.

According to local artist and writer Juan Antonio Frade de Villar (K-tono to his friends), every hidden street and avenue and bridge and streetcar line and bus and subway route in Bilbao leads you to San Mames stadium if you just know the way—and he did. From the moment I had landed in Bilbao, the inimitable K-tono—with his Quixotic beard, cape, and learned head forever covered by a *txapela* (typical Basque beret)—had guided me through the town's secrets. There was not a corner of the city that was unknown to his inquisitive eye, his passion for Athletic and its world reflected in a book of vignettes and sketches he liberally gave out to his friends like a Bible. Early in the day, K-tono had taken me to visit the magnificent Ibaigane Palace, which houses the club headquarters. Commissioned and owned by the Basque business magnate Ramon de La Sota in the early twentieth century, the palace was turned into a military headquarters during the Franco regime. "I remember my days as a conscript there, doing night guard duty in the garden, listening to the military governor, General Santamaria, standing on the balcony in his pajamas and barking orders before he rode out to exercise at *La Campa de los Ingleses*."

But it was his beloved San Mames—named after an early Christian martyr mauled by Caesar's lions—that had endured within him long after General Santamaria had been consigned to the dustbin of history. "I cut my soccer teeth kicking a ball in the nearby streets, and I've been going to that stadium for more than sixty years. I will also treasure memories of great triumphs and hundreds of games fought by legendary players, and the tears shed, sometimes from disappointment, others from pure joy."

Others began to chip in, pledging that they would remain fans to their dying day, even though these days the club did not produce teams like FC Barcelona and Real Madrid. Perhaps Athletic needed to loosen up a bit on its Basques-only policy, I suggested. I was told by one of the veterans present that the policy of restricting access to the team only to those born in the Basque Country had been applied only during Franco's time, not because the old dictator had any respect for Basque nationalism but because he thought only the Basques were pure Spaniards. Things had changed since democracy, and these days you could be born anywhere in the world and join the club as long as you had some Basque blood running through your veins. "In my humble opinion, the policy is more nuanced, and it has changed through history," suggested Iñigo Gurruchaga, a Basque journalist who lives between Bilbao and London.

It was then that Xavi, one of the younger guests, butted in rather drunkenly and accused them all of mythmaking. Suddenly, the tone of the gathering changed and threatened to become not just political but dangerously so. "The only reason we can't compete is because of Athletic's policy of recruiting only players with Basque blood in them. Athletic is the most xenophobic club in Spain!" It was the point at which the camaraderie began to disintegrate, as Xavi found himself having to fend off accusations of belonging to dark forces from

Madrid—a member of the center-right Partido Popular, or worse still an unreconstructed fascist and a closet Real Madrid fan—all of which he virulently denied. Later I stumbled into the night, well fed, well drunk, yet sensitive to the fact that no one had once alluded to the British connection—a reminder that Spanish soccer, whenever it was played, had achieved some kind of unilateral independence, and been given a further edge by local politics.

When it comes to Spanish soccer, I have been on a learning curve for a while now, and this was another lesson learned. A previous visit to the region was in 2003 when I was following David Beckham, during his first season at Real Madrid. I was struck by the radicalism of the local fans when the team played away in Pamplona against Osasuna. During Pamplona's famous bullfighting festival, the soccer fans ran the bulls and mocked the conservative families that occupied the best seats. At Osasuna's El Sadar stadium they occupied the stands behind the north goal, waved Basque nationalist flags, and chanted slogans in support of ETA, the Basque terrorist group, when not shouting abuse at Beckham and the other Real Madrid players. At one point a young ball boy threw a missile at Beckham while he was taking a corner. Beckham looked back and gestured like a teacher admonishing a wayward pupil. The gesture generated an uproar among the local fans. They weren't going to learn any lessons from Beckham, or any other *Inglés* for that matter.

Seven years later, in Bilbao, I sat in an old library in the city's British-style gentlemen's club, delving into old newspapers. I discovered that Basque soccer's declaration of independence came one spring day in 1894 when a group of *Bilbainos* published an advertisement in a local newspaper challenging the team of *Los Ingleses* to a soccer match. *Los Ingleses*—not just Englishmen but Scots-, Welsh-, and Irishmen too—won the toss and chose to play the first half with the

sun behind them. They played a very physical game—felling their opponents on several occasions with heavy tackles or barges that surprised and angered the *Bilbainos* and allowed *Los Ingleses* to secure a
two-goal advantage by the time the halftime whistle blew at approxi-
mately eleven o'clock.

At this point the *Bilbainos'* low spirits were lifted by the surprise
delivery to their locker rooms of eleven exquisitely roasted chickens, a gift from their opponents. The match was delayed to allow
the local team to enjoy their meal, just as *Los Ingleses* had planned.
By the time play resumed, the sun was setting, and it was still once
again facing the *Bilbainos*. Blinded by the light, pushed, and bruised,
and somewhat indigested, the *Bilbainos* lost 0–6. Only belatedly did
the *Bilbainos* realize the trickery of a team that boasted to be the
teachers of fair play. The locals pledged then and there to build a
team that would never again suffer such humiliation, either on or off
the field.

The year that game was played is mostly remembered by pres-
ent-day *Bilbainos* as the day Sabino Arana, the Basque Country's
most influential ideologue, founded his party, the Basque Nationalist Party (PNV). By the time he died nine years later, at the age of
thirty-eight, the PNV had become a significant force that was to
endure to the present day. Arana left behind not only an ideology
but also a flag, an anthem, and a name for a new and ancient nation,
Euzkadi.

Arana started off proclaiming the party's goal to be total independence from Spain, but before he died he ended up apparently accepting that "maximum autonomy" within the Spanish state was more
desirable. Despite such ambiguities, the spirit of nationalism that he
engendered had an impact on local soccer from its early beginnings.
In 1898, four years after the fateful chicken match, a group of Basque

soccer enthusiasts were confident enough about their own abilities to form their own soccer club, called the Athletic Club. By then soccer had spread from the Basque Country across northern Spain to Catalonia and up from the south to the capital, Madrid.

FC Barcelona: The first transport

CHAPTER 5

Catalans

It was in the fishing port of Palamós on Catalonia's Costa Brava in 1889 that a local merchant, Gaspar Matas i Danés, who had studied in England, formed the Palamós Foot-Ball Club. The Costa Brava, like much of Spain's coastline, has long been invaded and transformed by foreign tourists and property speculators. But the fish market and maritime museum are still there, dedicated to the generations of local men who risked their lives to keep the local traditions going. Palamós is one of the few towns along the Costa Brava that has managed to preserve its identity amid the plundering of the rest of the coastline by mass tourism.

Palamós's soccer roots are nonetheless discreetly stated on a fading plaque, well off the tourist track. Its history is hidden out of sight down a poorly lit inner gallery of a small, archaic English-style stadium built more than a century ago on its outskirts, one of the first such structures to be constructed on Spanish soil. It has endured to this day, like a long-abandoned church.

When I visited it, the place was not only unkempt but eerily silent. Despite repeated inquiries, I was told by a part-time volunteer secretary that no spokesman of the club was immediately available and would not be for several hours. She suggested there was not much they would enlighten me on anyway. She certainly had neither inclination nor time to help. Only a groundskeeper I found emerging from a rusty bathroom seemed marginally more forthcoming. He took me on a quick tour of the decaying stadium, bemoaning the lack of funds and cuts in public spending that were hitting local government following the credit crunch and the collapse of the property market. He was an immigrant from the Ivory Coast. "I like watching Barca, but Didier Drogba has always been my hero."

That a fellow Ivorian, Drogba, the captain of the Ivory Coast's national team who played for Chelsea, was marked out as his hero was hardly a surprise. Nor was the fact that he saw no contradiction in the fact that Barca was his favorite club. Another star fellow countryman, Yaya Toure, had only recently joined his brother Kolo at Manchester City after making a success of his time in the Catalan capital. Anyway, the presence of FC Barcelona just up the coast had long put Palamós in the shadows.

In the same year, 1889, that the Palamós FC club was formed, an occasion took place in Catalonia that was to prove altogether more providential. In a field in the neighborhood called Bonavona in Barcelona, the capital city and major Catalan port, a group of players kicked a ball around, dressed for the first time in the red and blue colors of what later became one of the world's great sporting institutions.

If soccer had come only belatedly to this part of Spain, it was because Catalans, regardless of class, were too caught up in local politics. There was a growing urban working class in Barcelona that had grown, as in Bilbao, from the region's early industrialization and a thriving business class that had profited from external commerce. But in the second half of the nineteenth century, Catalonia, and Barcelona in particular, became embroiled in a seemingly endless cycle of repression and violence that left little time to watch, let alone learn, an innovative sport. As for the middle class, while they enjoyed something of an economic boom in the last dozen years of the nineteenth century, their conservative society was threatened by escalating strikes and anarchist-inspired bombing campaigns.

Political and class divisions intensified following the final demise of the Spanish empire with the loss of Cuba in 1898. This provoked a great deal of soul-searching among some of Spain's politicians and intellectuals as to why the onetime empire had ended up being brought to its knees by a group of Latin American insurrectionists. No national consensus emerged around the diagnosis, still less any cure. In Catalonia it turned Catalanism—a belief that the region constituted a separate entity from the rest of Spain by virtue of its culture, tradition, and economic development, demanding special treatment—from a minority creed into a vehicle for generalized protest.

In such a nationalist atmosphere it was perhaps nothing short of miraculous that the majority of FC Barcelona's first-ever team were foreigners, notably Englishmen. The goalkeeper was called Brown, the club's first secretary Wild, and two key players Arthur and Ernest Witty, brothers in arms. Their father had emigrated to Barcelona in the middle of the nineteenth century and set up a shipping business, acting as an agent for the British merchant vessels that sailed in and out of the port city. As schoolboys the Wittys had been educated at Merchant Taylors, an English private boarding school with a long-established tradition of intelligent sportsmanship, or, as its legendary founder put it, "training the body as well as the mind."

In the spring of 1998, I went looking for Arthur Witty's oldest surviving descendant in a nursing home near the seaside resort of Castelldefels, south of Barcelona. Frederick Witty was hard of hearing and suffering from a cancer that would kill him a few months later, but he had retained a good memory and was happy to share it.

Frederick seemed the epitome of a postimperial Englishman abroad, with his tweed jacket and silk cravat and heavily accented Spanish and Catalan. We were surrounded by geriatrics holding on to their existence with the help of pills and tubes and the humanity of the nursing staff. So he was glad when I wheeled him out into the garden under a warm spring Mediterranean sun. He showed me old team photographs of his father, Arthur, a rather upright Colonel Blimp type with black hair and a heavy mustache, about five foot ten and strongly built. "When he was at school in England my father played rugby as a forward. Then he came to Barcelona and played soccer as a fullback," Frederick recalled. "To play rugby in Spain in those days was impossible because none of the sports grounds were fully turfed, whereas with soccer you could learn quickly enough to kick a ball around on any surface."

Only later did I think Frederick's comments might hold the key to offering another explanation as to why Spanish soccer had evolved the way it had. The Spanish landscape—its sheer geological variety and contrast—was one of the explanations of its political problems and economic underdevelopment. Spain has some regions where it rains like Ireland and others that seem an extension of the Sahara. It has regions covered in mountains and others covered in vast arid plains. It has fertile valleys and rivers that are dry for most of the year. One of the main still-unresolved challenges of Spain's evolution as a nation has been how to find ways of linking its diverse regions not just by roads, rail, and air but also constitutionally, in a way that shares Spain's development as a country while respecting political and cultural autonomies with their own historical identities like the Basque Country and Catalonia. Of course, modern methods of irrigation and power generation along with one of the boldest road and railway building projects since World War II have helped to make Spain more accessible both without and within, turf most stadiums, and allow more soccer fans to travel. But the landscape has yet to be fully tamed, and the playgrounds for the aspiring stars of the future remain varied.

But back to *El Inglés* Witty. We drank tea on the well-watered lawn of his nursing home, as the Mediterranean sun went down and his breathing became labored. Frederick shared a few more insights about his father. "He never did any specialized training—none of that stuff you see these days, with players having orders shouted at them by coaches acting like camp commandants. But he knew how to keep fit, and did so by going for long runs." He continued, "He played a lot of soccer between games of tennis. His favorite family outing was to walk all the way to the top of the Tibidabo, Barcelona's highest vantage point, and down again. In their styles, there was little to choose between him and the other early founders. They played with a combination of acceleration, toughness, ball control, and goal-scoring potential."

The Witty story came to be overshadowed in the mythology of FC Barcelona by the figure of Hans Gamper. He was the Swiss-born Barcelona businessman who helped assemble the early FC Barcelona players and was the club's founding president. Gamper proved himself to be a man well in touch with the social and political changes taking place in his adoptive country. He quickly learned Catalan and supported Catalonia's drive toward greater autonomy from Madrid. While the official history of FC Barcelona has it that the colors were imported by Gamper from Switzerland, the Witty version is that they were inspired by the maroon and blue of Arthur's old English school colors at Merchant Taylors. It seemed to me that Barca may have opted in later years to accept the Gamper version—with its prominence in neutral understated Switzerland—as a way of liberating itself from its British colonial roots.

Francisco Giner de los Rios: Sport is the essence of life

CHAPTER 6

Madridistas

The club that was destined to become Barca's eternal rival, Real Madrid, or Madrid FC, as it was called originally when it was registered for the first time in 1902, also had its early personality shaped by Englishmen, with its first book of rules imported from Manchester. The white colors that distinguish the club to this day were copied from those of the Corinthians, one of London's first amateur soccer clubs. Prior to the foundation of any soccer club in the capital, the first kick-arounds took place in a field near the old bullring, with participants using a room in a local bullfighting tavern as one of their meeting places. Spanish soccer from its early days, far from displacing bullfighting as a cultural and social phenomenon, coexisted with it. In time great players would join great toreros or matadors in the pantheon of popular mythology.

Yet even in premodern traditionalist Madrid, Spanish soccer owed much to its foreign roots. One of the first Madrid players was Arthur Johnson, a freethinking English businessman who shared his soccer skills and a similar philosophy of life with a group of young Spanish disciples of Francisco Giner de los Rios, one of the most influential of Spain's intellectuals at the end of the nineteenth century.

De los Rios founded the *Institución Libre de Enseñanza* (the Free Institute of Learning), dedicated to the ideal of a nonofficial, non-dogmatic education, which freed from the shackles of those conservative forces like the Catholic Church and the military would nurture a new generation of Spaniards capable of transforming postimperial Spain from a failed to a modern state. De los Rios was a huge admirer of Anglo-Saxon (post-Reformation) civilization and the Enlightenment. He encouraged the teaching of sport, alongside excursions in the countryside, as an essential element in the syllabus, first of his university and later the schools he developed, with mixed success, when the political extremes on the Left and Right took hold of Spanish politics in the early decades of the twentieth century. Nevertheless, de los Rios believed soccer, played according to its emerging set of rules, was a sport that would appeal across class lines and would in time come to overtake the popularity of bullfighting, which he considered a legacy of primitiveness and repression. To that extent he proved prophetic.

Real Madrid has kept a portrait of Johnson written by a Spanish friend of his. The writer contrasts Johnson's dedication and knowledge of the game with the chaos that characterized the play of some of the Spaniards in the first Madrid squad, not least the goalkeeper. According to the chronicler, Johnson "not only knew more about the game than anybody else," but was also *un inglés muy simpatico*—a very friendly Englishman. In 1902, the year after Madrid FC's foundation, the twenty-three-year-old Johnson was the veteran of a team whose average age was nineteen and whose youngest, sixteen-year-old Pedro Parages, had learned the game in England. "Johnson is the captain of the team—he distinguished himself with his tackling, agility and elegance of body. He plays in various positions, centre-half, centre-forward and goalkeeper." The rest of the team was made up of a former player from Athletic Bilbao, seven other Spaniards—two of them born in Cuba and one in Guatemala—and a Frenchman who had learned to play in England named Chalmandier. The Frenchman played at right half and distinguished himself by the great sense of self-confidence and elegance with which he played.

The first two administrators of Madrid FC, Juan and Carlos Padros, were born in Catalonia, a fact that sits awkwardly with the enduring rivalry between the two clubs. It is a curious paradox that serves as a reminder that beneath the myths created by the warring factions, or their apologists, the history of Spanish soccer, like the history of Spain, was never quite so easily delineated but subject to complex shades.

Partisanship has inevitably meant that the Padros brothers have been used by some Catalans to embarrass *Madridistas* about their non-Castilian roots, as when the Barcelona sports tabloid *Mundo Deportivo* in December 1992 boldly headlined an article: "A Catalan Founded (Real) Madrid!" The fact that the newspaper could claim an exposé nine decades after the event was the consequence of the refusal of Real Madrid's official historians to even mention the fact of Catalans being among the club's founding fathers. Yet whatever the myths and obfuscations, the Padros brothers were first and foremost motivated by soccer, not politics, and there is little evidence that they shared any particular sympathy for Catalanism as a separate political and cultural movement to the rest of Spain.

The Padroses—Carlos and Juan—were young children when their parents migrated to Madrid from Barcelona in 1876. Their father was a cloth merchant who spoke French and made frequent visits to the North of England to look at textiles. He was drawn to Madrid by the prospect of more business in 1876 when the Spanish capital was poised on the edge of political reform that promised to make civil war and military coups a thing of the past. The Bourbon dynasty had been restored under King Alfonso XII—father of the future Alfonso XIII—and one of Spain's greatest statesmen, Antonio Cánovas del Castillo, had helped draw up a liberal constitution that he hoped would make of Madrid a respected European capital of a country united under a constitutional monarchy.

It was Carlos, the oldest of the Padros brothers, whose idea it was to set up a small office to run FC Madrid's early affairs in a back room of his father's textile shop. Carlos was crippled in one foot from birth, so he grew up using an orthopedic boot and could never play soccer himself. Nonetheless, he had picked up an enthusiasm for the game when accompanying his father on his visits to England and France. In 1902 he temporarily overcame his disability and managed to referee the final of the first tournament in Spanish soccer club history to coincide with the celebrations surrounding the coronation of King Alfonso XIII.

The coronation tournament provided a good guide to the emergent soccer geography of Spain. The latest Bourbon to assume the Spanish throne was only sixteen at a time when modern sport was becoming internationalized. The modern Olympic movement had been founded six years prior to the coronation. Within four years of its taking place, Spain's northern neighbor, France, had organized its first major cycling tour and the sports car Gran Prix. The young King Alfonso—flush with the energy of youth and as yet uncorrupted politically, as he was destined to be—considered himself an open-minded, forward-looking king who was happy to give the "modern" game of soccer his blessing from the outset of his reign. The first championship, known as the Coronation Cup, was donated in his name by the mayor of Madrid, Alberto Aguilera. (The trophy was subsequently renamed the King's Cup.) It was played by two teams based in Catalonia, FC Barcelona and Espanyol; Athletic Bilbao, using the name of the Basque province from which the club emanated, Vizcaya; and Madrid

FC and another team, the New Football Club de Madrid, which had formed in the capital but would soon be absorbed by its rival and eventually named Real Madrid.

The games were played in the capital's hippodrome, which was then in open ground where today's Spanish ministry buildings are, near the modern Bernabéu stadium. The event drew an audience of between two and five thousand spectators, which was less than a quarter of the crowd that could fit into Madrid's main bullring. Nevertheless, it was the first mass gathering of soccer fans on Spanish soil and evidence of the sport's nascent popularity. Gamper's FC Barcelona beat Padros's Madrid 3–1 and then was beaten 1–2 by Vizcaya. All three teams played with English players but with a majority of Basque, Catalan, and other Spanish players. The trophy was taken back to Bilbao, where it has remained to this day in the offices of Athletic Bilbao, a club that went on to win four successive King's Cups and would remain central to the development of Spanish soccer in its early decades.

King Alfonso XIII: Soccer's King

CHAPTER 7

Growing Pains

Although many English fans can justifiably claim tribal loyalties dating back to Victorian times, the first Spanish soccer enthusiasts at the end of the nineteenth century and in the early twentieth century were in a small privileged minority, and to my knowledge my Spanish great-grandmother, resolved to spending her twilight years in the fading light of the island of Cuba, the Spanish empire's last colonial outpost, was not one of them.

Yet the hopes and dreams of early Spanish soccer fans contrasted with the incoherence of Spanish society as a whole. At the turn of the twentieth century, this was evident in the survival of traditional structures and attitudes that clashed with those pushing for reform. Spain still lacked a fully functional national railway system, and other communications were generally poor. Large swathes of rural Spain remained semifeudal, in the hands of local politically powerful landowners, caciques, with conditions of life among the peasant workforce comparable to the worst areas of Sicily and eastern Europe. Poverty was exacerbated by geology, with some regions beset by inadequate rainfall or poor soil or both. Many rural workers in parts of the South and Galicia in the North, for example, escaped from semistarvation by emigrating to South America or moving to the cities. By contrast, financiers and large-scale industrial entrepreneurs came to dominate the economic and social life of the towns of Bilbao and Barcelona on Spain's northern coast, along with a growing and increasingly militant urban working class.

Meanwhile, King Alfonso XIII in Madrid developed a taste for political intrigue, with an inflated belief in his capacity to ensure the stability and unity of the nation but ultimately incapable of conceiving a form of government other than a highly centralized one with the support of the military. Spanish politics was characterized by deeply rooted antagonisms between conservatives and progressive politicians, the enduring influence of a reactionary military and Catholic Church, and separate nationalist aspirations in Catalonia and the Basque Country.

Separate societies evolving within a country and markedly different rates of change were the common experience of Europe under the impulse of industrialization. Spain was distinguished by its tardiness, its sporadic incidence of development. At a more general level, unlike northern Europe, Spain lacked a well-rooted middle class, which eliminated a channel through which aristocratic taste could be distilled or primitive popular taste refined and diluted. Spain was a country were popular arts like flamenco, religious festivals, and bullfighting had triumphed and endured.

It is this cultural, social, and political context that explains the belated development of Spanish soccer into a mass sport in which both leading clubs and the national team came to be drawn into the political struggle between the nation and its regions. In spite of the attempts of Spanish reformers, the spread of soccer across class lines proved a protracted affair, its social inclusiveness made all the more complicated by the absence of a unified national consciousness.

The clubs that competed in Spain's early national tournaments could between them boast only relatively small numbers of supporters at a time when gates for big cup and league games in England were already regularly reaching the 20,000 mark. In 1901, the year before Spain staged its first club championship before a maximum crowd of 5,000 (some estimates put it at 2,000), the English Cup final between Spurs and Sheffield United at Crystal Palace drew a crowd of more than 110,000. Seven years later, long before anything resembling a Spanish national squad had been assembled, a Scotland-England match at Hampden Park drew more than 120,000, the largest ever for an international.

Nevertheless, in the first decade of the twentieth century a growing number of cities and regions in Spain acquired a focus of civic identity around their soccer clubs. The early pioneers in Huelva, Madrid, Bilbao, and Barcelona were followed by the foundation of clubs in Asturias (Sporting Gijon, 1905) and Galicia Deportivo La Coruna (1906). In Andalusia, Seville and Betis were formed within two years of each other (1905 and 1907, respectively).

An early anomaly in the geographical landscape was Atletico de Madrid, founded in 1903 in the Spanish capital by a group of Basques as a subsidiary of Athletic Bilbao. Both clubs agreed not to compete with each other in tournaments and shared players, an arrangement that persisted until the early 1920s, when Atletico became independent.

In Catalonia, the Sociedad Española de Football was founded in 1900 by a group of aristocratic university students who adopted the crest of Roger de Lauria, a medieval Sicilian-born warlord who served the crown of Aragon in its defense of Catalonia from the marauding French. Within a year it had been renamed Club Español de Fútbol before it became Club Deportivo Español. All these titles were a conscious reaction to FC Barcelona's identity as a Catalan club that was nonetheless open to other Europeans. Español's founding statute declared, "We create this club to compete with the foreigners of FC Barcelona." By foreigners it meant not just FC Barcelona's English and Swiss founding fathers, but its emerging brand as *the* club of Catalonia, a nation with a discernible cultural and political claim that separated it from the rest of Spain. Español made much of its claim that it was the first Spanish club to be made up exclusively of Spanish players, which included those born in Catalonia, although by 1911 it had three Englishmen playing for it. Español drew its fan base among Spanish civil servants, migrants, and pro-monarchist right-wingers who were happy to have Catalonia remain subservient to a centralized Spanish state headquartered in Madrid.

In 1912 Español was one of the Spanish clubs that were granted royal patronage by King Alfonso XIII and entitled to add the word *Real* to its name and put the crown on its colors. Others similarly ennobled in the Spanish sports world included Real Madrid, Real Sociedad, Real Club Celta de Vigo, Real Club Unión de Irún, Real Club Deportivo Mallorca, as well as Real Betis. The king appears to have aimed to broaden his popularity by extending his patronage of the game across regions. It is perhaps worth noting here that Español's existence did not stop the creation of a Catalan soccer league in 1901 and a distinct Catalan soccer association in 1904, both long in advance of the Spanish league and the Spanish Soccer Association.

King Alfonso XIII engaged with soccer fans more readily than any member of the English royal family at the time (it was only in 1914 that a British monarch appeared for the first time in the final of the FA Cup). But Spain being Spain, Real Madrid's and Español's royal appointments simply fueled regional political antagonisms and bitter rivalries that would endure.

Spain's neutrality during World War I meant that soccer faced no interruptions, and the popularity of the sport continued to grow after a group of small Basque businessmen and entrepreneurs funded the building and inauguration of Spain's first purpose-built soccer stadium, San Mames in Bilbao, in 1913, ushering in an extended period during which Basque players dominated Spanish soccer. Until that point soccer remained too incipient for it to be officially adopted by the Spanish state as a national sport, even as the first moves were being made north of the Pyrenees to regularize the game internationally.

Spain was one of seven countries that in 1904 attended an inaugural meeting in Paris of the Federation Internationale de Football Association (FIFA). The Spanish delegate was from Madrid FC, whose claim to represent the whole of Spain was questionable. FIFA was destined to spend its early years formulating regulations, providing referees, and deciding who could join and who could play rather than organizing any major international tournaments.

For its part Spain had neither the money nor the organization to attend the Olympics in London in 1908 or Stockholm in 1912. After that there had been no major international sporting event during World War I, and both the International Olympic Committee and FIFA went into cold storage. It was only at the first postwar Olympics in Antwerp in 1920 that Spain grasped for the first time an opportunity to test its soccer players in a major international tournament.

Rafael Moreno Aranzadi "Pichichi":
A Basque goal scorer

CHAPTER 8

Soccer with Cojones

The circumstances surrounding the Spanish squad's first major international test at the 1920 Olympic Games were far from ideal. The previous Olympics, due to take place in 1916 in Berlin, capital of the German empire, were canceled as a result of the outbreak of World War I. The 1920 Games were awarded to Antwerp to honor the people of that city after their suffering during the war. Participant countries struggled to come to terms with the spirit of sportsmanship after a conflict that had led to the death of 9 million soldiers. A total of twenty-nine nations participated in the Antwerp Games. In breach of the Olympic spirit, Germany, Austria, Hungary, Bulgaria, and Turkey were excluded, having been on the losing side of the war. Officially, they were not banned. But they were not invited, either. Also absent was the new Russian Soviet Republic, a revolutionary power that the West deeply distrusted. Instead, the dysfunctional Olympic family—using doves as a symbol of peace—embraced as new arrivals the newly created European state of Estonia and Czechoslovakia and the emerging soccer nation, Spain.

War had ravaged most of Europe so that these first postwar Olympics were organized on a shoestring and poorly attended. Soccer players, like the rest of the athletes, were housed in cramped conditions and slept on folding cots. Yet Spain had every reason to take them very seriously. Its presence in the Olympics signified an open door into an increasingly international sport. Thus, of the fifty-eight Spanish sportsmen who went to compete, more than a third were soccer players.

The most curious member of the squad was its coach, Francisco Bru. Born in Madrid, Bru had played for FC Barcelona and Español before becoming one of the country's more eccentric referees in 1916, choosing to carry a pistol attached to a holster whenever he officiated a match. Asked by a player why he needed to carry a gun, Bru answered deadpan, "I want tranquillity." Thankfully, he was never given cause to use it.

The squad was picked after a series of friendly matches across Spain between teams identified as "probables" and "possibles" by a triumvirate of officials who between them represented a consensual balance of power: one from Catalonia, one from the Basque Country, and one from Madrid. In early selection meetings, Basque officials argued successfully that the Olympic squad should be drawn mainly from the Basque Country, for it was there that the most successful soccer was being played at the club level at the time.

Among the players who went on the Olympic expedition in the end, thirteen players were Basque born and played for clubs based in the Basque Country, four were born in Catalonia or played for FC Barcelona, while three others were from Galicia. Northern Spain dominated the selection. The absence of any players from Madrid or the main southern region of Andalusia may have partly reflected the then general superiority of teams farther north. However, the selectors provided a further explanation. Unlike the North of Spain, soccer in Madrid and the South was still largely played on unturfed grounds.

Because the Olympics were to be played on grass, this—it was judged—disqualified certain players from selection.

The average age of the squad was twenty-nine years old, evidence that selectors had generally opted for experience and enduring popularity rather than taking a risk on young talent that had yet to be really tested in competitive terms. The youngest player on the squad was FC Barcelona's eighteen-year-old Pepe Samitier. Spanish club soccer was still some ways off from making its mark on the international scene, so expectations of Spanish success in the Olympics of 1920 were not high.

Spain began the tournament by beating Denmark 1–0 and was then beaten in the quarterfinal by Belgium, 1–3. But an unexpected opportunity came its way when the Belgium versus Czechoslovakia final failed to secure a legitimate runner-up. The English referee of the final so upset the Czechs with his handling of the game that they walked off the field in the forty-third minute and refused to return. A field invasion bizarrely led by Belgian soldiers ended all hope of the match being restarted, and the Czechs were eventually disqualified. Thus, Spain found itself playing for a runner-up medal, beating first Sweden 2–1 and then Italy 2–0 and finally taking the silver when it beat the Netherlands 3–1.

That Spain achieved what it did in the end by a mixture of luck and default mattered little. Spain's achievement was legitimately governed by the rules at the time, under the so-called Bergvall system. This was named after Eric Bergvall, a pioneering Swedish journalist and Olympic sportsman (he played water polo) who wanted to give strong teams defeated in the earlier rounds a further chance to remain in the tournament and fight for second and third places. Thus, a fair distribution of medals would be secured and with a minimum of matches, according to Bergvall. Besides the usual knockout method, teams defeated by the eventual winner could compete for second place and those defeated by the second-place winner could continue to compete for third place.

Spain found the system made to measure. By winning a silver medal in their first major international tournament, Bru's squad achieved mythical status in the annals of Spanish soccer history. It was one of only two medals won by Spanish sporting teams in those Olympics but easily the most important. The soccer silver was widely celebrated back home, by contrast to the other silver—for polo— which barely penetrated the collective consciousness.

Soccer became established as the country's most popular sport and was on its way to generating a mass following on a par with bullfighting. And this was in part thanks to the legend that was built up around one goal in particular, José María Belauste's winning shot against Sweden that set Spain on the course for its medal. It was one of those moments of soccer history forever embedded in the collective memory of a people thanks to the literary imagination of a participant. The writer with the power of the pen in this case was Manolo de Castro, a popular soccer journalist who wrote for a Spanish newspaper under the pseudonym Handicap. De Castro wrote:

> When play resumed after half-time, Spain seemed to rally behind a call to battle and launched an attack of such ferocity that within two minutes it had secured a free-kick just outside the penalty spot. Sabino was about to take the kick when Jose Mari [Belauste], in a predatory advanced position amidst the Swedes, with his back to the goal screams: "Sabino, give me the ball and I'll wipe them out!" And that's what happened. Sabino kicked the ball upwards, a Swede tried to reach it but only to find Belauste head the ball with such strength that he and various Swedes tumbled together into the goal. It was a really herculean goal!

In time the story of the goal—not subject to any action replay but at the mercy of every soccer pundit's imagination—became elaborated.

Thus, in a book of memoirs written ten years later by the Spanish goal-keeper Zamora, it was claimed that Belauste drove the ball into the goal, the ball balanced on his chest, and with four Swedes clinging to his shirt. By then a mythology had already been born—that of *La Furia Española*, or Spanish Fury—a particularly muscular and aggressive style of soccer, blessed with a nobility of intent and execution over which the Basques at the club level had already claimed a kind of copyright but which was absorbed into the broader national psyche. Curiously, the first recorded use of the phrase *La Furia* is not to be found in any Spanish media but in a Dutch newspaper, which reported the day after Spain's victory by drawing an analogy to the fearsome tactics used by Spain's imperial sol-diers when they sacked and pillaged Antwerp in November 1576.

From those Olympics, a few members of the Spanish squad became legends. The first was the captain, Belauste. The ninth child born into a family with Basque nationalist leanings, Belauste studied law at Deusto, the prestigious Jesuit University in Bilbao, founded, like the city's first soccer field, on the banks of the river Nervión. Contemporary photo-graphs of Belauste barely hint at his relatively comfortable upbringing. They show a gentle giant, bruised and battered by endless battles. With a bandaged knee, a broken nose, heavily shadowed indented eyes, and large ears clasped back by a four-cornered white handkerchief—tightly bound to protect him from an incipient alopecia—the six-foot-three Belauste was 210 pounds of pure square-shaped muscle that had nobly endured countless injuries.

Belauste was by all accounts a down-to-earth guy who shunned stardom. His favorite hobby was practicing *palanka*, the traditional Basque rural pastime of throwing a metal bar, otherwise known as "the miners' sport." It was a game that tested an individual's physical re-sistance to the fullest. But it was on the soccer field that the Basque showed himself a worthy captain of the national squad, mobile and visionary enough to order play from midfield when not using his

strength and height to create or deliver goals up front. He began playing for Athletic Bilbao at the age of fifteen and retired in 1922, aged
thirty-six, to pursue a career as a lawyer. It proved a turning point in his
life, drawing him increasingly into Basque nationalist politics in a way
that would overshadow all else, including his love of soccer.

Another famous Basque from that Olympic side was Rafael Moreno
Aranzadi, nicknamed Pichichi, the little duck. He and Belauste formed
the key ingredients in making Athletic Bilbao one of Spain's leading clubs
in the years 1911–1921. In the days before the creation of the Spanish
league, Pichichi was Spanish soccer's first great goal scorer. He scored
seventy-seven goals in 89 Copa Del Rey matches and two hundred goals
in 170 matches in total, most of which came in the northern regional
championship. He played in 6 Copa Del Rey finals and was a major contributor to winning 4 of them. From a highly literate Basque family (his
great-uncle was the internationally respected philosopher and author
Miguel de Unamuno)—Pichichi's intelligence as well as skill in the
field more than made up for his generally diminutive body. He was five
feet in height and weighed just under 115 pounds. He too played with a
tied handkerchief covering his head. He said it was to better protect
himself from a ball that in those days was stitched in panels, like a jig-
saw. If you failed to avoid heading the ball at the laced bit, you ran the
risk of a cut or a headache. The handkerchief minimized the cuts.

Like many Basque players, Pichichi developed a love of soccer as a
young boy in a private school run by a Catholic religious order imbued
with the discipline and sporting ethos of a British public school. This
connection contrasts with the ideology of some of the early players in
other parts of Spain who experienced a lay education and saw soccer as
liberation from traditional Spain, of which they saw the Catholic
Church playing an inseparable part. The strong links that Basque soccer has with Catholicism reflect those between Basque culture as a
whole and the cult of Saint Ignatius of Loyola, the sixteenth-century

Basque soldier who became a hermit and then founded the Jesuit order. Joseba Zulaika, a leading Basque academic, lay great emphasis on the religious formation of Basque nationalists and in particular what he saw as the metamorphosis of religious vocation into an ideology predicated on commitment and action. Zulaika argued that this in turn has also had a decisive influence in reinforcing the Basque cultural tendency to see complex issues in antagonistic black-and-white terms.

Zulaika's subject of examination is Basque nationalism in its most extreme form, which is that of the Basque separatist group ETA, founded—he argues not coincidentally—on July 31, 1959, the feast day of Saint Ignatius. Saint Ignatius may also be partly responsible for laying the seeds of *La Furia* among the Basque players who had such a formative influence on Spanish soccer.

But to return to Pichichi, his first games as an adolescent were played in the Campa de los Ingleses, near the river Nervión. Legend has it that the nickname—a derivative of *pichon* or *puichin* and a term of affection usually accorded to small people—was first used on him in these early kick-arounds and that it stuck when he was later spotted by a club scout.

Pichichi joined Athletic in 1910 when the team was shedding some of its British roots and developing a Basque identity by restricting the recruitment of players to those of Basque stock. Here was born the notion of *la cantera*; literally translated as *quarry*, the word draws on a mining term to describe the source of a player's heritage. In its early Bilbao version it applied, as it still does, to a certain extent to a cultural and racial precondition, although over the years the term has been used more widely to apply to youth academies across Spanish soccer.

Pichichi was Basque born and bred. His playing days on the first team of Athletic and Spain's national squad coincided with the club presidency of Alejandro de la Sota, a Basque nationalist politician and businessman whose more famous brother, Ramon, rented half his shipping fleet to the British in the First World War and was honored with a knighthood.

A fitness fanatic, Pichichi used his pace and dribbling skills to get around the often brutal stratagems of Basque defenders much bigger and stronger than himself, while proving himself a hugely effective striker of the ball. He managed to score a great many goals with his feet, and not a few with his head. Local journalists called him *el Rey Del Shoot*, the Strike King. One of his most faithful fans was his cousin Alfonso Moreno, a Jesuit priest and a soccer writer in his spare time. It was said at the time that if you were young and lived in the Basque Country, your best career paths lay in the Society of Jesus or with the Athletic Bilbao. In fact, both organizations locally shared recruits and philosophies to the point of being indistinguishable—they were both militant Catholics and fervently Basque.

Of Pichichi the player, Father Alfonso wrote:

My cousin "Pichichi" is the best player in Athletic and the best player in Spain. He's a tremendous striker, with a low level of gravity and very powerful, so that there isn't a goalkeeper capable of stopping him. But above all he dribbles better than anybody and goes from one end of the pitch to another with the ball stuck to his feet and without anyone taking it away from him, until he has scored his genius goal. He also has an extraordinary ability to head the ball, particularly in set play, off corner kicks. When things are going badly for the team, the crowd expects Pichichi to remedy the situation. . . . The only criticism is that that he sometimes plays like an individual and loses sight of the team. Nevertheless there are various English teams who would like to take him away from us even if Rafael has no thought of leaving Bilbao.

As Athletic's star player, Pichichi generated the kind of popular passions that until then had been mainly the preserve of top bull-fighters. A certain element of self-belief mixed with vanity pushed him to continue playing long after he lost form, something for which the fans did not thank him. During his last three years at Athletic, which included playing as an international, Pichichi was often jeered and criticized by the home crowd. The silver medal he obtained with the Spanish team was the swan song of a star player already in decline. He retired in 1921, the year after the Olympics, having scored his last goal in a match against West Ham. He briefly embarked on a new career as a referee but found the profession lacking excitement. He was saved from growing old and bitter by an early death. After a meal of oysters, he was struck down by typhus and died in 1922, only aged twenty-nine. His last words were whispered to one of his former teammates, Aquilino "Chomin" Gomez Acedo: "Chomin, mind you look after my wife and daughter," he pleaded.

Pichichi's reputation grew after his death, and he achieved certain immortality among his fellow Basques as a romantic hero, thanks to the large mural-like paintings that were made of him by leading Basque painters. The most popular were created by the artist Aurelio Arteta, who idealized a Basque culture he believed was threatened by the advance of industrialization. In perhaps the most famous and arguably most striking painting ever done of a soccer player, Arteta painted an elongated Pichichi, darkly handsome and powerful in club colors, courting a beautiful young woman in a white shirt and similarly fashionable long skirt and shoes—modeled on his young wife, Avelina—against the backdrop of a Basque rural landscape. Painted the year before Pichichi's retirement, Arteta called it *Idilio en Los Camps ode Sport* (An Idyll in the Sporting Fields). Today the painting hangs in the president's office of Athletic's administrative headquarters, the magnificently decorated Ibaigane Palace, although copies—whether in poster or postcard form—remain best-sellers of Athletic's illustrated history.

The figure of Pichichi has another enduring symbol in a small bust of the player installed in the San Mames stadium in 1926 and thereafter a place where teams visiting the stadium for the first time lay a bouquet of flowers. The bust was erected in memory of the player who scored the first-ever goal in one of Spain's oldest built stadiums (as distinct from the oldest surviving professional playing field, El Molinon, the site of Sporting Gijon's stadium in Asturias) on August 21, 1913, the inaugural game against Racing Irún.

Finally, Pichichi was given a central place in *La Liga* thanks to the decision made by the sports newspaper *Marca* in 1953 to introduce the Trofeo Pichichi, an annual award for Spain's top scorer that remains to this day. Ignored in the numerous books about Athletic published in the Basque Country is any attempt to explain why *Marca*, a newspaper allied with Franco from its early days and supportive of Real Madrid, should have opted to celebrate a Basque player in such a high-profile manner. The reasons lie in the fact that Basque nationalism is not the only party guilty of playing highly charged political games in the Basque Country.

Spanish right-wing nationalists, like Franco, have traditionally been sympathetic to the idea that the Basque Country contains the seeds of "true Spanishness," inseparable from Catholicism and Spain's history of empire, conquest, and surviving against the odds in a hostile environment. The Basques fit into this worldview essentially as members of Spain's warrior class or Spanish militarism whose essential values, steeped in virility, are bravery, self-sacrifice, obedience to leaders, and a sense of honor.

It is not a coincidence that the Pichichi prize came into being when Athletic was enjoying a postwar resurgence in its fortunes and after being temporarily purged of Basque nationalist sentiment by a right-wing presidency handpicked by the regime. Franco was quite at ease with himself in celebrating Athletic as a Spanish soccer team of blood, guts, and attitude. Indeed, it was his favorite Spanish soccer team, in the days before Real Madrid became great. As for Pichichi and the other prominent Basques who also played for Spain, they could be seen through the myopic prism of Francoism as true patriots in the tradition of those Basque soldiers who were prominent in the Christian reconquest of Islamic Iberia and the subsequent "discovery" and conquest of Spanish America.

Two other personalities that featured in Spanish soccer's first major venture onto the international stage are worth mentioning here. They were close friends as well as FC Barcelona teammates. The first was Pepe Samitier, who traveled to the Olympics in Belgium only a year after being signed by the Catalan club, aged seventeen, on May 31, 1919.

Of Samitier, one can say that his alleged humble beginnings belied his early transformation into a star, on and off the field, with the story of his early triumphant years as a player eventually the subject of the first mass-circulation Spanish soccer biography. As Uruguayan author Eduardo Galeano has written, "Samitier was the team's ace player and his biography was on news-stands all over the city. His name was on the lips of cabaret *chanteuses*, bandied about on the stage and revered in sports columns where they praised the Mediterranean style 'invented by him.'" Samitier, "a striker with a devastating shot, stood out for his cleverness, his domination of the ball, his utter lack of respect for the rules of logic, and his Olympian scorn for the borders of space and time," wrote Galeano.

Although he initially played in defense, there was no position off-limits to him, as he feinted and dribbled his way from one end of the field to the other, baffling his opponents and often leaving his teammates to purely supporting roles, shifting their own positions to accommodate his talent. El Sami was also blessed with an extraordinary ability to defy gravity, not least with his trademark kick while flying through the air—arms and legs splayed—which earned him the nickname "the Lobster Man."

I was fortunate that I was able to gain some insight into the man and the player from someone who had known El Sami in his early years and had lived long enough to tell me the tale before he died. In 1997 I met El Sami's longest-living admirer, the former Barca vice president Nicolas Casaus. Aged eighty-four at the time, Casaus shared his memory of meeting Samitier in 1922, when the player had turned twenty and he was nine years old. "They'd organized a friendly between Barca and Igualada, and Samitier came to play. In those days you had to pay twenty-five cents to get into the stadium, but I couldn't afford it. So what the boys and I did was organize ourselves into porters. When the team bus arrived we ran along and offered our services. I had the good luck of picking up Samitier's suitcase. He thought I was a funny kid—fat and small as I was then—but he made me a member of the club there and then." Those were the days when players could still fuel a popular following without being millionaires.

It was the same with Zamora, who perhaps more than any other goalkeeper achieved the title of "great" during the 1920 Olympics. He was "the pearl [of the Spanish team]," in the opinion of one of Spain's most distinguished soccer writers, Alfredo Relaño. It was during the Olympics that he was consecrated by the emerging critics of international sport as a superstar (*supedotado*), the destiny of his team quite literally in his hands. Zamora had made his debut as a major club player with Espanyol in 1917, aged sixteen, before moving to FC Barcelona after a row with one of his early bosses. In Belgium he was the youngest on the squad and among the least experienced, but his physique (he was tall and strong) and emerging talent as a player had already made Zamora a personality. He wore a broad tweed cap in deference to the memory of the early English pioneers and a white polo-neck sweater for no other reason than that he believed he should be dressed as elegantly on the field as off.

During the Olympics Zamora showed himself to be strong, courageous, and skillful. He used his acute sense of anticipation and timing to block attacks while his extraordinary vision of play had him launching counterattacks well beyond his own goal line, often leading the charge himself. He also used his height to good effect, winning cross balls or reaching up and out to deflect an attempted header at the goal. No other goalkeeper had yet appeared in Spanish soccer with his talent, and after the Olympics his reputation grew in such a way that he came to be considered one of the great Spanish sportsmen of all time. In Spain fans across the club divide nicknamed him El Divino, the Divine One. Of Zamora, the lyrical if not always precise South American Galeano has this to say: "He sowed panic among strikers. If they looked his way they were lost: with Zamora in the goal, the net would shrink and the posts would lose themselves in the distance. For twenty years he was the best goalkeeper in the world"—and that despite a daily diet of three packs of cigarettes, an occasional cigar, and a cognac or two.

On the Spanish team's return from the Olympics, Zamora's teammates decided they would play a joke on him, stuffing his suitcase with contraband liquor and cigarettes without his knowledge. When the train reached the Pyrenean border, the French gendarmes discovered the load and arrested him. Zamora spent the night in a cell before the Spanish authorities convinced their French counterparts that one of the great stars of the Olympics was no criminal but the victim of a cruel hoax by unknown conspirators.

Once reunited, Zamora together with the rest of the Spanish squad received a hero's welcome across the country. In time his name would be immortalized on the annual trophy given to the best Spanish goalkeeper. For Spanish soccer, the Olympics proved a point of arrival as well as departure. Spain had gained international recognition, and the stars who won that silver medal would be forever celebrated in the collective memory. But it would be many years before a national squad would again prove to be as collegiate or successful.

Fred Pentland: The eccentric Englishman

CHAPTER 9

The Magic of Mr. Pentland

Bilbao's Athletic, the club that had contributed the most players to the 1920 Olympic squad, was plunged into a management crisis during the 1921–1922 season with the departure of its English coach, Billy Barnes—but it proved short-lived. The son of a London dock-worker, Barnes had played as a seventeen-year-old with Thames Iron Works—the club that would later become West Ham United—before signing for Sheffield United and later playing for West Ham, Luton Town, and Queen's Park Rangers. While his brother, Labour MP Alfred, chose a life in politics, later becoming a minister in Clement Atlee's postwar government, Willy retired as a player in 1914, at age thirty-five, and sailed to Bilbao, initially to escape the Great War and pursue a career as a coach.

In England as in much of Europe, war brought professional soccer to an effective halt, symbolized by the fact that Britain's pioneering Football Association had its London headquarters requisitioned by the War Office. Soccer players across the Continent were among the first to volunteer and then increasingly to be conscripted because of their youth and fitness.

By contrast, Spain, though still without a professional league, kept its young men away from the trenches, having declared its neutrality in the war. Soccer continued as a growing popular entertainment, and Spain became a land of opportunity for any retired former player–turned-coach. Englishmen, because of their historical connections as the harbingers of the game in Spain, were in the pole position to offer themselves up for hiring.

Athletic was pursuing its policy of Basque-only players, but of all Spain's clubs it remained the most Anglophile. Its main financial backers—the family-owned de la Sota industrial and shopping conglomerate—supported the Allies, with whom they continued to have business dealings throughout the war. Barnes was the latest in a line of imported English coaches.

Barnes took the club to victory in the Spanish Cup over his first two seasons, after which he returned to Britain and briefly signed up for military service. He returned to Bilbao in August 1920 for a further short stint. Soon after his arrival, he told a local journalist, "Basque soccer has progressed a lot since I was last here. When I first came it was a patient, slow game of short passing—elegant to watch but totally unpractical, Scots style. I introduced at Athletic a fast game with long passing, taking the ball from wing to wing, and fast players in the centre capable of scoring goals. Today I find most clubs have a tendency to play this way whereas Athletic seems to have lost its way."

Barnes stayed on for another season, at the end of which Athletic once again won the King's Cup, beating Atletico de Madrid 4–1 at San Mames in 1921. His departure provoked a tortuous search for a suitable replacement. Advertisements placed in the *Daily Mail* and *Sporting Life* drew hundreds of enthusiastic but unsuitable applications from demobbed British aficionados. The success of one applicant, who went by the name of "Mr. Burton," proved short-lived. He had inhaled so much mustard gas in the trenches that he lasted two months in his new job before his lungs collapsed. For a short period the club struggled under a temporary emergency management committee of limited organizational ability made up of two former players, Juan Arzuaga and Luis Iceta, and the captain, German Echevarria. Then another Englishman, by the name of Fred Pentland, came to the club's rescue.

Pentland was born in Wolverhampton in 1883. He played for the Blackburn Rovers, Brentford, Middlesbrough, Halifax, and Stoke and won five caps for England. After retiring as a player, Pentland traveled to Berlin in 1914 and took charge of the German Olympic soccer team. Within months, the First World War broke out, and he was interned in a civilian detention camp at Ruhleben. Famously, Pentland helped to organize hundreds of prisoners—some of them professional players—into teams to play an informal league championship. After the war he coached the French national team before moving across the Pyrenees to Spain and taking on the job of coach at Santander's Racing.

Since its foundation in 1913, Racing had developed a reputation as one of Spain's better teams, with a proven record of playing an attacking style of soccer. Several of its young players "graduated" to bigger clubs such as Real Madrid. The strategy and tactics of the team improved still further with the arrival of Pentland. He was an advocate of the short passing game, focused on technique and the ball skills he had learned at Blackburn. Pentland dissuaded his players from copying the long-ball and rough tactics Spaniards associated with *Los Ingleses* while encouraging them to pursue the courage and determination on the field that had earned the Spanish national squad its first major victory on the world stage at the 1920 Olympics.

In Bilbao Pentland took on the airs of the archetypal English gentleman, smoking cigars and wearing a bowler hat—on and off the field—for which he earned the nickname *El Bombin* (the Man in the Bowler Hat). One of Pentland's first initiatives at Athletic was to instill a new dress code. Photographs of that time show a somewhat stern, mustachioed figure in a dark suit and impeccably folded pocket handkerchief. He taught his players how to tie their shoelaces correctly ("Get the simple things right and the rest will follow" was among his favorite mantras). He was not a man who took himself too seriously so that even in his sternest poses there was a hint of an ironic smile beneath his mustache and unyielding stare. He was happy to tell his players early on that they could celebrate a famous victory by collectively stamping on his hat as he had a good stock he could replenish it from. The fact that he went through several hats was an enduring testimony to his success at the club.

Pentland became the most successful manager ever to sit on the bench at San Mames, taking Athletic, in two spells at the club, to five cup wins and two league championships, and in the process becoming the first manager in the history of Spanish soccer to win *La Liga* and Spanish Cup double. His "records" include taking Athletic to a 12–1 win over FC Barcelona in 1931, the worst defeat ever suffered by the Catalan team.

Two years earlier Pentland helped coach the Spanish national squad to its first significant international achievement since it had won the silver medal in the Olympics in 1920—and it was in a game against England. His appointment followed a spell at Atletico de Madrid, which he had guided to victory in the Campeonato del Centro, central Spain's regional championship, a rare achievement for the historically underperforming "other" Madrid team. Pentland had a unique insight into the game, gathered from his personal experience of both British and Spanish soccer, and he was adept at picking teams that could combine virility with style and speed.

The Spanish national team that played England on May 15, 1929, drew more than half of its squad from Real Madrid. There was a dominating presence of Basque-born players who had moved to the Spanish capital or continued to play for regional clubs such as Real Sociedad and Osasuna. The backbone of the team was formed of players who were destined to distinguish themselves in one of Real Madrid's most successful periods in the early 1930s. They included Basque-born Jacinto Quincoces—a champion *pelota pala* player—who with Ciriaco formed one of the most skilled and toughest defenses in Real Madrid's history, helping the club secure two successive league championships between 1931 and 1933 and then winning two Spanish Cups (as the King's Cup was known in the years of the Second Republic) after ending up in second place in the league.

The match against England at Atletico de Madrid's Metropolitano stadium was held in the same year that Barcelona hosted FIFA's historic meeting at which member countries agreed on the staging of the first-ever World Cup. Spain was being taken seriously as a soccer nation. With tickets sold out two days previously, some forty-five thousand fans gathered to watch a match that although a "friendly" also had national pride at stake. England went into the match on the back of a 4–1 win over France and a 5–1 victory over Belgium, but with true form under scrutiny following a number of questionable refereeing decisions. "The Englishmen played none too well. They lacked speed and will have to play better if they are to beat Spain, who a month ago beat France by eight goals to one," reported the *Daily Sketch and Graphic*. Significantly, one of England's star players, the Middlesbrough forward George Camsell, had been injured in the match.

It was the 167th international match England had played since 1872. Spain, by contrast, was playing only its 32nd game since its first major foreign engagement in 1920. Only a year earlier it had suffered a humiliating 1–7 defeat at the hands of Italy in the Amsterdam Olympics. In the preceding 24 matches against non-British teams, England had won 23 and drawn 1, scoring a total of 121 goals and conceding only 27. All the major European national teams had been crushed by the seemingly invincible English squad: Austria (three times), Hungary (three times), Bohemia (once), Belgium (seven times), France (six times), Sweden (twice), and Luxembourg (once).

Hardly surprising, Spain's chances of success were poorly rated by the British media. Their perception of Spanish players was that while capable of passing the ball around neatly enough, they lacked the drive and ruthlessness of Anglo-Saxons in front of the goal. Spain was viewed by the British media, somewhat patronizingly, as a soccer nation whose star was rising and with the potential of being the best on the Continent, but not up to the standards maintained by the English.

Early on, the match seemed to prove the pundits right, with England gaining a clear superiority of two goals within the first twenty minutes. The first had Leicester City's outside right, Hugh Adcock, beating several Spaniards before finishing off with a fine cross that Jose Carter of West Bromwich Albion delivered on. A similar movement from both players led to the second goal within a few minutes.

Then, just when a lesser team might have collapsed, Spain rallied in what the Spanish media would later portray as a heroic fight back, worthy of the best fighting spirit of *La Furia*. Real Madrid's Gaspar Rubio headed their first goal before his club teammate Jaime Lazcano scored with what the *Times* correspondent conceded was a "brilliant shot." The two teams were level by halftime.

In a match that enraptured the stadium and was conveyed live nationally across Spain on radio for the first time, both teams returned to the second half determined to do battle. According to the *Times*, England rallied first after their goalkeeper, Ted Hufton, had thwarted a Spanish attack and the forwards swept down "in fine style," leaving it to Joe Bradford to put them ahead. "With the game drawing to a close England looked like good winners," the *Sporting Life* reported. Then Spain drew level with a goal in the seventy-ninth minute by Lazcano, followed by a third by the only amateur in the squad, Severino Goiburu, eight minutes before the final whistle. "I never thought I would live to see the day when 11 Spanish players humbled the might—more or less—of English soccer," wrote the correspondent of the *Daily Express* days after the game, although that paper, along with most English papers, had not bothered to cover the game on a major scale.

As soccer writer Jonathan Wilson has noted in his forensic historical analysis of the match, the underreporting by the English was perhaps one of its most striking aspects from a modern perspective, given the historical ties and animosity between the two nations. As Wilson notes, "Among the stories deemed more important than England's first defeat to foreign opposition were the presentation of a grandmother clock to Wally Hammond, Tottenham's 2–0 victory over the Army on a tour of Malta, Portsmouth signing William Hill from Scunthorpe United and the fact that the final of the British Women's

Open gold was to be contested between Miss Joyce Wethered and Miss Glenna Collett."

At the international level, Spain's national team revived some of the glory of the early Olympic days. Its 4–3 victory on May 15, 1929, at home against England, was the first time the English team had ever lost a match outside a Home Championship. As far as the Spaniards were concerned, the man in the bowler hat had come up aces.

However, any hopes that Spain might have had of replacing England's hegemony in international soccer proved premature. When the two sides met again at Highbury in 1931, Spain was thrashed 7–1. Prior to the game the Spanish had picked up some more impressive victories over Italy, Yugoslavia, and Portugal and had just one defeat, to Czechoslovakia. But as the Austrian Willy Meisl, one of the leading sports journalists at that time, wrote, "What the English could not know was the incredible inferiority complex under which these early Continental sides labored when they stepped on to a British soccer field. For them it was sacred soil. They were so over-awed they hardly dared put a foot down. If they were hit by an early goal, let alone by a couple, their strained nerves were shattered and they were beaten before they had a chance to get going." And that is exactly what happened. With only four minutes into the game, Spain already found itself two down, with goals from Portsmouth's Jack Smith and Everton's Tommy Johnson (formerly of Manchester City), and from then on it was all downhill, or almost. After conceding the seventh goal, Spain got a small consolation: Athletic's Gorostiza, the Basque-born outside-left, nicknamed *la Bala Roja* because of his red hair and fiery shooting, hit a powerful strike that the England goalkeeper, Hibbs, could not stop.

The Spaniards struggled to control their dribbling and passing play in the muddy turf conditions and were overwhelmed by the physicality of the English players. England's defenders were content to pump the ball forward for the strikers to chase. The ease of the victory restored the myth of England's superiority and a perception among English fans that the earlier defeat of 1929 was an aberration, caused by the Spanish heat, the poverty of the Spanish soil, and the absence of England's best players. Nevertheless, in Spain's former colonies new ideas were being embraced that would in time provide new life to Spanish soccer.

Uruguayan captain José Leandro Andrade

CHAPTER 10

The South American Connection

Both the shortcomings of Athletic, one of Spain's most successful soccer clubs, when faced with foreign competition in the first decades of the twentieth century and the emergence, by contrast, of a new soccer power outside Spain were only too evident during a South American tour by a group of Basque players in the summer of 1921. The players, many of them Spanish internationals, including Belauste, the Olympic goal scorer who had become a national legend, set off by ship from Lisbon on June 27. The team arrived just over two weeks later and were received like heroes by a large and enthusiastic Spanish (mainly Basque) immigrant community in the port of Buenos Aires.

Their first match was against a selection of players from the Argentine capital. Most came from the working-class neighborhood of Barracas, where Alfredo Di Stéfano was born five years later. The visitors were overwhelmed by the superior style and skill of their hosts. The Argentines put on an extraordinary display of *tiqui-taca* soccer: control, possession, and quick, short movements of the ball.

In Argentina soccer had escaped from the manicured fields of the rich and discovered new roots in the slums, on barren earth and against makeshift walls. It delivered a new language that connected the local underclass with the poor immigrants who arrived from southern Europe, northern Spain, Italy, and the Middle East. As South American novelist Eduardo Galeano has written, "A homegrown way of playing soccer, like the homegrown way of dancing, came to be born. Dancers drew filigrees on a single floor tile, and soccer players created their own language in that tiny space where they chose to retain and possess the ball rather than kick it, as if their feet were hands braiding the leather. . . . On the feet of the first *Creole* virtuosos *el toque*, the touch, was born: the ball was strummed as if it were a guitar, a source of music."

The Basque team lost 0–4. They recovered some of their honor in the following games played in the cities of Rosario in Argentina, Montevideo in Uruguay, and São Paolo in Brazil, but this did not turn into the triumphant tour that they had expected. The final tally was two victories, one draw, and five defeats.

Whereas Spanish club soccer had mixed fortunes when it faced the emerging power of South America, Spain's national squad simply found itself humiliated. The squad returned from the 1924 Olympics, effectively a world championship, empty-handed, with Uruguay taking the gold. It was Uruguay that was set to place South America firmly on the map of world soccer when its team swept down on the Paris Olympics and crushed all opponents.

Other South American countries, Germany, and the United Kingdom were absent from the Olympics, yet soccer confirmed itself as one of the world's most popular sports, with thousands of spectators watching twenty-five matches over a two-week period. Uruguay beat Switzerland 3–0 after demolishing Yugoslavia, the United States, France, and Holland. French writer Gabriel Hanot reported on the arrival of an exciting new soccer-playing nation: "The principal quality of the victors was a marvelous virtuosity in receiving the ball, controlling it and using it. They have such a complete technique that they also have the necessary leisure to note the position of partners and team mates. They do not stand still waiting for a pass. They are on the move, away from markers, to make it easy for team mates." Hanot went on to compare the Uruguayans with the early English pioneers who had such an early influence on Spanish soccer: "The English are excellent at geometry and remarkable surveyors. . . . They play a tight game with vigor and some inflexibility." By contrast, the Uruguayans "are supple disciples of the spirit of fitness rather than geometry. They have pushed towards perfection the art of the feint and swerve and the dodge, but they know also how to play directly and quickly. They are not all ball jugglers. . . . They create a beautiful soccer, elegant but at the same time varied, rapid, powerful and effective." Hanot's conclusion left little room to doubt that a revolution on no small a scale was sweeping through international soccer. "These fine athletes are to the English professionals like Arab thoroughbreds next to farm horses."

In a press conference attended mainly by French journalists, the Uruguayan captain José Leandro Andrade, said that his players had trained by chasing chickens on the ground. The early influence of Latin Americans on Spanish soccer had a magical quality to it, verging on the fantastical. The skills involved were real enough, however, and foreshadowed some of the great figures of Spanish club soccer, from Di Stéfano to Maradona and Ronaldo and later Lionel Messi.

Andrade himself was an emblematic figure with the La Celeste Olimpica, as the Uruguayan team came to be known. He was also the first black player to earn respect at the international level, despite his off-field extravagances. When the Paris tournament was over Andrade stayed on for a while in the French capital, enjoying a bohemian lifestyle and becoming a popular figure of the nightlife cabaret scene—dressed in a top hat, striped jacket, silk scarf, and bright-yellow gloves and carrying a cane with a silver handle.

Four years later he won his second Olympic gold medal, when Uruguay faced a strong challenge from Argentina in the final, and in 1930 again he was instrumental in the Uruguayan team's success, this time conquering the first-ever World Cup to be organized by FIFA. Thirteen countries took part in the tournament hosted by the two-time Olympic champions, only four of them from Europe—Belgium, Romania, Yugoslavia, and France. In common with other countries that absented themselves, Spain argued that taking its team across the Atlantic in the midst of a growing recession was something the country could not afford, a poor excuse given that Uruguay agreed to cover all the costs, including travel.

In reality Spain was struggling to come to terms with the humiliating fact that its former Latin American colonies were producing as good if not better soccer—the old colonial master was in danger of reverting to pupil status. The Black Marvel, Andrade, was not the only player to dazzle fans with his exquisite plays. Another of the cast of South American legends was Ramón Unzaga, the inventor of the bicycle kick, or *chilena*, in tribute to his nationality, which was first used on Spanish soil by a fellow national, David Arellano, during a tour of the country by his team, the Chilean team Colo-Colo, in 1927.

By then the growing superiority of Latin American players showed in their ability to bring down to earth some of the great myths of Spanish club and international soccer history. For example, in a home game played between Uruguay's Peñarol and Español of Barcelona, the thirty-six-year-old veteran Uruguayan striker José

Piendibene managed to completely outfox the great goalkeeper Zamora with a typical display of masterful ball control. Galeano takes us through the moves:

> The play came from behind. Anselmo slipped around two adversaries, sent the ball across to Suffiati and then took off expecting a pass back. But Piendibene asked for it. He caught the pass, eluded Urquizu and closed in on the goal. Zamora saw that Piendibene was shooting for the right corner and he leapt to block it. The ball hadn't moved. She was asleep on his foot: Piendibene tossed her softly to the left side of the empty net. Zamora managed to jump back, a cat's leap, and grazed the ball with his fingertips when it was already too late.

People still talk about that goal in Uruguay, although the suggestion that Piendibene was given a new house as a prize for beating the greatest soccer player in the world proved false. He was given a gold medal instead. After the Basque squad and Español, other teams like Barca and Real Madrid toured the Southern Cone. The experience for a while raised the standard of play in the nascent Spanish league, formed in 1926. However, the promise of Spanish soccer as epitomized by Spain's victory over England three years later foundered amid the growing political instability in the run-up to the country's civil war.

FC Barcelona President: Josep Sunyol

CHAPTER 11

Gathering Storms

When in the early 1920's the dust had temporarily settled on the cata-
clysms of war, revolution, hyper-inflation and austerity, there was in all
these societies a profound need and desire for hedonism and escape,
for pleasure and for play, from the fabulously rich to the appalling poor.
Soccer was one of these pleasures.

—DAVID GOLDBLATT, *The Ball Is Round*

Spain was not immune to the transformation of the political and social landscape that impacted most of Europe as a result of the First
World War. If the development of its soccer still lagged behind that of
several other countries on both sides of the Atlantic, it was because its
development as a country too seemed out of step, out on a limb, and
seemingly permanently in crisis.

Between 1921 and 1922, the emerging giants of Spanish club soccer, FC Barcelona and Real Madrid, each inaugurated a new stadium.

Of the two, FC Barcelona's Les Corts, built a few blocks away from Barca's current stadium, the Camp Nou, had the biggest capacity, with seating for twenty thousand and a covered stand for a further fifteen hundred. Real Madrid's Chamartín stadium, constructed on the very site where the Santiago Bernabéu stadium stands today, had a capacity of only fifteen thousand.

Although there can be little doubt that attendance records generally for Spanish soccer matches had been increasing up to and during the First World War, the growth was still of a lower order of magnitude to, say, that of England during the early twentieth century or during this time of the emerging nation-states in central Europe. For example, in 1922 the crowds of that year for the most popular game— that between Austria and Hungary—had swollen in just four years from fifteen thousand to sixty-five thousand.

The following year the young Spanish prince Don Gonzalo marked the inauguration of Real Madrid's stadium by kicking the ball of honor and in a boyish voice crying out, "Hala, Madrid" (Let's go, Madrid). The phrase would be adopted as the club's official rallying cry and echoed by generations of fans to this day. Just four months later, on September 13, 1923, Captain-General Miguel Primo de Rivera staged a bloodless military coup and shut down parliament, claiming that party politics had become corrupt and the monarchy ineffectual while making a token gesture to the aristocracy by leaving Alfonso XIII as a symbolic king without power.

Prompted into action in part by the politicians' mishandling of a protracted Spanish colonial war in Morocco, Primo de Rivera was an emotional Spanish patriot of the old school, believing that Spaniards should be Catholic and united. He considered atheism, including all its manifestations such as Marxism, to be a mark of the devil. His greatest enemies were Spaniards who called themselves anything but Spaniards and toyed with the idea of becoming more separate from

Madrid, by pursuing their own devolved government and speaking their own language.

Among Spain's most powerful regions, it was Catalonia that posed the greatest threat in the eyes of the dictator, with its nationalist movement becoming increasing radicalized and lurching to the left. A clash between the new military government and Catalonia's potent sporting symbol, FC Barcelona, seemed inevitable, and so it proved.

June 14, 1925, came to be a date remembered in the collective memory of Catalan nationalism and many Barca fans as a day of infamy. The occasion was a fund-raising game FC Barcelona had organized for the Orfeo Catala, a choral society set up to carry on the work of the father figure of Catalan music, Josep Anselm Clavé. At halftime the crowd whistled as a band of English marines from a visiting Royal Navy vessel played the first notes of the Spanish national anthem. When the marines abruptly stopped and then struck up again, playing the English national anthem, the crowd broke into spontaneous applause. The demonstration had been fueled by Primo de Rivera days earlier banning the public use of the Catalan language and closing down local government offices. Now the Madrid government moved in with a vengeance, with Barcelona's newly appointed civil governor, Joaquín Milans del Bosch, fining the Barca directors and imposing a six-month ban on Barcelona's activities as a club and as a team.

A majority of Spaniards were immensely relieved when the increasingly ineffectual Primo de Rivera resigned and left Spain in January 1930. But the dictatorship had also alienated popular support for a king who had passively acquiesced in the authoritarian regime. King Alfonso XIII was forced to abdicate and go into exile when Spain's new Republican government was proclaimed by a group of liberal intellectuals.

Newsreel film of those heady days shows thousands of Spaniards taking to the streets of Madrid and Barcelona following the proclamation on April 14, 1931. Suddenly, after centuries of political instability fueled by dynastic struggles and military interventions, there seemed to be the possibility of a truly democratic Spain. It proved a pipe dream, as a succession of increasingly radicalized, short-lived left-wing and right-wing elected civilian governments struggled with the reality of Spain's continuing economic and political underdevelopment: vast disparities between rich and poor, particularly in the countryside; unresolved tensions between centralists and the regions, as Catalan and the Basque nationalists pressed for increasing autonomy from Madrid; bitter quarrels among groups of democrats about how far left, anticlerical, and decentralized the new Republic should be; and all against the enduring presence of two traditionally powerful institutions—the military and the Catholic Church—that saw its privileges under threat.

In Barcelona politics and soccer turned into an increasingly volatile mix. In 1928, as the Primo de Rivera regime was entering its death throes, a young radical lawyer named Josep Sunyol became a member of FC Barcelona's governing board and president of the Federation of Associated Catalan Football Clubs.

Sunyol used his newspaper, *La Rambla*—which split its coverage between sport and nonsport items—to appeal to a new social order where soccer and politics formed an essential part of a new democratic society. While the perspective of soccer through the prism of a reformist political agenda seemed to mirror the enlightened ideals of the early founders of Real Madrid, Sunyol's politics was firmly rooted in Catalonia, with FC Barcelona as a role model. In an early manifesto, Sunyol explained what he meant by his slogan, "Sport and Citizenship." He wrote, "To speak of sport is to speak of race, enthusiasm, and the optimistic struggle of youth. To speak of citizenship is to speak of the Catalan civilization, liberalism, democracy, and spiritual Endeavour."

As a lawyer and a journalist, Sunyol tried to present himself as, first and foremost, a Catalan patriot rather than a party dogmatist and a true soccer fan. In July 1935 he was elected FC Barcelona's president.

In his acceptance speech he declared that he would endeavor not to let politics get in the way of his work for the club. But for all his love of sport, Sunyol was primarily a politician and regarded the soccer of FC Barcelona as a means to an end rather than an end in itself. Three years earlier, in the summer of 1931 after the proclamation of the Second Republic, he had been elected as a deputy to the new parliament in Madrid as a representative of Esquerra Republicana de Catalunya, a new pro-independence party.

In October 1933, in reaction to the emergence of a conservative government in Madrid, Sunyol's party was among those who backed the unilateral proclamation of a Catalan government—a "Catalan state within the federal republic of Spain." The initiative was blocked by Madrid, only to be revived and enacted after a Popular Front coalition of socialists and communists was swept to power in February 1936 when Sunyol and other Catalan radical nationalists once again took center stage.

For all the political effervescence, this was not a period of sporting success for FC Barcelona, under Sunyol's presidency, and the club failed to win either the new league championship or the Spanish Cup in the 1930s. By contrast, Real Madrid on May 6, 1934, ended a seventeen-year drought in the Spanish Cup championship, beating Valencia 2–1 in the final and ending Athletic Bilbao's run of uninterrupted success in the tournament. The final against Valencia was played in Barcelona. When the Madrid team arrived back at the Spanish capital's Atocha station, they were greeted with a rendering of the "Himno de Riego," the new national anthem of the Republican government after the demise of the Primo de Rivera dictatorship and the abdication and exile of King Alfonso XIII. The club had dropped *Royal* from its title in deference to the political situation.

Two seasons later, on June 22, 1936, Madrid played FC Barcelona in their first-ever Spanish Cup final clash. The game was played in

Valencia's Mestalla stadium. Madrid was leading 2–1 when Zamora threw himself full-stretch toward the left-hand goalpost and blocked a last-ditch attempt at an equalizer by the Catalan striker Escola. Within minutes the game was over, and Zamora, El Divino, was raised on the shoulders of his joyous fans. The team received an even more ecstatic welcome when they returned by train to the Spanish capital, as Madrid fans once again converged on the Atocha station.

By then, however, no amount of celebration could hide the fact that Spain was on the verge of disintegration, the incompatible politics of the Left and Right lurching out of control toward civil war in a context of increasing violence. A day after the Madrid-Barcelona match, General Francisco Franco, then the captain-general of the Canary Islands, wrote to the Spanish prime minister, Casares Quiroga, warning of growing military unrest. Franco had yet fully to throw his hat into the ring with the plotters of military officers and right-wing civilians, but it was just a matter of time before he did. The conspirators, concerned about the violent anticlericalism and the growing militancy of industrial and agricultural workers, and what they saw as the breakdown of order, were plotting a coup to stop the country from lurching further toward socialism. On July 18 the military uprising began, and the country's history of failure, division, and frustration gave birth to its ultimate despair, the Spanish Civil War.

Chamartin stadium during the Spanish Civil War

CHAPTER 12

Soccer Against the Enemy: Part 1

On July 19, 1936, the day after the military uprising had been initiated in the South, local fans in the northern Galician city of
Corunna turned up in the thousands to watch a match in the Riazor
stadium between the local team Deportivo and their regional rival,
Celta. A game-day report in the local newspaper *Voz de Galicia* commented, "In these times in which emotions are stirred in all sorts of
different ways, a soccer match is a welcome event because, while it
might seem paradoxical, it can act as a sedative to our shattered nerves."

Initial support for the military uprising varied from region to region. Thus, while Madrid and much of Catalonia resisted the coup,
other parts of Spain, such as Andalusia, fell to the insurgents. Galicia
was one of the areas where the initial coup was successful and remained in Nationalist (Franco's army) hands through the Civil War.

Although there were no pitched battles, the calm in Galicia proved deceptive. As in the rest of the country, Galicians—many of them no doubt soccer fans—were soon killing each other for reasons that ranged from personal vendettas to ideological beliefs.

As the Civil War deepened and the military rebels captured increasing amounts of territory, the political map of Spain became like an abstract patchwork, with soccer mirroring the new reality of tactical alliances and severed ties. In Galicia, in deference perhaps to Franco's own Galician roots, further games were organized between locally based clubs once the region had been taken over by rebel forces in the early days of the conflict. The next major game between the old rivals Deportivo and Celta was played before thousands of pro-Franco fans in Vigo as a testimonial to General Millán Astray, the controversial founder of the Spanish Foreign Legion. An extreme right-wing fanatic, Millán Astray had lost his left arm and right eye in a previous military campaign in Morocco, earning him the title Glorioso Mutilado (Glorious Amputee.) His most popular war cry was "Viva la muerte" (Long live death). Millán Astray was a grotesque caricature of the Quixotic myth of heroic noncompromise, the personification of violence, cruelty, and fanatical obsession with death that hangs over much of Spanish history.

For a while, soccer in some parts of Spain proved a social palliative, one of the few public acts of the Civil War where the participants treated each other with respect. Other teams that took part in the Galician championship while the Civil War raged elsewhere included Lugo, Racing del Ferrol (the club of Franco's birthplace), and the Pontevedra club Eirina. Isolated games were also played in parts of Andalusia, where Seville and other towns fell earlier on to the military insurgents, and in the Levante region, where a Mediterranean championship involving Valencia, FC Barcelona, and Espanyol (the club's name had been Catalinized under a new pro-Republic administration) was played under the control of the loyal government forces. Elsewhere in Spain's regions, Navarre and Aragon sided early on with the military uprising so that local teams Osasuna and Zaragoza reorganized themselves under the auspices of the Francoist authorities.

But the perception that the world of Spanish soccer could continue much as before proved delusional, as events in the Spanish capital were to show. By the end of November 1936, the initial military uprising in Madrid had been thwarted and the capital city had settled into a long siege. For its own safety, the Republican government moved its headquarters to Valencia, leaving Madrid in the hands of communist and anarchist militias. Days were punctuated with the sound of air-raid warnings and the revolutionary propaganda that spewed from loudspeakers in squares and main avenues. At night and at daybreak came the sinister sound of isolated bursts of machine-gun and rifle fire as Francoist suspects were rounded up and shot.

Since its foundation in 1902, Madrid (whether Real or simply FC) had survived the various changes of regime, adapting to political developments and managing to continue to grow as one of the country's most popular sporting institutions. But now the club faced a major challenge to its organization and sense of identity, with its members, players, and officials dragged unwittingly into the bloodiest civilian strife the capital had ever experienced. The moderate president of the club, Rafael Sánchez-Guerra, was unceremoniously sacked by a workers' committee headed by two Soviet-style commissars. Later there would be further political intervention in the club's affairs by a communist army officer, Lieutenant Colonel Antonio Ortega, who took his orders from the Soviet secret police.

Thus, Madrid (its royal status had been ditched under the Republic, as had that of other clubs), which over the years had increased its popularity across the social divide, was monopolized by a bunch of revolutionaries. One of their first acts was to order a review of the club's membership lists to identify political enemies. Sport in the besieged capital, to the extent that it could be played at all, became a crude propaganda vehicle. Chamartín, the Madrid stadium, was used for parades by militias and Soviet-style mass exhibitions by the youth of the newly created "Spanish Battalion of Sport," which aimed to project an air of revolutionary discipline and health. In the final stages of the siege of Madrid, the stadium's benches and fences were torn up and burned for fuel, bricks and other building materials pilfered, and the turf turned into a rough collectivized vegetable plot to help feed an increasing starving population.

But by then any concept of a national soccer league had been lost in the fog of war. FC Barcelona, for example, rejected a request from Madrid FC and Atletico de Madrid that they be allowed to compete in the Catalan championship in areas of Spain that remained in Republican hands. Barca officials argued that the involvement of clubs from central Spain would undermine the traditional "Catalan" spirit of the competition. The Catalan championship went ahead nevertheless in the first year of the Civil War with six "Catalan" teams instead of the usual twenty: FC Barcelona, Espanyol, Gerona, Jupiter, Badalona, and Sabadell. It proved short-lived, however.

Catalonia resisted the military uprising for much of the Civil War. Nonetheless, these were turbulent and unpredictable times, not least in the Catalan capital, Barcelona, where the chaotic and violent revolutionary atmosphere was being documented by the English volunteer soldier and author George Orwell for his masterly work *Homage to Catalonia*. Orwell would write of his time in Barcelona: "During all those weeks that I spent there, there was a peculiar evil feeling in the air—an atmosphere of suspicion, fear, uncertainty, and veiled hatred. . . . At the Red Cross aid centre on the corner of the *Placa de Catalunya* the police had amused themselves by smashing most of the windows. . . . Down at the bottom of the *Ramblas* near the quay, I came across a queer sight: a row of militiamen, still ragged and muddy from the front, sprawling exhaustedly on the chairs placed there for the boot blacks."

For a while FC Barcelona endured as best it could, given the circumstances. A reduced number of local members kept coming to the stadium, and occasional games were played by conscripts on leave. But the club, in the hands of another "workers committee" was drawn into the increasingly radicalized politics of the city. By the spring of 1937, politically moderate FC Barcelona officials and those players who had not been conscripted were looking for a way to escape. It came in the form of an invitation from a Mexican benefactor, basketball player–turned-businessman Manuel Soriano. He invited FC Barcelona to travel to Mexico and play a series of soccer games with leading local teams. The deal was that he would pay Barca fifteen thousand dollars in cash, with an up-front payment of eight thousand dollars deposited in the loyally pro-Republican Spanish consulate in Mexico City. He would also cover the cost of travel and all other expenses.

FC Barcelona's coach at the time was Patrick O'Connell. A former captain of Ireland, O'Connell had had a distinguished career beginning in Belfast before playing in England for Sheffield Wednesday and Manchester United. O'Connell's Spanish soccer career started in 1922 when he replaced Fred Pentland as coach of Racing Santander. The Irishman impressed the club's owners by building on Pentland's methods, encouraging the native skills of dribbling with the ball, while training his defenders in the long upfield passing and crosses that he had learned as a young player in Ireland and Britain. He also placed great emphasis on fitness, discipline, and teamwork. This represented a cultural shift for many Spaniards, on and off the field.

The seven years O'Connell spent at Racing were formative years for the club. O'Connell's own experience as a defender proved hugely valuable when during the 1926–1927 season a new offside rule was introduced. He trained his defenders in moving forward so as to catch the other side's attacking forward and leave him offside when he gathered the ball from a pass. His main achievement, however, was in establishing Racing's rightful claim to be treated as an important soccer club by its loftier rivals. Thanks to O'Connell, Racing was able to successfully challenge an attempt by a small group of clubs led by FC Barcelona, Real Madrid, and Athletic Bilbao to restrict the access of smaller clubs to the new Spanish league. The so-called minimalists wanted the Primera Liga to be composed only of them and three Basque clubs, Real Sociedad, Arenas, and Real Club Unión de Irún. The "maximalist lists" made up of all the other smaller Spanish clubs organized a parallel championship, which Racing won. A subsequent compromise agreement led to the creation of an expanded Primera Liga in which Racing was among those allowed to play.

Having secured Racing's place in top Spanish soccer, O'Connell spent two seasons as manager of Real Oviedo in Asturias, helping to mold the newly created club into a competitive sporting institution. O'Connell then spent a further three seasons at Betis where he became a popular figure with the Andalusians and developed a love of flamenco.

O'Connell, or Don Patricio, as he was now popularly referred to, had become accustomed to his expatriate status and was seemingly content to maintain a distant if dutiful relationship with the family he had left in England, sending them regular bank transfers drawn from the income he earned as manager. He spent these turbulent years in regions of Spain with a strong tradition of industrial and rural militancy that surfaced in the run-up to the Spanish Civil War. His Irish background had left him better prepared than most expatriates for the volatile atmosphere of Spanish politics, and he fitted in well with a club that was proud of its populist roots.

Under O'Connell, Betis achieved considerable success on the field. After becoming the first Andalusian club to qualify for the Primera

Liga, Betis went on to win the championship on April 28, 1935, with a crushing 5–0 victory over Racing. The night before the game, which was played in Santander, O'Connell visited the Racing squad at the hotel where they were staying. Racing was way down in the league table and had no chance of winning the championship, regardless of the outcome of the game. By contrast, Betis was at the top of the table but had to win if it was not to be overtaken and lose the championship to its main rival that season, Real Madrid. O'Connell shared a drink or two with his former club colleagues and then suggested that they might do him a favor. "You've got nothing to play for tomorrow. You won't kill yourselves to beat us, will you?" he asked. The answer from one of the leading players was unequivocal: "I'm sorry, *mister*, but Madrid wants us to win. Our president, José María Cossio, is a Madrid fan himself and is offering us 1,000 *pesetas* per (Racing) player if we win."

It was perhaps just as well that O'Connell left the matter to rest there. To have pursued the conversation with an offer of a counter-bonus (or bribe) would, if found out, have risked tainting his reputation and possibly curtailing his career. Instead, he went on to become manager of FC Barcelona. The timing of his arrival in the Catalan capital suggests that behind O'Connell's ambition to manage one of Europe's leading teams lay the politics of a man not prepared to remain indifferent to the Spanish Civil War. O'Connell took his new job after Catalonia had emerged as one of the regions in Spain where there was a significant proportion of the population determined to defend the Spanish Republic from the right-wing plotters and their friends in the military.

O'Connell arrived in Barcelona in the summer of 1935, days after the soccer club had elected as its president the radical Catalan nationalist Josep Sunyol. Nevertheless, rather than stick it out in revolutionary Barcelona, O'Connell happily volunteered to go on FC Barcelona's tour of Mexico. The team was composed of players who had played with mixed success in the prewar Spanish championship under the tutelage of the Hungarian goalkeeper-turned-coach Franz Platko. They included some of the club's legends such as Balmanya, Escola, Ventorla, and Zabalo, an Anglo-Catalan born in South Shields, England, who had played for Spain in the 1934 World Cup. The team's physiotherapist was Ángel Mur. I caught up with Mur, the only surviving member of the squad, many years later. I was fortunate in finding him a lucid and amusing interviewee, with a good memory.

Mur recalled how he had been working as a gardener at the club's Les Corts stadium when El Mister (O'Connell) told him that he was looking for a replacement for the masseur who had just quit. When Mur said that he only knew about looking after the turf of soccer fields, O'Connell reassured him that he would quickly learn something about the human body. "And that's how I ended up going to Mexico with a suit I was given by one player and a suitcase I was given by another player," Mur told me. "I bought myself a couple of books on the anatomy of the human body and got to learn something about the vulnerable parts."

In Mexico City, the team was given a warm official reception by the authorities and local media. But on the team's first night in the capital, the politics of the civil war came back to haunt them. Arriving for dinner at a Spanish dining club, they saw the monarchist flag used by Franco's forces flying over the entrance. Then some of the players found themselves barracked by a group of Spanish businessmen who criticized them for being anti-Francoist.

FC Barcelona went on to play six games against local opposition, of which it won four. One local newspaper report in *El Universo* reported that the team did not play the best soccer in Spain (such an accolade was left at the time for the Basques) but that the tour itself had left a "good taste," because the players had "behaved like true gentlemen." After Mexico the expedition moved north of the Rio Grande and had an unbeaten run of four games in New York against teams that ranged from a US "selection" to others put together separately by the Hispanic, Jewish, and Irish communities.

By the end of September 1937 Barca had run out of places to escape to, and Rosendo Calvet, the club secretary, gathered everyone to a crisis meeting. The "tourists" were offered a stark choice: they could return to Barcelona and face whatever uncertain outcome awaited them, or they could stay away from Spain, effectively as exiles. Of the sixteen players, seven chose to follow Calvet, O'Connell, Mur, and the team doctor back home, while nine decided to stay in Mexico— including Ventorla, who had fallen in love with the niece of the Mexican president, Lázaro Cárdenas. When the rump of the team returned, FC Barcelona struggled to stay afloat, as Calvet had taken twelve thousand dollars in clear profit from the tour and transferred it to an account in Paris.

On January 8, 1939, a Barca reserve team played the last soccer game in Spanish territory held by the Republic against a minor local team called Martinenc and won 3–1. Eighteen days later, Franco's army entered the city of Barcelona, and the streets and balconies lining the city's main artery, the Diagonal, filled with cheering supporters. On March 27 Franco took Madrid, the last major city held by Republican forces.

Basque refugee children, Southampton, England, 1937

CHAPTER 13

Soccer Against
the Enemy: Part 2

On May 22, 1937, the Spanish Civil War had nearly another two years to run when nearly four thousand refugee children accompanied by teachers and priests arrived in the port of Southampton on board the SS *Habana* after crossing the Bay of Biscay from northern Spain. The ship had left a day earlier with its human cargo—the biggest single influx ever of child refugees into Britain—from Bilbao, as the Basque port faced conquest and occupation by the besieging forces loyal to General Francisco Franco. The children had been evacuated to escape the horrors of the conflict. Amid much political controversy back at home, Britain had waived its policy of nonintervention and agreed to escort Basque refugee ships to safe haven.

Conditions aboard the SS *Habana* were cramped and depressing, exacerbating the children's feelings of distress from being separated from their families and sent off to a foreign land and an uncertain future. As the ship tossed and turned in the rough seas, children cried in the night, calling out for their mothers and fathers. Among them were fourteen-year-old Raimundo Lezama and his brother Luis from Bilbao's industrial suburb of Barakaldo, the sons of a ship worker who had been detained in the Republican-held port of Sagunto and would spend much of the Civil War in prison.

While Mrs. Lezama was left caring for her only remaining child, a young baby girl, the two boys were thrown into an extraordinary new environment on arrival on English soil. Waiting for them were hundreds of volunteers and government officials with a relief operation that in its generosity exemplified the deep popular emotions stirred in Britain by the Spanish Civil War. Tumultuous scenes greeted the *Habana* as it berthed in the Southampton dock. The next day, the local newspaper the *Echo* headlined with the words "Basque Children Cheerfully Taking to Camp Life" and commented on "the excitement of feeding the multitude" in the temporary relief camps set up nearby. Hundreds of sympathizers converged on the town from around the UK, bearing gifts and food. A Salvation Army band played and a BBC crew filmed, all amid bunting left over from the coronation of King George VI that had taken place less than a fortnight before and had been deliberately left hanging to give the occasion a festive air. Later one of the children would recall, "When we entered the bay of Southampton, we thought we had entered a wonderland. Every little house lining the bay had its own pretty garden, well-tended, and all decorated to celebrate the coronation. Everything was bunting, flags, music playing, and people waving their handkerchiefs at us."

It was not quite so idyllic as it appeared, however. Fearful that the children might be bearers of typhoid or some other potentially deadly infectious disease from the war zone, the Home Office insisted that each child be meticulously examined by health officers and disinfected in public baths. The camp where the children were initially taken and housed in tents soon turned into a muddy quagmire after two violent thunderstorms. Inexperienced volunteer aid workers struggled to communicate with children who spoke only Spanish and in some cases Basque. Yet the adults tried to keep the young amused with excursions, film shows, and a representation of Shakespeare's *Midsummer Night's Dream*. But Southampton's North Stoneham facility was only ever envisaged as a transit camp, and by September 1937, the Lezama brothers along with the other children had been dispersed to private homes and government-run residences.

Raimundo Lezama, separated from his brother, stayed in Southampton. He was given shelter, food, and rudimentary English lessons in a hostel run by nuns called Nazareth House, about a half mile away from the Dell, the stadium of Southampton FC. Raimundo was fed well by the nuns and subjected to a relatively benign regime that included music and outdoor activities, mainly soccer. While still a teenager he was scouted by Southampton FC, progressing from the schoolboy to the club's "B" team and making his first-team debut as a goalkeeper on June 1, 1940, ten months after the outbreak of World War II. A few months later, and after a brief period working as a driver for the Royal Air Force, Raimundo was reunited with his brother, and both returned to Spain, where Franco had emerged victorious in the Civil War a year earlier.

In March 1937, about the time the Lezama brothers boarded the *Habana*, local politicians redefined Athletic Bilbao as the matrix of a national team representing the Basque Country called El Euskadi. The cause of the new national team had as one of its most fervent supporters and organizers José Antonio Aguirre, the first *lehendakari*, or president, of Euskadi (the Basque lands of Spain not including Navarre) during the Spanish Civil War. Aguirre in his youth had himself played for Athletic. Although he never made his mark as a player, Aguirre had developed a politician's instinct. He had a keen sense of the club's popular cultural roots and of the growing propaganda value of soccer as it developed into an international mass sport.

Aguirre's Basque government was formed at a time when most of the region it claimed to represent was already occupied by the military rebel troops, except for the region of Vizcaya with Bilbao at its heart. After setting about creating a Basque army to fight for the Republic's survival, Aguirre hit on the idea of having a soccer squad from the region go on a foreign tour to raise funds and international support for his cause. At the end of March 1937, with the Civil War reaching new levels of brutality on both sides, and at a time when the national soccer league was no longer functioning, a group of players responded to Aguirre's call to arms by presenting themselves for training and selection at Bilbao's San Mames stadium. There were some key reinforcements. Among them two Basque-born leading Spanish internationals, the brothers Luis and Pedro Regueiro, who had spent the years leading up to the Spanish Civil War playing for FC Madrid, and Isidro Langara from Real Oviedo in Asturias. While playing at the Asturian club, Langara became a three-time winner of the Pichichi trophy, awarded to the top scorer in the Spanish league. The striker became the figurehead of the celebrated *delanteros electricos* (electrical forwards) whose youthful talent and speed with the ball steamrolled opponents.

Among the other Basque players who traveled from other regions of Spain for the historic gathering in San Mames were Enrique Larrinaga from Racing Santander and two of the best Spanish defenders of the 1930s. One was Pedro Areso, an FC Barcelona player formerly of Betis whose ability to disrupt even the best-laid attack from the opposing side earned him the nickname El Stop. The other was Serafin Aedo, who played alongside Areso at Betis during the 1934–1935 season when the Sevillian team won the Spanish *Liga* for the first and only time in its history. Aedo was hoping to follow his friend Areso and pursue his professional career at FC Barcelona when the outbreak of the Civil War frustrated his plans after playing only one friendly with the Catalan club.

As part of the Basque Diaspora, the bulk of the volunteers were Athletic players who had played on the Spanish national squad during the Republic: Gorostiza, Blasco, Iraragorri, Cilaurren, Muguerza, Echevarria, Zubieta, Aguirrezabala. The players had also been involved in the trophy hunting of one of the strongest and most successful clubs in prewar Spanish soccer. This was the Athletic team that between 1930 and 1935 racked up the extraordinary record of two Pichichis (twice won by Gorostiza), a Zamora Prize for the best goalie (Blasco), the biggest thrashing in the history of the Spanish league (12–1 victory over FC Barcelona in 1931), two Copas del Rey, and four league championships. The squad was coached over a period of nearly a month at San Mames—and prior to the start of the extended siege of Bilbao—by a veteran Athletic center-forward of the early 1920s, Manuel Lopez Llamosos, nicknamed Travieso (Artful Dodger) for his mischievous wit, cunning, and restless unpredictability. Travieso took good care of the players, including supervising the tailoring of the team colors. However, for reasons that remain a mystery, he decided not to join them the day they set off on their foreign tour with a squad of eighteen.

His place as coach was taken by Pedro Vallana, a former Spanish international who had played for the Arenas Club de Guencho before becoming a referee. He was accompanied by Athletic's massage therapist, Periko Birichinaga; a sympathetic local journalist, Melchor Alegria; and two officials, Ricardo Irazabal, vice president of the Spanish Soccer Federation under the Republic, and former Athletic president Manuel de la Sota, a member of one of Bilbao's richest industrial family dynasties.

The squad was captained by Luis Regueiro. Such was the propaganda value of the former (Real) Madrid player and Spanish international that pro-Franco military rebels spun a story that he had disappeared after being executed by forces loyal to the Republican government. Regueiro's sympathies were clearly with the Basque cause. He recalled many years later, "With Franco's revolt under way it was no longer possible to play soccer [in Spain]. There was however a huge need to bring home to the rest of the world that we Basques were different to what some wanted to make us out to be. It was this idea that inspired us both in and outside the stadiums we played in abroad, winning games on the pitches, and generating sympathy and friends beyond them."

Not every player was equally enthusiastic about the tour. Some hoped that, like the Civil War, it would prove short-lived. Both turned out to be protracted, fueling divisions that were exacerbated as the Spanish Civil War turned in Franco's favor. One of the players, Zubieta, recalled years later: "We became nomads with our soccer as our only arm. . . . We had embarked on a new life, without knowing where we were heading, and I think that when we crossed the frontier into France, our hope was that we would return soon."

The squad arrived in Paris in the spring and, after being greeted by local representatives of the Basque government, laid a wreath wrapped in the Basque national colors at the Tomb of the Unknown Soldier. In their first game, against the French Racing Club, on April 24, 1937, in the Parc des Princes stadium they won 3–0, with Langara scoring a hat trick. Celebrations over the victory proved short-lived, however, as news came in over French radio of the bombing by the pro-Franco Luftwaffe of the Basque town Guernica. While the bombing and the ensuing mass fatalities among the civilian population became an important propaganda tool for the Republican government, it raised concerns among the players for the safety of the families they had left behind, while also making them think more deeply about where their true political loyalties lay, as Franco moved to extend his control across the Basque Country.

From Paris the tour continued through Czechoslovakia and Poland before reaching Russia, where the squad stayed for two and a half months. Authorized accounts of the tour were written later by individual players, most of which were published during the censorship of the Franco years, when the cause of Basque nationalism became mythified by exiles. They focus on the soccer success of El Euskadi, with a majority of games won against national as well as local club teams and the occasional defeats blamed on a lack of that "fair play" that the Basques had learned from the English. Thus, of the 4–2 defeat against a Czech team in Prague, Langara recalled, "It was an outright robbery. They beat us on penalties. The referee, who seemed to be nervous because of an accident he had suffered just before the game, whistled penalties against us to calm his nerves. And whenever our goalkeeper Blasco blocked the ball, he insisted that the penalty had to be taken again, claiming unjustly that Blasco had moved."

In Moscow the squad was not short of photo opportunities. They were filmed visiting a school and residence where Basque children who had been evacuated were being cared for. But the propaganda seemed to serve Stalin's Russia rather than the cause of the Basque Country. Another player, Zubieta, recalled: "Playing soccer, drinking vodka, and staying in the hotel was how we spent our time in that far away and strange land and we had no contact with anything other than the world of sport." The games played in Moscow drew large crowds of loyal Communist Party officials and members in a display of international solidarity as news reached the squad that the city of Bilbao had fallen to Franco's troops. In Moscow the Basque soccer team's local minders appear to have ensured that the visitors be screened from local political realities, not least the terrible political repression that was then reaching a particularly brutal point in Stalin's Russia. The year 1937 may still be remembered by Basque nationalists as the year of the heroic expedition abroad of El Euskadi—a noble high point in the history of Spanish soccer—but this was also the most tragic and fateful year in the history of the Soviet Union. It was also the year when Stalin extended his "terror," with the aim of physically annihilating the substantial socialist opposition to his bureaucratic and repressive rule.

Nevertheless, such awkward coincidences were ignored when memoirs of the tour were published after Franco's death. Thus, the journalist who accompanied the players, Melchor Alegria, recalled in 1987, "Moscow was a huge success. All the games were played in a magnificent atmosphere, which was also very moving as it showed the understanding that the Russian people had for the suffering of the Basque nation. What proved particularly gratifying was when we were in Leningrad and were asked to stay in Russia at the request of the trade unions and other organizations."

Such a rose-tinted view of the tour was not shared by everyone in the soccer community. The growing influence within soccer's nascent international body, FIFA, of officials sympathetic to the Franco cause meant that some national soccer federations like Argentina's tried to make life complicated for the Basque squad, canceling some planned games. When El Euskadi eventually returned to Paris, some of the players were secretly contacted by Francoist emissaries who told them that they were embarked on a lost cause and urged them to defect.

Only a very small minority of the squad broke ranks, but they were of sufficient standing to prove helpful propaganda tools for Franco during the final two years of the Civil War. The first to quit and sign up to the Franco cause was Athletic's legendary Gorostiza, whose lightning speed as a left-wing forward earned him the nickname Bala Roja, or Red Bullet. He was followed by another Athletic star player and international, the midfielder Echevarria, and by the massage therapist,

Birichinaga. Days later, on a windy autumnal day in October 1937, what remained of the squad boarded a transatlantic French liner, *Ile de France*, in Le Havre and sailed via Cuba to Mexico, where during the 1938–1939 season El Euskadi was allowed to compete in the local national competition, ending as runners up in the league table.

Soon afterward, when the Civil War ended in Spain with Franco's victory, El Euskadi was disbanded, with each player receiving a payment of ten thousand pesetas. A year earlier their coach, Vallana, had left the tour in controversial circumstances. Before departing, he secretly negotiated a payoff equivalent to a two-month salary when his players had not yet been paid a cent. The incident did nothing to enhance a reputation damaged years earlier when in the 1924 Paris Olympics Vallana scored a disastrous own goal in a game against Italy that ended with Spain's early exit from the competition. Rather than return to Franco's Spain, Vallana chose to live in exile in Uruguay, where he worked as a sports journalist after retiring from soccer.

The majority of the team chose to spend the rest of their playing years in other countries in Latin America, thus contributing unwittingly to the soccer cross-fertilization between Spain and its former colonies that continues to this day. In Argentina, Zubieta, Langara, Iraragorri, and Emilin signed with San Lorenzo de Almagro, while Blasco, Cilaurrane, Areso, and Aedo joined River Plate. Others were signed up by the Mexican clubs Asturias and—ironies of ironies—España. Luis Regueiro and Aguirrezabala retired but settled, respectively, in Mexico and Buenos Aires. Although some of these players, such as Iraragorri, returned quietly to Spain after the Franco regime had long been established, the myth of the defiant squad with a strong sense of its separate cultural and political identity endured. As Manuel de la Sota, one of the financial backers of El Euskadi wrote in a prologue to a book on the team published after Franco died: "Bad luck had united us, but that luck turned out to be one of the most fortunate in my life. For thanks to it I came to know examples of our race who as well as being artists of a sport which they taught foreigners to play, were also standard bearers of the dignity of a small people whose name was Euzkadi."

Months before Luis Regueiro played his first games abroad with the Basque national team, another former (Real) FC Madrid player, Santiago Bernabéu, whose name would in time grace one of the great stadia of world soccer, had enlisted in the Franco forces. Whereas Regueiro's Republican sympathies had left him unharmed after the initial military uprising was frustrated in the Spanish capital, Bernabéu's right-wing leanings had put him immediately at risk. Bernabéu was saved from a Republican firing squad thanks to the intercession on his behalf of another Madrid FC supporter and friend, the socialist Spanish ambassador in Paris, Álvaro de Albornoz. Thanks to the diplomat, Bernabéu was granted asylum by the French embassy in Madrid before being smuggled across the Pyrenees. He returned a few months later, in 1937, crossing into Spain from France at Irún and enlisting right away with the Franco forces that had taken the Basque town.

Bernabéu's arrival in Irún, in the midst of the Civil War, was like a chronicle foretold, for it was here during the early 1920s when while playing as a young Madrid player that Bernabéu had famously suggested to his teammates in a game against Real Club Unión de Irún that they should celebrate each goal they scored with the cry "Viva España," a phrase that the Franco forces later adopted as one of their rallying cries. With the passage of time it was reinvented as a popular chant by Real Madrid fans and came to have wider use whenever the Spanish national team played.

There is an old photograph of a still relatively young if already somewhat corpulent Bernabéu, as a corporal in the Franco army, dressed in military cloak and fatigues and smoking a pipe. He is strolling along the streets of the Basque seaside resort of San Sebastián, looking somewhat content with life. And he was. The original photograph was taken after Bernabéu had earned his first military medal for contributing to the rout of the pro-Republican units in the Pyrenean town of Bielsa on June 6, 1938. A few months later, just before Christmas, the first "national" sports newspaper to be published under Franco's rule hit the streets of San Sebastián and other towns "liberated" by the military rebels. It was called *Marca* (brand or mark) in deference to the neo-fascist worship of totemic symbols. The tabloid newspaper, published initially as a weekly and later as a daily, served two interrelated purposes: to act as the official organ of the Franco authorities on sports matters and to turn the mass following of soccer that had been developing since the 1920s from the Left to the Right of the political spectrum. While adopting from the outset a clearly identifiable propagandist tone, it came to mirror the profound changes in the organization and politics of Spanish soccer that deepened as the Civil War reached its end and paved the way for a dictatorship.

Marca's first front page appeared heavily influenced by the racist obsessions of Nazi Germany, which from the outset of the Civil War had helped arm the military insurgents and provided further military assistance. It had a photograph of a blonde girl making the fascist salute in tribute to "all the Spanish sportsmen and women." In fact, the Civil War had meant that individual soccer players were no longer respected by either side for their skills, but supported or condemned depending on what side of the political divide they were perceived to be on. This would do long-term damage to the evolution of Spanish soccer, although Bernabéu himself would reap a good harvest from Franco's victory because of his enduring loyalty to the Generalissimo. During his billeting in San Sebastián, Bernabéu was profiled in *Marca* as an iconic figure. The article paid homage to him as a man who in the 1920s had given Real Madrid some "great days of glory" as a player before serving as a director and then resigning in order to devote himself to "The (anticommunist) Cause." *Marca* dramatized Bernabéu's departure from Madrid, describing his "escape from the ferocious persecution of the red hordes" and noting that while he had sought asylum "in an embassy" (no mention of the French or the Spanish socialist ambassador who had saved his neck), his deliverance into safe hands came only after a series of further dramatic twists in the story of his heroic bid for freedom. The alleged dramas included taking cover as a patient in a general hospital and hiding in a chicken run before escaping through a trapdoor.

The newspaper profile included some memorable quotes from Bernabéu. In one he defined what he saw as the essence of sport in the New Spain that would emerge with Franco victorious: "The spectacle of a few sweaty youths must disappear and give way to a youth that is healthy in body and spirit under the direction of specialist trainers." The article concluded with a final fawning tribute to its subject, noting that it was not just the character of players that was destined to change in the New Spain, but also the fans of Real Madrid, many of whom had supported the Republican government. "If we can count among them [the fans] people like our interviewee, the club's resurgence will be rapid," the article's author stated.

The writer was none other than El Divino himself, Ricardo Zamora, the onetime goalkeeper of FC Barcelona who had transferred to Real Madrid before making one of the most spectacular saves in the history of Spanish soccer. The fate of clubs, players, and fans was sealed as much by where organizations or individuals happened to be as by an ideological preference, with conflicting loyalties resolved by death or the threat of it. At the outbreak of the Civil War, Zamora was confronted by an anarchist militiaman, brandishing a knife and condemning him as a right-wing extremist for contributing occasionally to the conservative Catholic newspaper *Ya*. Zamora, so he related later, had little doubt that his assailant was bent on killing him. But to his surprise the militiaman suddenly dropped the knife and embraced him after identifying himself as a Madrid FC fan. During the ensuing dialogue over the relative merits of Spanish clubs and their star players, the militiaman praised Zamora for all the great saves he had made and for helping his club become champions.

The two men parted company, now the best of friends. Zamora remained suspected by others of being pro-Franco. He was arrested days later and imprisoned without trial in Madrid's Modelo jail. While he was there, a military broadcast from the Andalusian capital of Seville, which had been occupied within hours by forces loyal to Franco, reported that the "nation's goalkeeper" was among dozens of well-known personalities who had been executed by the "reds." The rumor was initially taken seriously enough for masses to be organized in Zamora's memory in towns that had fallen to the Catholic rebels. But it was pure invention, part of the propaganda war.

In the Modelo prison Zamora was periodically paraded by his captors in front of visiting officials as if he were a prize possession. To be called out from your cell in those days was to confront the real prospect that you were on your way to a firing squad. Zamora later recalled that his legs would physically tremble every time he was summoned. However, he was able to survive mentally and physically thanks to the occasional soccer games that jailers and their prisoners played with each other in the Modelo's main yard. Zamora was eventually released after an international campaign was mounted on his behalf in France, and he took refuge in the Argentine embassy in Madrid, where arrangements were made to transport him, his wife, and young son out of Spain. By then Zamora had decided that his best interests lay in remaining unrecognized by the public, at least until he was safely across the Pyrenees. So one day, once his escape plan had been formed, he emerged from the embassy wearing dark glasses and having grown a beard. The disguise did not fool the militiaman who was on sentry duty. "Hey Zamora, *hombre*, what you doing with the beard?" The interrogator turned out to be another FC Madrid fan, so safe passage was ensured.

Zamora made his way to temporary exile via the ports of Valencia and Marseille to Paris. While in the French capital, Zamora gave an interview to the newspaper *Paris Soir* in which he described himself as a "one hundred per cent Spaniard." While carefully avoiding expressing on what side his patriotic sympathies lay, Zamora said he believed he deserved to be better treated by some of his compatriots than to be made to fear for his life. He then journeyed to Nice, where he played for a time with his old friend Pepe Samitier, El Sami, the other star soccer player who had transferred from FC Barcelona to FC Madrid before the Civil War. El Sami's escape from the "reds" also entered the mythology of the conflict, thanks to the newly created sports paper *Marca*. It gave full coverage to Samitier's narrow escape from arrest, his days in hiding, and his eventual arrival in French territory "with two suits, a lot of hunger, and exhausted."

There were other stories of escape and survival. For example, Spain's star international soccer player Jacinto Quincoces served in the pro-Francoist Navarra Brigades and returned to his old club, Real Madrid, after the Civil War. Paulino Alcantara, the FC Barcelona star of the 1920s who retired from soccer to become a doctor, was on a death list for his alleged right-wing sympathies but managed to escape Republican-held Catalonia, the day after the military uprising, and made it across to France, before eventually returning to a life of retirement under Franco's rule following a brief and uneventful spell as coach of Spain's national team in 1951.

Not everyone, by any means, had such luck. Nearly 1 million Spaniards died in the Civil War. They included soccer officials and players who were executed or shot in battle, mostly not because they had worn the colors of any particular club but because they were associated with the enemy side. The victims came from clubs across the divided landscape. They included Gonzalo Aguirre and Valero Rivera, former vice president and treasurer, respectively, of Real Madrid; Damien Cabellas, secretary of Espanyol; Angel Arocha, the Spanish international and FC Barcelona player; and Ramon "Mochin" Triana y del Arroyo, who played for Atletico and Real Madrid. Other "disappeared" players included Oviedo's Gonzalo Diaz Cale and Deportivo La Coruna's Barreras and Hercules FC's Manuel Suárez de Begoña, a former player and coach. In addition, at least four club locations suffered major damage: Real Madrid's Chamartín stadium, Betis's Heliopolis stadium and administrative offices, Oviedo's stadium, and FC Barcelona's social club and archive.

Few personal stories in the history of Spanish soccer sum up the tragedy of the Spanish Civil War as that of Josep Sunyol, elected member of the Catalan parliament and president of FC Barcelona. His last act as club president was on July 30, 1936, a few days after the outbreak of the Civil War, when he presided over an emergency meeting of FC Barcelona's management board. He then drove south to Madrid and up into the nearby Guadarrama hills. He was visiting some Catalan militias who were defending the Spanish capital from the military insurgents when he lost his way and drove into hostile territory. Sunyol was detained and shot on August 6, and his body was thrown into an unmarked grave.

Although his body was never found, Sunyol was posthumously prosecuted for "political crimes" on September 28, 1939, by the Francoist state that had emerged victorious from the Civil War. Two months later an official report condemned Sunyol the politician and president of FC Barcelona for being anti-Spanish.

Franco and Doña Carmen at the Santiago Bernabéu stadium

CHAPTER 14

Franco Rules

A mong the thousands of Republicans summarily executed after the surrender of the Spanish capital to Franco's forces was Lieutenant Colonel Ortega, the former head of security who had for a while taken over the running of Madrid FC as a Soviet-style workers' federation. The new regime moved rapidly to take control of all soccer institutions across the country. A super sports ministry with overarching power over the Spanish Soccer Federation was staffed mainly by right-wing Falangists. Its chief was General José Moscardó, one of Franco's most loyal officers. Major sporting events, including soccer competitions, resonated to the sound of the old Civil War rallying cries "Arriba, España" and "Viva Franco." The fact that both were echoed in the same breath showed the extent to which the old battle cries of Spain's imperial warriors evoking one nation and its patron warrior-saint Santiago (mythified as an anti-Muslim warrior as well as an apostle of Christ) had been subsumed into the public discourse of the Franco dictatorship. Spaniards were expected to put the Civil War behind them while absorbing a war ethic in which military values transcended the level of mere personal valor and were placed in the service of the Francoist state.

Athletic Bilbao was ordered to drop its traditional English title and stick to the Spanish Atletico. The regime resurrected the phrase *Furia Española* (Spanish Fury) as its favorite sporting mantra. Franco held up Basque soccer players as examples of how the game should be played, while stripping the Basque nation, along with Catalonia, of its rights and freedoms. Franco dusted off the image of the ideal Spaniard and of traditional Spain and transferred it to the soccer stadium, there to share company with Don Quixote, in the spirit of non-compromise. No matter that in time such inflexibility might tilt against Quixote's self-interest and against reality. His hopelessness and failure could be forgotten beside the nobility of purpose. Thus, the quintessential virtues of the Spanish soccer player were destined to be bravery, honor, and pride in his endeavor to conquer the enemy. The myth of a deluded Castilian knight had been walking across much of Spanish history, leaving behind a trail of stereotypes and conditioning an entire aesthetic of the Spaniard. But it was given fresh stimulus by the Spanish right-wing militarism fueled by the Spanish Civil War.

It was in the town of Salamanca, turned by Franco from one of Spain's great centers of academic learning into his military headquarters, that a new hybrid soccer emerged from the trenches. It was there in 1937 that a young noncommissioned officer called Francisco González picked the best soccer players among his soldiers and, during their periods of rest from military duties, trained them as a team called Aviacion Nacional, or National Air Force. It competed in an embryonic Copa del Generalissimo with teams from other towns occupied by Franco forces such as Zaragoza and Real Sociedad of San Sebastián.

Aviacion played in blue shorts and trousers, the same colors as the Spanish Falange. It included German, Vazquez, and Campos—young recruits from the Canaries who had learned the ball skills associated with Latin Americans—and some veterans of the old Atletico de Madrid team such as Mesa, Gomez, and Machin, who played a more aggressive game, with some flair. A coherent style of play was not a priority. What mattered was the spirit,

The old Atletico had been relegated to the Second Division prior to the military uprising and was encumbered with a debt estimated at 1 million pesetas. Eight of Atletico's players were killed while fighting in the subsequent Civil War. Once the conflict was over, Atletico was forced into a merger with the nascent Aviacion. The new club, called Club Athletic de Aviacion, was officially launched in October 1939. It was initially deeply unpopular with Atletico's traditional fans. Atletico had originally been founded by three Basques and grown up in the working-class outskirts of the capital, near the river Manzanares. The appearance of Aviacion came to symbolize the control that the emerging Franco regime wished to exert over soccer. The merger was forced through by the newly appointed high command of the Spanish Soccer Federation as a precondition for Aviacion's registration as a First Division club.

The merged club agreed to play in Atletico's colors—red and white stripes and blue shorts—as a token concession to tradition. But its senior management was composed of military men and civilian officials who had fought for Franco. They had firm views about soccer's political usefulness and how the game should be played by Spaniards. In 1947 the club reverted to the old name of Atletico de Madrid and in subsequent years developed a reputation as the capital's "badlands," less establishment than Real Madrid and less rich.

In *Una historia de una fabula* (A book of fables), Spanish journalist and Atletico fan Carlos Morino Benito imagines the impact the hard-line and dogmatic Francoist mentality has had on the ethos of a club that had always taken pride in its creativity and unpredictability. In one episode, loosely based on oral history passed down through generations of fans, an unnamed Francoist officer barks instructions at Ricardo Zamora, the legendary goalkeeper who was appointed the new club's coach in its first full postwar season 1939–1940. "I'm telling you no, Ricardo, I don't want to hear your excuses or justifications—your team is not playing well, and you know it. What's lacking in this team, Richard, is cojones, a lot of cojones. . . . [T]he team has to run more and throw everything at the opposition. Zamora, stop trying to please so much. . . . [A] coach needs to have a bit of spunk, impose discipline, use the whip now and again," shouts the officer.

This was soccer played as if it were another battle of the Civil War, blood and cojones, and fury, with no room or time for discussion, debate, let alone finessing technique and individual skill as part of a harmonious whole. It says something nevertheless for the quality of some of the players and the personality of Zamora himself that Atletico Aviacion went on to win the first two seasons of the postwar Spanish league. Then Zamora was unceremoniously fired after several military officers linked to the club complained, falsely, that he had not been as loyal to the Franco forces as he should have been during the Civil War. But such was El Divino's popular standing that Zamora soon returned to the fold of Spanish soccer as coach of the national team. It proved the biggest challenge of his career.

Spain had not played in the 1938 World Cup, immersed as it was in its Civil War, but the Franco regime was anxious to see the national squad make up for lost time and gain a veneer of diplomatic acceptance. So while the outbreak of World War II effectively disrupted international soccer and the cooperation of FIFA member states, Spain's soccer authorities organized a series of friendly matches. With the exception of a game played against neutral Switzerland in Valencia, all the national-squad matches were played against representatives run by extreme-Right dictatorships or their collaborators: Portugal, Vichy France, Nazi Germany, and Italy's Mussolini.

After beating a team of French Nazi collaborators in Sevilleon April 12, 1942, Spain played against the Third Reich's Germany in Berlin's Olympic Stadium in front of a crowd of more than eighty thousand. The game was widely reported by the Spanish print media and broadcast live by Spanish radio. The Spanish news agency Efe reported, "On the occasion of this sporting act, we recall the great friendship and solidarity that exists between Germans and Spaniards, who today fight united in Russia with the aim of annihilating criminal bolshevism." Such solidarity contrasted with the reception the German team had gotten when it played in the 1938 World Cup prior to the outbreak of World War II. When Switzerland played Germany in the opening game in Paris's Parc des Princes, French soccer fans jeered the Nazi salute and pelted the German players with bottles, eggs, and tomatoes throughout the match.

In Berlin most of the stadium, more than sixty thousand of the seats, for the Germany-Spain game were taken up by Germans. Of these fourteen thousand were reserved for the German army, six thousand for schoolchildren and Nazi youth, and another five thousand for uniformed Nazi officials and their guests from the Spanish Falange. The remaining tickets were taken up by Spaniards working for Nazi Germany. They included wounded and resting soldiers from the Division Azul (Blue Division), the volunteer military force Franco had sent to the eastern front to fight alongside the Germans against the Russians.

The Spanish players who lined up before the start of the game alongside their German counterparts and joined in the Nazi salute symbolized the extent to which they had become political pawns in terms dictated from on high. They were acting under the orders of new manager Eduardo Teus, the former Real Madrid goalkeeper-turned–sports journalist with strong right-wing political views. Teus had been tasked by the Franco regime with the specific mission of "reconstructing *La Furia*"—the soccer of cojones first mythologized during the 1920s Olympics that, encouraged by the Spanish military, would become part of the national soccer culture during the long years of the Franco regime.

Teus, in consultation with sports minister General Moscardó and other military officers, had selected a team of loyal patriots. The players were expected to show the dedication of crack units storming the enemy trenches. The coach was Ricardo Zamora, his reputation as a national icon restored after his brief banishment from soccer's front line. Zamora led the team in chants of "Franco, Franco, Franco" and fascist salutes before the opening whistle.

The Spanish squad included several players from the newly created Athletic Aviacion: German; Gabilongo; Campos; Arencibia; Real Madrid's Jesus "Chus" Fernandez; two from Español (now renamed in Castilian), Martorell and Teruel; a couple of survivors from the Basque team that had toured South America, Juan Ramon and Gorostiza; and Epifanio Fernandez Berrido, "Emilin" whose club Oviedo had had its stadium destroyed by anti-Franco forces during the Civil War.

One of the veteran Spanish internationals was the striker Campanal, a leading scorer in the Spanish league. Campanal was part of the legendary Stuka forwards on the Sevilla team named after the lethal ground-attack aircraft that made its combat debut in 1936 as part of the Luftwaffe's Condor Legion intervention in the Spanish Civil War. With its infamous Jericho-Trompete (wailing siren), the Stuka became the propaganda symbol of Nazi airpower and the Blitzkrieg victories of 1939–1942. Sevilla in the 1940–1941 season ended in fifth place after pulverizing FC Barcelona, 11–1, the biggest win in the history of the club in the Primera division. Campanal scored five goals.

The Spanish Stuka was little in evidence in Berlin. Instead, the Germans took an early goal, within twelve minutes by Decker, before the visitors scored, ten minutes from the end after a strange free-kick call by the referee, suggesting that the match may have been fixed beforehand. Certainly, the final score, a 1–1 draw, suited both sides politically and diplomatically.

"Spanish soccer, dexterously ruled by the Falange, will give many days of glory to the [Spanish] Empire which now is reborn under the mandate of *Generalissimo* Franco, the Spaniard's immortal *fuehrer*," declared a statement from the Third Reich's sports organization, the Nationalsozialistischer Reichsbund für Leibesübungen. The Spanish media were no less enthusiastic, with the Barcelona-based *El Mundo Deportivo* declaring, "The Spanish team has provoked a demonstration of affection that breaks through the strict boundaries of sport and enters the realm of mutual respect and passion."

Before the week was out, the Spanish squad played against Italy in the San Siro, in Milan. The game, refereed by a German, was watched by another massive crowd, this time made up of pro-Mussolini Italian soccer fans and black shirts. Italian soccer was still basking in the glory years of the 1930s when it won two World Cups in succession (1934 and 1938) and won a gold in the Olympics in 1936. As in Hitler's Germany, and Franco's Spain, soccer in Mussolini's Italy was used to shape public opinion, inculcate mythical nationalist values, and develop the country's standing in the international arena. The Spanish squad was outclassed by the Italians and beaten 4–0. The defeat prompted recriminations against the Spanish squad when it returned home, with the media accusing it of not having fought bravely enough to defend the country's reputation.

At the club level, Atletico Aviacion regained some national honor when it beat a visiting side from the Italian air force in Christmas 1942, 6–2. The game was played in the Metropolitano stadium, which had been rebuilt after suffering major damage during the Civil War. Its design and construction under military management were held up as examples of Franco's urban regeneration, rising, like Real Madrid's Santiago Bernabéu stadium, from the ruins of war.

Elsewhere in Spain, the renamed Athletic Bilbao had regrouped and was posing the biggest challenge to the supremacy of the new pretenders in Madrid. The club had re-formed with a new pro-Francoist administration itself and the rump of the Basque Diaspora. Among the players who had returned voluntarily to Franco's Spain rather than join their colleagues in exile was Lezama, who as a young teenage Civil War refugee had started playing for Southampton as a goalkeeper.

In 1940 Lezama joined the Second Division Arenas Club de Getxo. A year later he signed with Athletic Bilbao and made his *Liga* debut on September 27, 1942, in a 5–0 win over Real Betis. After initially struggling to reassert itself after the Civil War, Athletic recovered some its former glory, thanks to a team that included three emerging young internationals: Telmo Zarra, José Luis Panizo, and Agustín Gaínza.

Athletic won the league championship, three points ahead of Sevilla, and the Copa del Generalissimo when it defeated Real Madrid in the final. The club and its supporters marked both occasions with huge celebrations on the streets of Bilbao that seemed to be free of any political overtones. Whatever outpouring there was of Basque pride, it was suppressed, since the use of Basque political activity, language, and flags was banned by the regime.

When the partying was over, the players were taken by club officials to Bilbao's University of Deusto to there undertake a discreet spiritual retreat at the hands of a Jesuit priest. The relationship between the club and the Jesuits, whose founder, Ignatius, one of the Spanish church's great saints, was born in the Basque Country, was destined to strengthen throughout the Franco years, helping to deepen the mystique of Athletic's Basque cultural roots while offering it a measure of protection from the officially Catholic regime. Although at one point ETA tried to claim Saint Ignatius as their icon, the Jesuits were never as intimately involved with the terrorist organization as some priests were and often spoke out publicly against violence.

The Basque Country's strong religious identity is deeply embedded in its mountainous landscape, as is Athletic's training ground and youth academy outside Bilbao, named Lezama in memory of the Basque refugee boy who returned to the fold. From the great spine of the Pyrenees to the multiple ribs of the Cantabrian Cordillera, the Basque Country is dotted with shrines, small chapels, and churches, with the most famous sanctuary being the Virgin of Aranzazu, in Gipuzkoa, to whom Saint Ignatius made his vow of chastity more than five hundred years ago.

The postwar period saw the virtual beatification of another Basque legend: the Basque player Zarraonaindia, better known simply as Zarra. As French journalist Enrique Terrachet has written in his history of Athletic: "To talk of Zarra is to write another history exclusively dedicated to him. Zarra's popularity, even among those who were not soccer fans, and among his own colleagues, was extraordinary. Zarra was the symbol of *La Furia*, of courage, of pride, of heart." It is interesting here that Terrachet introduces the word *heart*, thus humanizing as well as softening the definition of *La Furia* in a way that frees it from the rhetorical clutches of Spanish fascism. The spirited center-forward became a prolific goal scorer in his fifteen seasons at the club, winning the Pichichi trophy in six of them, a record unbeaten to this day. He scored more league goals (252) than any other player in Spanish soccer history and an additional 81 cup goals. He also shared the record for most goals scored in a season: 38 in 1950–1951.

Tall for a Spaniard of his generation at five feet eleven, strongly built like many of his Basque countrymen, Zarra was a powerful and versatile striker, with a devastating left foot and equal ability to win balls in the air. But he was loved by Athletic fans as much for his personality as for his sporting talent. He always volunteered to play even when badly injured and led by example in his civility toward opponents, often offering a conciliatory handshake or stopping play whenever he felled an opponent.

Beneath his tough exterior lay a sensitive human being, as when he cried with a sense of injustice after being sent off for the only time in his career. It happened during a hard-fought final of the Copa del Generalissimo against Valencia at the Montjuïc stadium in Barcelona. The referee accused Zarra of hitting back after being kicked in the mouth by Valencia's defender Alvaro, at the time one of *La Liga*'s hard men with a reputation for ugly tactics. Zarra himself claimed that Alvaro had come into him hard with the intention of eliminating him from the match but in the process injured himself. "At that point, when Alvaro was on the ground, Gaínza came along and told me, 'Telmo, go ahead and stamp on his headband,' so I feigned a stamp," Zarra later recalled.

After his expulsion, Zarra sobbed uncontrollably in the locker room while the two teams continued head-to-head at 2–2 until in extra time Irionda struck home Athletic's winner off a deflected shot by Gaínza. During the ensuing celebrations in Bilbao's main square, fans demanded Zarra step out on the mayoral palace's balcony alone, not just once but twice, so they could honor him. Such was Zarra's popularity that in the following season fans were happy to adopt a moving ritual at San Mames, on his suggestion. This was the use of specially trained messenger white doves to signal to the patients of the nearby sanatorium of Santa Marina whenever Athletic scored goals.

Sadly, such gestures contrasted with the vindictiveness and repression that characterized the Francoist regime. In 1942 Franco traveled to Barcelona to celebrate the third anniversary of his military victory. Three thousand doves were released in his honor as thousands of soldiers and Falangists marched along the city's main avenue. Franco wished to be seen as Spain's beloved leader who had not only won his nation's war but also secured the peace. For all this show of public self-confidence, Spain was a country politically divided within itself, and soccer provided an escape valve for suppressed emotions.

A year later the Francoist image of national unity was badly dented during two volatile games that Real Madrid and FC Barcelona played against each other during the semifinals of the Spanish Cup, renamed La Copa del Generalissimo. The first leg was played in Barcelona's Les Corts stadium, with the home crowd spending most of the game booing and whistling the visitors and the referee between huge celebrations every time Barca scored. Real Madrid was beaten 3–0.

In a postgame report in *Ya*, one of the main national newspapers, a former Real Madrid player, Eduardo Teus, accused the Catalans of a deliberate conspiracy against the state. Further inflammatory statements were made in the Madrid media and free whistles handed out to Real Madrid fans in the run-up to the second leg. Then, minutes before the game was due to start, the FC Barcelona players received an unexpected visit in the locker room from the count of Mayalde, Franco's director of state security, who warned, "Do not forget that some of you are playing only because of the generosity of the regime in forgiving you your lack of patriotism." His comment was interpreted by the players as a veiled threat against at least three of them who had left Spain during the Spanish Civil War and who despite returning to Franco's Spain were suspected of being secretly opposed to his regime. They included Escola—dubbed El Rojo (the Communist One) by right-wing Francoists. The Barca player was forced to spend the first leg on a stretcher after being kicked in the stomach by a Real Madrid player.

The second-leg game went ahead with FC Barcelona this time finding itself at the receiving end of verbal abuse from the home crowd. Physiotherapist Ángel Mur's memory of the event remained photographic many years later when I caught up with him in the Camp Nou locker room. He was long retired but still working for the club as a volunteer. He told me:

> The night before the game we had to change our hotel, and even then we didn't leave it all evening because we thought we would be lynched. Then when the game started our goalkeeper was so petrified of being hit by missiles that he spent most of the game as far forward from his goal as possible, allowing the Madrid players to get near our goal from all directions. Not so far from where we were sitting, there was a man dressed in military uniform who kept on screaming throughout the match, "Kill these red Catalans, kill these Catalan dogs." At one point I interrupted him and said, "Look, I may not have been born in Catalonia, but I feel I belong to it, and I will go on working there because it is different from the rest of Spain." The officer shouted, "You separatist son of a bitch!" and told me I was under arrest for sedition. It was at that point that the marquis of Mesa de Asta, the president of Barca that Franco had appointed, intervened, telling the officer to leave me alone. The marquis was a distinguished aristocrat and a close friend of General Moscardó, the sports minister. But the officer did not recognize him. "Who do you think you are?" the officer asked angrily. Then the marquis showed his identity card and told the officer to accompany him.

FC Barcelona lost the match 11–1. Journalist Eduardo Teus described the result as the "most resounding victory in the history of Real Madrid." But another observer of the event provided a different version of the game, after using his pro-Franco political credentials to evade the censor's pen. He was Catalan-born Juan Antonio Samaranch. The future president of the International Olympic Committee, a keen roller-hockey player as a young boy, had been conscripted as an eighteen-year-old medical orderly by the Republic during the Spanish Civil War, escaped to France, and then returned to nationalist Spain under Franco and enrolled in the Falange.

Samaranch covered the game as a sportswriter with the conservative *La Prensa* newspaper. In his article, he condemned the violent atmosphere surrounding the match and concluded that the intimidation of FC Barcelona not only was unprecedented in the history of Spanish soccer but had made it impossible for there to be a fair game. Samaranch accused the referee of playing to the crowd when early in the first half he sent off one of Barca's key players, Benito. The decision proved a turning point in the match. From that moment the ten Barcelona players faced an avalanche of goals and seemed either unable or unwilling to put up much resistance. Samaranch wrote:

> Perhaps if the final result had been 4–0, it would have been possible to blame this or that player. But a ten-goal difference is too incredible for there not to be an alternative explanation. If Barca had played really badly, the result would have been different. But it was not a question of playing badly or well. Barca simply ended up by not playing at all. Individual players were fearful of making even the most innocent of tackles because of the crowd reaction and therefore hardly touched their opponents. . . . It was frankly sad having to watch the spectacle of a Barcelona team forcefully reduced to impotence by the coercion of the crowd. . . . I won't

deny there was some merit in Real Madrid's playing. Its midfield was marvellous, and the team as a whole dominated the match, but on reflection, one has to admit that it's not difficult to look great if you haven't got anyone playing against you. A children's team would have probably had more of an impact than Barcelona did in this match.

Samaranch's report drew such an outraged reaction from Real Madrid and its supporters that it cost him his job at the newspaper. A privileged and successful career still awaited Samaranch as a sports minister, deputy of parliament, and, after Franco's death, as the chairman of Catalonia's biggest savings bank, La Caixa. He reached the pinnacle of his career as the International Olympic Committee's top man, responsible for the Olympic community's first major television and sponsorship deals and bringing the Russians in from the cold. Among Catalan soccer fans Samaranch would be remembered, somewhat generously given his political affiliations, as a true sportsman.

Ramallets: "The Cat of Maracana"

CHAPTER 15

World Cup, 1950

In 1946 the United Nations imposed sanctions on Spain while both the United States and the United Kingdom withdrew their ambassadors from Madrid in protest at the authoritarian nature of the Franco regime and its past ambiguous relationship with Nazi Germany. Ernest Davies, parliamentary undersecretary of state for foreign affairs in the postwar Labour government, insisted that Britain would abide by the 1946 UN embargo resolution because the Franco regime remained "repugnant."

In response Franco rallied his countrymen around him, exploiting their rather skewed sense of patriotism and turning to his own advantage the nation's sense of injustice. An indignant Franco attributed British hostility to Masonic plots and communists in the British Labour movement who had fought against him in the International Brigades during the Spanish Civil War.

Within four years, FIFA staged soccer's World Cup, the first to be held since 1939 because of World War II and its aftermath. Spain was not among the favorites—England and host Brazil were—but its presence in the high-profile sports tournament had a strong political dimension to it. It presented the Spanish national squad with an opportunity to come in from the cold of their country's diplomatic isolation.

Spain's pool match with England generated excitement in both countries, although it was the Franco regime that approached it in propagandistic terms, determined to be seen to hit back at his diplomatic detractor and to stir up nationalist feelings over Spain's historic claim over Gibraltar. The recovery of the British colony, long considered by Spanish nationalists a part of Spain in foreign hands, was an ambition long cherished by Franco, who always liked to emulate the great warrior conquering heroes of Spanish history. Just as the Catholic kings had expelled the Moors, he wanted to expel the Brits from Gibraltar—or at least defeat them on a soccer field.

The government-controlled Spanish media had little difficulty in stirring up anti-British feeling among Spanish soccer fans, portraying Spain as a courageous underdog against an English squad that was among the favorites to win with players like Wright and Ramsay, Finney and Mortensen, Mannion and Matthews.

England and Spain won their opening games, against Chile (2–0) and the United States (3–0), respectively. But then in a surprise result, England lost to the United States 0–1, while Spain beat Chile 2–0. The Spaniards thus faced the English with an unbeaten record in the competitions so far and needing only a draw to enter the final stages. Despite their shocking defeat to the United States, England was in a confident mood. Reports had reached the English camp that the Spanish backs played square and were therefore vulnerable to the through pass and the speed of Matthews and Finney on the wings. The English were further encouraged by the decision of the Spanish coach to gamble on Ramallets, one of their reserve goalkeepers, a rising star in FC Barcelona but as yet untested on the international stage.

But the Spaniards were up for a fight. FC Barcelona and Athletic Bilbao provided the majority of players on a squad that was not short of spirit or talent either. Apart from Zarra and his club colleagues Gaínza, Panizo, and Nando, Spain counted on the Barca stars Basora and Cesar and Real Madrid's Luis Molowny, known for his quick precision passing, skillful ball control, and lightning-fast attacking soccer. Molowny was born in the Canary Islands, a part of Spain that had always considered itself geographically and in spirit between the old continent of Europe and the new continent of Latin America. If the Spanish media came close to seeing the game as some kind for revenge for the Armada, Guillermo Eizaguirre, the Spanish manager, seemed well suited for the job, not so much because of any special talent for the job but because he was a loyal Francoist. Eizaguirre had been something of a legend in his own time, dubbed the "Flying Angel" during his heyday as goalkeeper with Sevilla in the run-up to the Civil War when the Andalusian club became Spanish Cup champions. Eizaguirre then volunteered to fight for Franco and ended up serving as a captain in the fanatical Spanish Legion and received a medal for bravery on the field of battle.

Spanish media coverage of the game was heavily biased in keeping with the political circumstances, not least the national radio coverage that thousands of Spaniards tuned in to hear. The only Spanish live radio commentator was Matias Prats. Utterly loyal to the Franco regime, Prat's portentous turns of phrase and excitable tone made him a hugely popular figure among listeners and a useful propaganda arm of the regime. Fourteen minutes into the game Milburn headed Finney's center past the Spanish goalkeeper, Ramallets, but the goal was disallowed by Italian referee Signor Galeati. Newsreel photographs show a Spanish defender putting Milburn onside. Prats described it "as clearly offside." But with the second goal, there was no dispute. Three minutes into the second half, Ramallets stepped well

off his goal line and launched a counterattack, throwing the ball to
Gonzalvo, who passed to Panizo, who back-passed to Puchades. The
next move—an attempt to pass to Gaínza again—was intercepted by
Wright, but the ball went loose and fell at the feet of Gabriel Alonso,
who found Gaínza. His header was met by Zarra, who volleyed it
home with his right foot. It was the winning goal. Prat's extended
"*Goooool*" went on for the better part of a minute and enthralled thousands of Spanish listeners. As Prats later recalled, "Zarra put the goal
in the net, and I put the goal in the mind of all Spaniards." Thanks to
Prats, it became another of those mythical goals in Spanish soccer.
The Armada had prevailed after all. With that goal, Franco's Spain
had not only defied England but also reasserted its imperial honor.
As author Vazquez Montalban would later recall with his character-
istic sharp sense of irony, "Thanks to Prats, the land of Bread and
Bulls became the land of Bread and Soccer—that GOOL is the origin of 'We Count on You' (the slogan used by the Franco regime to
unify Spanish youth through the practice of sport), of the development of tourism, of Massiel's triumph in the Eurovision song contest . . . and of the Seventh Development Plan." In other words,
Franco felt he had found his national squad worth showcasing, a
priceless support at home and abroad. At home, it would give
Spaniards a new sense of pride. Abroad, it was a ticket toward diplomatic recognition, or so he thought.

In his postgame interview, the president of the Spanish Soccer
Federation, Armando Muñoz Calero, a veteran of Franco's Blue Division who had fought alongside the Nazis against the Russians on the
eastern front, told Prats, "We have defeated the Perfidious Albion," a
remark that infuriated the Foreign Office, and unsettled FIFA, but
delighted Franco and his supporters. In deference to FIFA and the influence within it that the English FA exercised in those days, Muñoz
Calero later, somewhat disingenuously, claimed that he had actually

used the word *blond* instead of *perfidious*. However, it was his early re-marks that had set the jingoistic and triumphalist tone of the Spanish media and sharpened the sword of Spanish diplomacy. "England de-feated!" screamed the headline in *Marca*. It reported, "Zarra scored the goal of the most glorious Spanish victory. . . . [W]e have taught a sub-lime lesson to the alleged masters . . . a splendid demonstration to the whole world that the traditional Hispanic virtues of passion, aggres-sion, fury, virility and impetuosity have been completely recovered in the 'New Spain' born out of that bloody conflict—the Civil War."

The Spanish coverage included an invented quote from the Eng-lish team manager, Walter Winterbottom, predicting that Spain would go on to win the World Cup. As things turned out, in the round-robin final format, Spain drew first against Uruguay and on July 13, 1950, was swamped 1–6 by Brazil and then 1–3 by Sweden. The Spanish team failed to qualify for four of the next six World Cups and per-formed badly in the two that it did play. Spain had to wait sixty years before winning the tournament.

Nevertheless, the year 1950 represents a "before and after" in the history of modern Spain and its soccer. By that year the worst of the post–Civil War repression was over, and what had been consolidated was an authoritarian, conservative Catholic regime with Franco at its apex. Tarred with the fascist brush and linked to Hitler's Germany and Mussolini's Italy, Franco's Spain was initially cold-shouldered by the international community in the wake of the Second World War. This isolation allowed Franco to stoke an exaggerated feeling of nationalism based on a traditional view of a single Spanish identity, the myth that Spain was a nation inhabited by a population that felt itself to be Spanish and shared a similar loyalty to a single political center, the capital, Madrid.

A sustained anti-Spain campaign might have threatened Franco's survival early on in his regime. But instead Spain became a player in the

Cold War between the West and the Soviet Union, its uncompromising anticommunism supported by the United States. The postwar UN embargo was lifted in the year of the 1950 World Cup and three years later Spain agreed to the setting up of US military bases on Spanish territory in return for substantial economic aid. Meanwhile, the Spanish coastline, which until then had been characterized in the main by a succession of little fishing villages and untenanted coves and beaches, experienced the arrival of the first charter flights filled with tourists in what in time would turn into a mass invasion of foreigners less interested in the country's politics than they were in a cheap holiday under the sun.

The Franco regime lasted for much longer than anyone foresaw and from the 1950s onward, as the economic situation improved, gradually grew somewhat more liberal. Thus, while the country as a whole remained culturally hamstrung, Spanish soccer did indeed begin to act as a bridge to the outside world. The performance of the Spanish team in Brazil in 1950 was judged of sufficient significance to transform Spain from a postwar diplomatic outcast into a full member of the international soccer community. Spain was voted for the first time onto the executive committee of FIFA with the support of South American countries.

Of that 1950 squad, Zarra was one of two players who gained a very special place in the hearts of Spanish soccer fans. The other was Ramallets. He had been nicknamed the "Cat of Maracana," for it was in Rio's stadium that he showed his agility in the air and his intelligent distribution of the ball. He was also strong and brave and played without gloves. Spain may well have never won its mythical victory were it not for his defiant defense of his goal line. But for that "offside" goal the English found him unbeatable. Ramallets's achievement was all the more remarkable given that he was neither the first nor the second choice goalkeeper but the third, so that he entered the tournament belatedly, and by default rather than choice.

I caught up with Ramallets many years later. It was the autumn of 2010, a few weeks after the World Cup. I had thought that Ramallets, like so many veterans, would choose the safe territory of the club offices (in his case FC Barcelona's) for the interview. But instead he asked that I visit him at home. This was no palatial residence in a leafy neighborhood of Barcelona, but a small stone cottage in Mediona, a village in the rolling wine county of the Alt Penedès. Ramallets belonged to the last generation of Spanish soccer players who weren't able to enrich themselves through their profession. On retiring he had embraced the austerity of a hermit. "Ask at the old pensioners' bar, and they will give you the final directions to where I live," a rather croaky old man's voice had told me over the phone.

His tiny house was along a narrow street beyond which you could see the open country and then the foothills of the Pyrenees. Ramallets himself, at eighty-six, had a face weathered by the years, his skin as wrinkled as a plowed field. But he still stood tall, with only a slight suggestion of a stoop. What struck me most, apart from his simplicity, was his mental alertness and just how big his hands were and how strong his handshake was. Time had been kind to his gifted assets. We sat by an open hearth surrounded by photographs and newspaper clippings donated by friends of his days as a player when he inherited Zamora's title as the best goalkeeper in Spain and became a source of inspiration for other great number 1's, from Iribar and Zubizarreta to Reina, Valdes, and Casillas.

We began talking about goalkeeping, that most undervalued of positions in sport but that in Spain has produced some of its most loved, respected soccer players, from El Divino Zamora to La Roja's Iker Casillas, with other legends along the way, like Iribar and Zubizarreta, as if this country, so torn throughout its history by violence and betrayal, had a need of good, reliable saviors. "Zamora is a legend from whom all the others follow. He was a man who personified, like no other, the solitary figure of the goalkeeper in all its potential for greatness: a strong personality who saw the imperative of limiting failure. The goalkeeper depends on his teammates. But only he can win or lose a match, and that's what makes him such a key figure."

Perhaps it is true, as Peter Chapman argues in his book *The Goalkeeper's History of Britain*, that soccer around the world has waged war against the goalie—from the early days when a striker could bundle a keeper across the goal line and score to the more contemporary indignities of the pass-back rule—and it is a universal truth that the best of us is to be found in our struggles to "keep a clean sheet." But just as Chapman goes on to suggest that Britain's character as an island nation finds its sporting embodiment in the shape and stance of the man between the uprights, may I also venture a similarly whimsical premise to explain Spanish goalkeeping. And that is that the Spanish goalie—and I am talking in particular about one who has risen to play in the national squad—has inevitably been caught up in the enduring figure of Don Quixote. He personifies those high ideals that were supposed to make Spain great, a bastion against the enemy as well as an excuse for failure.

The goalkeeper would carry the destiny of the Spanish squad on his shoulders long after Franco died in 1974. Ten years later, after his death, Spain reached the final of the European Championship against France, where the Spanish captain, Real Sociedad's Luis Arconada, famously smothered a free kick by Michel Platini under his chest in a diving save, only to fumble the ball, which slid off under his body and rolled into the net. The blunder was blamed for Spain's eventual defeat in a competition it thought it could win.

Rather than ponder on such demons, Ramallets recalled the 1950 World Cup and *that* game with the English. "The tournament wasn't easy for us. I guess we were not as fit as we should have been, and it was very hot. We ended up in fourth place. But we beat England, who were one of the favorites and who played a fast and attacking style of soccer. The English refused to give up after we scored and kept coming at me, forcing me to make saves or clear the ball even after they'd run into my net. They had a great team. I know they had Matthews, but the player I remember most of all was Finney, who played on the left wing and was really fast." That first English goal? "It was clearly offside. The fact is I saw it and lifted my arm to appeal even before the referee blew his whistle."

Born into a poor family, Ramallets was just twelve when the Spanish Civil War broke out. He spent most of it in Barcelona, digging earth to help build bomb shelters. For someone who had suffered Franco's bombs, what was it was like playing for his national squad? "We were all good friends and felt pretty separate from politics. I'd get on well with the Basques but also with the Real Madrid players and those from other clubs. If you were selected, you just became part of a team; you felt part of it. We all felt equal," he said.

I asked whether the mood changed once they crossed the frontier. "Wherever we went, we had Spanish immigrants or exiles giving us a good reception—I think it was because they felt true Spaniards. They would ask us, 'When is the regime going to change?' This was what concerned them, more than the soccer we played. They wanted to know how and when they could return."

So what happened to Spanish soccer over those years of dictatorship? I asked. Ramallets paused, briefly closed his eyes, and then said, "I think the Civil War produced a gap in the development of our soccer. . . . Many players were killed, and it took many years to reorganize the national game. I think soccer in Spain began to become something from 1950 onward. I think we learned from the foreigners who came in. I think it was these foreigners who marked a before and afterwards in the history of Spanish soccer."

Francisco Seijas: Argentine star

CHAPTER 16

The Boys from Almagro

The neighborhood of Almagro in Buenos Aires boasts a colorful history of enterprising Basque and Italian immigrant workshops, street brawls, and tangos—"Neighborhood of my soul, where I spent my youth and spent nights of love," the great tango singer Gardel would sing in the 1930s.

Almagro is west of the center of Buenos Aires, a city where I worked and lived for several years, in pursuit of the Argentine soccer legend Diego Maradona. Long before Maradona—otherwise known as the Hand of God—came to play for FC Barcelona in the early 1980s, Buenos Aires, thanks to Almagro, earned a place in the history of Spanish soccer because of the lesson a neighborhood team gave when they toured Spain in the winter of 1946–1947. The lesson is foretold in the development of Spanish soccer from the mythological beginnings of *La Furia* so beloved of the Franco regime over many years to the refinement of *La Roja*, the national squad that won Spain's first-ever World Cup at the start of the second decade of the new millennium.

This story has its beginnings in the early 1900s, when a street gang based in the Almagro neighborhood would invite gangs from other neighborhoods to play street soccer by painting walls with the legend *Los Forzosos de Almagro Desafían* (Almagro's Strongmen Dare You). Almagro was by then crisscrossed by streetcar and bus lines, so playing soccer was a risky business. When one day a young boy was run over by a streetcar, a local Catholic priest, Father Lorenzo Massa, took charge and hosted soccer games in the backyard of his parish church in the Avenida de Mexico. It was there that the first organized teams of San Lorenzo de Almagro came into being, becoming with the passage of time one of Buenos Aires's top clubs, along with Boca Juniors, Independiente, River Plate, and Racing. San Lorenzo recruited from the immigrant Basques, with their tradition of tough, physical soccer, and from a mixture of Italians, Spaniards, and mixed-blood Indians drawn from the provinces, players known as *los gauchos*, like the wild, lawless cowboys who roamed the extensive plains known as the pampas.

The Basques, with their seemingly unquenchable physical reserves and uncomplicated, aggressive play—tough tackling, then heading, crossing, and occasional long balls—drew some of their inspiration from the English. But the backstreets of Buenos Aires and the dry state of the turf that came to characterize Argentine soccer stadia contributed to a productive melting pot of styles, with an emerging native culture putting a greater emphasis on individual trickery and dexterity.

Such soccer had its precursor in the 1920s, when Argentina's neighbor Uruguay won two Olympic gold medals in succession, an achievement writer Eduardo Galeano (a Uruguayan) has described as the Second Discovery of America. "The English . . . had perfected the long pass and the high ball, but these disinherited children from far-off America didn't walk in their fathers' footsteps. They chose to invent a game of close passes directly to the foot, with lightning charges of rhythm and high-speed dribbling," wrote Galeano.

South American soccer players were destined to have an important influence on the evolution of Spanish soccer. An early pioneer, if unsung hero, was Francisco Seijas, one of the rising stars of Argentine soccer players who signed up with Celta Vigo in 1930. I stumbled on his story, by chance, some years ago when I visited for the first time what would become one of my favorite eating places in London—an Argentine meat restaurant called El Gaucho. It was owned and run by Luis, a retired dancer who in his youth had shown off his tango skills in Hollywood and Las Vegas before marrying a very beautiful Chilean woman, a dancer like himself. One night Luis showed me two faded photographs. The first showed him dressed as a gaucho when he worked with a circus troupe. The other showed someone remarkably similar to him but dressed in a suit and a fedora hat and surrounded by adoring women on the quayside of some old port. "That's my dad, Francisco, when he was about to board the ship for Spain—the first professional Argentine soccer player to leave for a European club," Luis told me proudly. An enduring friendship was sealed then and there, with El Gaucho becoming an unofficial watering hole for Maradona fanatics like myself. "Back then Francisco Seijas would not have dreamed of the kind of fame that Maradona achieved and other Argentines since, like Messi. For him it was an adventure, a challenge, but without the celebrity, or the money," his son told me.

The Galician club Francisco chose to play for was one of the late arrivals on the Spanish soccer scene, having been founded in 1923. Despite inaugurating the impressive Balaidos stadium in 1928 in anticipation of a more professional era, Celta was struggling to make its mark in Spain's Second Division. Within weeks of his arrival, Seijas had established himself as the club's leading goal scorer, after scoring four goals in his debut against Athletic Bilbao. Because of his short height, Seijas had a low center of gravity that gave him near-perfect ball control and an ability to glide past defenders. He was not the first or last Argentine to have such qualities, but he had a unique claim to have helped Celta on its way to promotion.

The migration of players like Seijas to the Spanish *Liga* slowed during the 1930s. Argentine soccer belatedly became professionalized, while Spain was thrown into economic and political turmoil. As David Goldblatt has written, "Cut off from the carnage, freed from the imperatives of war and survival, Argentinean soccer could create a distinct blend of instrumentalism, art and entertainment," with the Argentine media articulating a "working mythology of a unique national playing style."

This rich alchemy of styles was what San Lorenzo de Almagro brought with them when they toured Portugal and Spain in 1946–1947. The team had just won the Argentine League title, thereby breaking the River Plate hegemony of the legendary La Maquina (The Machine). This was the name given to the relentless and well-oiled attacking soccer exemplified by River Plate's legendary forward quintet—Muñoz, Moreno, Pedenera, Labruna, and Lousteau. After dethroning River Plate, the Iberian tour was a high mark in San Lorenzo's history. San Lorenzo arrived at Madrid's newly enlarged Barajas airport four days before Christmas 1946 in an Iberia DC4, after refueling in the Canary Islands. First to walk down the steps to the tarmac was Bilbao-born Ángel Zubieta, who had stayed in Argentina after touring with the Basque squad during the Spanish Civil War. Zubieta was greeted by his mother and sister. The emotional reunion between the returning onetime Spanish international, now playing for the Argentine champions, and two seemingly happy

Basque citizens of Franco's Spain served its political purpose in the regime's favor.

In the following weeks, local soccer fans, encouraged by the extensive coverage provided by the Spanish soccer media, marveled at the play of the Argentine visitors. What they saw was the best of the attacking soccer made famous by La Maquina and now made part of an intricate display of quick short passes and turns, skillful flicks and lobs, and magical goals. The team came to be known as El Ciclon (The Cyclone) because of the speed and artistry with which it mesmerized and ran circles around most opponents. "What occurred between the 21st December and the end of January 1947 seemed unreal and inexpressible," commented the Spanish newspaper *El Pais* in a tribute published on the fiftieth anniversary of the tour. "The daily press and the magazines doubled their normal soccer coverage. San Lorenzo, despite playing in the cold, snow, and intense rainfall of that winter, caused a sensation."

In their first game in Madrid's Metropolitano stadium, with most of their players still recovering from an exhausting transatlantic flight, San Lorenzo beat host Atletico Aviacion 4–1. Two days later the Argentine club played in the same stadium and lost by the same margin to Real Madrid. On the eve of the game, San Lorenzo's captain, the Basque Zubieta, was overheard telling a friend that he hoped his team would double their scorecard against the winners that season of the Copa del Generalissimo. "Beating Real Madrid will be the real marker for the whole tour because they are well known in Argentina and are today Spanish champions," Zubieta said. The boast prompted the Madrid captain, Ipiña, another Basque, to rally his players. At a meeting on the eve of the game he told them, "I am prepared to bust a gut tomorrow, and I expect the same from all of you. What on no account must we do is fight with the same arms as them." Ipiña proposed quite simply that the team focus on closing down San Lorenzo's game and beating them on the counterattack. The strategy would include

man-to-man marking and a solid midfield being able to count on the
speed on and off the ball of Molowny and Belmar, strong defenders
who could also be lethal in attack. And so it proved. The trickery and
patient buildup play of the visitors was smothered by the stoic defense
of the Spanish champions. San Lorenzo's passing game was typically
fluent, but all too often played in front of the Real players rather than
behind them.

On the few occasions the Argentines had a sight of the opposing
goal, the attacking player was crowded out. Real was quick on the
break, with Pruden scoring two goals and Belmar a third by halftime
after lightning counterattacks down both sides and lethal finishing. It
was a fiercely fought encounter for a friendly. Ipiña was carried off injured after a bruising tackle before Alsua struck home the winning
fourth goal. But although Real Madrid would make much of its victory, the game barely dented San Lorenzo's reputation.

For the rest of the tour, the visitors proved unbeatable, with three
players in particular, Farro, Potoni, and Martino—the so-called *trio de
oro* (golden trio)—playing hugely entertaining soccer. Potoni was offered a contract with FC Barcelona but turned it down, while Martino
ended up playing with Juventus.

San Lorenzo beat FC Barcelona and drew with three other Spanish clubs, Athletic Bilbao, Valencia, and Sevilla. Of the three, the game
that made the biggest impact on local fans was played at Bilbao's San
Mames, where the popularity of San Lorenzo's captain, Zubieta, had
endured, while that of Athletic's Panizo had always been questioned.
Whereas Zubieta's Basque workmanship and team spirit were held up
as examples, Panizo found himself criticized by Athletic fans for playing with the ball too much. But when the crowd watched the San
Lorenzo players show off their ball-control and passing skills, word
went around San Mames with a newly discovered sense of admiration: "But they all play like Panizo!"

It was, however, against the Spanish national squad that San Lorenzo pulled off its most assertive victory, winning by 13–5 over two games. As Jaume Olive, the coach of FC Barcelona's youth team, put it many years later, "There was a before and after in Spanish soccer which was delineated by the San Lorenzo visit. The Argentine champion left a deep imprint . . . an elaborate soccer of short passes, of triangulation, in contrast to the more direct soccer of a Spain where to talk about tactics was regarded as heresy. The Argentines believed in making the best use of the ball and strategy—against this Spaniards could only respond with *La Furia*, and improvisation."

Alfredo Di Stéfano: A Real Madrid legend

CHAPTER 17

Di Stéfano

The Argentine club's tour laid the seeds for one of the most exciting periods of Spanish soccer club history, with Real Madrid in particular showing greater respect for foreign imports than its triumphalist tones, on beating San Lorenzo, had suggested.

Among those who had watched Real Madrid's victory over San Lorenzo in that winter of 1946 was Santiago Bernabéu, the Spanish club's first postwar president and one of the great figures of international soccer. Bernabéu, as well as being a former player and a hugely enthusiastic soccer fan, was a man of ambition and vision, if not opportunism, who managed to harness his allegiance to the Franco regime so as to benefit his club. In 1943 Bernabéu took advantage of Spain's neutrality in World War II to draft plans for a new stadium as part of Madrid's post–Civil War urban regeneration. Bernabéu had little trouble in convincing Franco and his ministers that the stadium—planned as one of the largest in the world—once populated with star players, would draw to it Spaniards of diverse social backgrounds and act as a bridge to the outside world.

Bernabéu saw his opportunity to seize on South American skills at the end of March 1952 when as part of its fiftieth anniversary celebrations Real Madrid played against the Colombian team Millonarios in their new stadium along Madrid's Castellana Avenue. Of the players that played that day, one in particular, Alfredo Di Stéfano, caught Bernabéu's eye because of his evident versatility and skill as well as strength on and off the ball. Although billed as a center-forward, Di Stéfano showed an extraordinary work ethos, at one moment tracking back into defense, the next leading a fast counteroffensive, and striking with disarming accuracy. "This guy smells of good soccer," Bernabéu remarked after watching him play.

Di Stéfano, the son of working-class Italian immigrants, was born in Argentina, a country that, like Spain, had learned to play soccer from the British but had developed a style of its own, fast, magical, and mischievous. His first home was just a few yards away from the Boca Juniors stadium, in the port of Buenos Aires, where Argentine soccer's earliest teachers, the English sailors and merchants, had first made their mark. He learned to play street soccer with the school kids of his barrio while his father earned enough money as a foreman in the local market to buy some land. It was against walls and on hard surfaces, whether on the dusty pavements or on dry grass, that Di Stéfano discovered his talent in dribbling and passing while developing his skills as a sharpshooter with his left and right feet.

Di Stéfano grew up amid the *potreros*—the small yards and fields of the sprawling metropolis of Buenos Aires, where large groups of kids would often find themselves fighting for the ball with adult men. It was there that he learned to use his individual instincts while fighting for his team. One of the first teams he played for in the barrio was called Unidos y Venceremos (United and We Will Win). It was with them that he learned not only to fight to defend, but also to play to win. He first made his reputation playing for River Plate during the late 1940s when Argentine club soccer enjoyed one of its golden periods, as La Nuestra—"ours, meaning our (Argentinean) style of play"—came into its own.

Di Stéfano in his memoir recognized what he and many others owed to the early pioneers. He wrote, "We should pay tribute to the English, who went all over the world with their railways, but also with their soccer. . . . They went to America, to Asia, to Africa. . . . In Spain, in Huelva, *Rio Tinto* they were also the first to introduce soccer. . . . [T]hanks to them, we have become a [soccer-playing] family." But while La Nuestra owed its beginnings to the British Empire, it forged its identity in the social context of postcolonial South America. The soccer came to claim a style of its own, creative and surprising, with players turning into magicians. Their range of tricks included bicycle kicks and scissors kicks, incredible flicks and back-heels, individual juggling and the collective painting of elaborate tapestries with quick, perfectly controlled passes. Such soccer was both elegant and mischievous; it mesmerized and brought smiles to people's faces, as much ballet as circus, as the players dribbled and passed the ball between each other, each move an attempt to up the entertainment, each goal a surprise.

While playing at River Plate, Di Stéfano's trainer and inspiration was Carlos Peucelle, who in his days as a player was nicknamed Barullo (Mayhem) because of his tendency to play all over the field in no defined role other than as a constant threat or bulwark. Of Di Stéfano himself, perhaps the best evocative portrait has been written by Galeano, who wrote of the Argentine's days at Real Madrid in *Football in Sun and Shadow*:

> The entire playing field fitted inside his shoes. From his feet the
> pitch sprouted and grew. . . . [H]e ran and reran the field from net

to net. He would change flanks and change rhythm with the ball from a lazy trot to an unstoppable cyclone; without the ball he'd evade his marker to gain open space, seeking air whenever a play got choked off. . . . He never stood still. Holding his head high, he could see the entire pitch and cross it at a gallop to prise open the defence and launch the attack. He was there at the beginning, during, and at the end of every scoring play, and he scored goals of all colours.

Di Stéfano signed with Real Madrid on September 15, 1953, after protracted negotiations, made all the more controversial by thwarted counterbids made by FC Barcelona, which the Catalans blamed on dirty dealings in Madrid aided by the Franco government. What is beyond doubt is Bernabéu's ambition to make Di Stéfano the central actor in Real Madrid's transformation into one of the world's great clubs. Three months before the Argentine's arrival, Bernabéu signed Paco Gento, a young winger from Santander, one of several players who would blossom thanks to Di Stéfano's inspiration and support.

Gento was lackluster and came close to being dropped from the team in his first season with the Merengues—as Real Madrid was affectionately nicknamed by the popular Francoist radio commentator Matias Prats, for no other reason than that he saw a resemblance between their white colors and one of his favorite desserts. But he survived because Di Stéfano argued, quite rightly as time would prove, that Gento was a winger with extraordinary pace who needed to improve tactically—something that could happen only by playing alongside more experienced players like himself.

Undoubtedly, Gento grew as a player thanks not just to Di Stéfano but to the array of, mainly foreign, talent that Bernabéu brought to the team. It was courtesy of Di Stéfano's advice that Bernabéu enlisted José Héctor Rial, the Argentine inside-left, who had also played in Colombia. Di Stéfano wanted someone who could help him build up an attack from midfield with a series of quick one-two passes. But Rial also contributed to the team by connecting with Gento, a traditional left-winger, with his long passes, thus widening the team's attacking options. Rial helped improve Gento's timing and control while making full use of his speed to tear into defenses. Gento soon earned the nickname Supersonico.

Rial was joined at Real Madrid by other foreigner stars—the Uruguayan José Santamaría, the Frenchman Raymond Kopa, and last but by no means least the Hungarian Ferenc Puskás. "People say of those days that it was soccer played by five or six attackers and defended by the rest—but that's an outrageous misrepresentation," Di Stéfano told the Spanish journalist Orfeo Suarez on the eve of the 2010 World Cup. "What we had were wings that moved up the pitch, and forwards that tracked back in defence. It was a collective effort. I was taught that soccer is all about touch and mobility."

Not everyone had the genius of Di Stéfano. He was ahead of his time. Of all the stars of Real Madrid's Golden Age, it was unquestionably that of Di Stéfano that shone the brightest. Without him there would have been stars but no firmament. Di Stéfano's greatness lay in his ability to combine his individual skill with his talent for organization. Miguel Muñoz, his first captain at Real Madrid, once said that with Di Stéfano on your side, it felt like having two players in every position. Di Stéfano was responsible for casting a whole club in his image in a way that impacted the development of Spanish soccer as a whole. He created a whole mythology around Real Madrid's invincibility that others struggled to emulate and that unwittingly came to contrast with and highlight the underachievement of Spain's national squad and his inability to inspire it to greatness.

Ladislau Kubala: Cold War hero

CHAPTER 18

Kubala and Other Hungarians

R eal Madrid's glory years of the 1950s were the product of its hands-on president Santiago Bernabéu's policy of having his managers periodically renovate the team with new stars, even though Di Stéfano remained the central figure throughout this period.

Among the other star foreigners, Puskás had already earned a special place in history as a member of the Magic Magyars, communist Hungary's national team that had dominated European soccer in the early 1950s, crushing the English 6–3 at Wembley on November 25, 1953, with a superb display of innovative passing and tactical sophistication. Hungary, captained by Puskás, was the first national squad to break with the fifth forward of conventional soccer formations, withdrawing the number 9, or center-forward, into a midfield that had already been depleted by one player playing deeper. Meanwhile, the role of the two remaining midfield players was primarily organizational and attacking, supporting interplay and passing among the forwards. This was called 4-2-4.

During his time playing for Hungary, Puskás was dubbed the Galloping Major because of his rank in his country's army. As journalist Brian Glanville recalled, he was "the star of stars, a squat little Budapest urchin-figure, plastered hair parted down the middle, with superb control, supreme energy, and above all a left-foot shot which was unrivalled in the world, dangerous from a distance up to thirty-five yards." At Real Madrid, where he arrived aged thirty-one in 1958, Puskás won enormous affection and respect for all these qualities, despite the paunch that never left him in all his playing days.

One of my favorite Puskás tales involves *la barriguita*, or little stomach, as it was diplomatically referred to. One day Antonio Calderon, one of the club directors under Santiago Bernabéu, called in the then trainer, Camiglia, to inform him that the club had signed Puskás. "Is that so? Well, what are we going to do with that stomach of his?" asked Camiglia, making it clear that he was not pleased. Calderon answered, "That stomach is your responsibility to get rid of." Hours later Puskás trained with the team for the first time. Then Calderon asked Di Stéfano what he thought of his new teammate. Di Stéfano replied, "He controls the ball better with the left leg that I do with my hand." No one ever raised questions about Puskás's *barriguita* ever again, and he came to be known instead as *Canoncito* (Little Cannon).

During his time at Real Madrid, Puskás scored 20 or more goals in each of his first six seasons in the Spanish league and won the Pichichi four times. When he retired, at age forty, he had secured a place in the history books as one of the most prolific scorers in soccer history, 514 goals in 529 matches in the Hungarian and Spanish leagues.

The golden years during which Real Madrid conquered Europe was also a period when FC Barcelona refused to let up as the country's other major club, aping Santiago Bernabéu's grand architectural ambition and moving into its own huge stadium, the Camp Nou. The expansion was principally aimed at accommodating the impact of Ladislau Kubala on the club's fortunes. Kubala arrived at FC Barcelona after an epic escape from his native Hungary where he had played for three clubs—Ferencvaros, Slova Bratislava, and Vasas of Budapest. Soccer and politics had restarted in Hungary in 1946 following the end of World War II in the shadow of the Soviet armed forces. By 1948, as the division of Europe was being finalized, the Communist Party edged its conservative and social democrat coalition partners out of power and began to tighten its grip on all aspects of society, including soccer. On January 25, 1949, Kubala fled from communism to the West, initially to a US military zone in Austria and then to Italy, where he played for a while with a local team called Pro-Patria in the town of Busto Arsizio.

The Communist authorities denounced Kubala as a delinquent and a cheat. He had in fact hurriedly escaped while the ink was still wet on a contract he had signed with and been paid for by Vasas for whom he had only played for a short while. The Hungarian Soccer Federation issued a formal extradition request on account of alleged financial crimes, his leaving the country without authorization, and his failure to engage in military service. While the extradition request was ignored by the West, Hungary's growing influence as an emerging postwar soccer nation within FIFA secured a one-year international ban.

Kubala once again packed his bags, this time moving with his young wife to a refugee camp in Italy under US military administration. There he met up with some fellow Hungarians who had similarly fled their country and formed a soccer team called Hungria. That summer he traveled to Spain on what was to prove the most defining journey of his soccer career.

I caught up with Kubala many years later in Barcelona. It was in late May 1998, and Kubala was playing in a veterans' match on a small field near the Camp Nou, under a blazing midday sun. My first glimpse of him was that of an old man in shorts, bare chested and holding a T-shirt likes an emblem in one hand. Kubala seemed to be working harder than all the others, and suffering too, his bow-legs barely carrying his weight. Yet at one point this geriatric hero managed to conjure some energy from a mysterious inner reserve and dribbled from his back line the length of the field before delivering a perfectly angled shot into the goal.

I struggled to understand this motivation so late in life, and Laszi gave me an explanation of sorts later when I interviewed him in the veterans' office. No sooner had we begun talking when he lifted his suit trousers to the knees to reveal a close-up of scarred skin. "Look at this. . . . That's seven operations—and still things aren't quite the way they should be. . . . The older one gets, the more problems, but I go on playing because I don't want the other 'granddads' knowing about it, because if they found out they would give me nothing but trouble. So they don't know anything, and that means we are all happier when we play together," he said, speaking Spanish rapidly with the clipped accent of an Eastern European.

My team was called Hungria because we were four or five Hungarians playing in it, but there were also Czechs, two or three Croatians, a few Russians. . . . [T]hey'd all escaped from communism. . . . We traveled to Madrid to play in a friendly with the Spanish squad that was getting ready to play in the 1950 World Cup. Pepe Samitier, who was the Barca coach, was in the stadium, and he watched me play. Afterward he came up and said, "Why don't you come with us to Barcelona?" and I told him, "I would love to, but FIFA does not allow me to play as a professional and

I've left my country without authorization." Then he said, "Don't worry, we'll fix it."

Samitier's endeavors to draw Kubala away from the clutches of Real Madrid, which had expressed an interest, were helped by Kubala's extraordinary capacity for hard drinking. According to a well-sourced account I heard from Enrique Llaudet, a senior official of FC Barcelona at the time, El Sami's seduction of Kubala verged on the farcical. It certainly endures as one of the most extraordinary transfer stories in Spanish soccer history.

Kubala came to Spain thinking he was going to be signed by Real Madrid, but because he was half pissed he didn't really know whether he was coming or going. If Kubala had one weakness it was that he drank too much—whiskey, wine, whatever he got his hands on. Well, as things turned out, there was real confusion on the train that took him from Madrid to Barcelona, with Kubala at one point turning to Samitier and saying, "Hey, we are going toward Madrid, aren't we?" and Samitier saying, "Sure we are," then Kubala insisting, "But the sign says Barcelona," which is when El Sami said, "Don't you worry. We are going to the club now." And that is how he brought us Kubala.

As things turned out, Kubala struck a hard bargain when he signed with FC Barcelona. When he sat down to negotiate, Kubala took out a copy of a draft contract Real Madrid had prepared and insisted he wanted something similar or more. The contract he signed with FC Barcelona made him the highest-paid player yet in the history of the club. Next to him the best-paid member of the Barca squad was the team's new Czech coach, Daucik, Kubala's brother-in-law, whose hiring formed part of the deal El Sami had helped negotiate.

The ban on Kubala's playing professional soccer was lifted by FIFA on April 2, 1952. Subsequently, Kubala was given Spanish nationality, his status fast-tracked through Spanish bureaucracy thanks to friendships Samitier had with members of the Madrid political establishment and the personal intervention of the Francoist president of the Spanish Soccer Federation, Muñoz Calero. That they found sympathetic ears at the highest level of the regime was hardly surprising. Kubala's story of escape from communist repression and delivery into the friendly hands of Spain perfectly suited Franco's efforts to exploit the developing Cold War to break out of his diplomatic isolation. Kubala's life story was given its crudest treatment in propaganda terms in a filmed dramatization, *The Stars Search for Peace*, which became a box-office hit in Spain.

Although unwittingly used for a while as a political pawn, Kubala undoubtedly contributed to lifting the quality of Spanish soccer during the 1950s. He brought to FC Barcelona a combination of skills and strength that Spanish clubs had until then rarely seen in one player. Kubala was quick on and off the ball, demonstrated extraordinary control when dribbling, and showed a good vision of the game, knowing when to pass. He was also a consummate goal scorer, devastatingly accurate with both feet and a master with the dead ball, with his curling ball often defying even the best-constructed walls. His great rival Di Stéfano would pay a generous posthumous tribute to the Hungarian when he died in May 2002. "Kubala was one of the best there has ever been. His game was pure, crystalline, a real joy for the fans," Di Stéfano said. "He was potent, technical, fast, and a great goal scorer."

In truth little separated the sheer quality and creativity of both men. Together they provided so many examples of sheer brilliance that others in more modern times from Maradona and Ronaldo to Zidane and Messi would follow. Many soccer fans would retain an enduring memory of a game Spain played Belgium in 1957, when Di Stéfano dived full-length before scoring with a back-heel from the air off a cross-kick from Miguel. Di Stéfano had a habit of scoring goals like that. Any open net was an invitation for a goal, and much of the time he executed it ruthlessly.

Spanish soccer fans were given a tantalizing glimpse of what might have been on January 26, 1955, when both players played alongside each other wearing the FC Barcelona colors in a charity match and delivered an extraordinary exhibition of soccer skill and imagination, beating Italy's Bologna 6–1, with their combined goal-scoring power. "The trick with Alfredo," Kubala told me, "was that you had to give him complete freedom of movement and a colleague who knew how to back him up. We would take turns going forward, but always supporting each other. We were constantly changing positions. This meant that we were always with the ball, and always creating problems for our adversaries, particularly when they tried to mark us. Alfredo and I were always two against one, and that made the game easier." So what was Di Stéfano's defining gift? I asked Kubala. "He had speed, technique, and a great vision. He also knew how to sacrifice himself for the good of the team."

I guess soccer stars, like any competing artists, get nicer about each with old age; its their way of reconciling themselves with life. Certainly, Di Stéfano and Kubala were kinder to each other as old men than as young players—they never really got along—and both men played a great many more games against each other than they did as teammates. Circumstances beyond their control meant that these players came to be embroiled in the history of enmity between Spain's two biggest rival clubs.

Perhaps what gave Di Stéfano the edge in soccer was his portentous presence on and off the field in contrast to Kubala's somewhat Rabelaisian eat, drink, and be merry way of living. What is certainly true is that personality, politics, and fate conspired to keep both players from forming an enduring partnership either at the club or at the international level.

Neither Di Stéfano's nor Kubala's help was sufficient to enable Spain to qualify for the World Cup in Sweden the following year. Curiously, it was a tournament in which another of Bernabéu's foreign stars, the Frenchman Raymond Kopa, seemed to flourish when playing with his national squad. At Real Madrid, he had been banished to the wing, not his natural position, in order to accommodate Di Stéfano's domineering presence. But with France, he flourished anew as an attacking midfielder, in control of the orchestra just as Di Stéfano was at Real Madrid. Kopa scored more goals per game for the national team than he did for his Spanish club.

It was Di Stéfano's ego and Kubala's undiscipline together that in the end excluded them from any enduring presence in the national squad once each player had separately taken on Spanish nationality. Some Spanish commentators criticized Kubala early on for playing rough, using his elbows too often, and with a tendency to monopolize the game. But his colleagues and the huge following of fans that he generated saw only the best in Kubala—a hard worker who sweated through his shirt in every game and inspired the whole team with his unique talent and incurable, if naive, generosity. Bernabéu used to say that Kubala had a hole in the palm of his hand where he kept the money he wanted to give to the people he thought needed it.

Despite being one of Spain's best-paid players, he shared with others as much as he spent on himself, supporting less fortunate Eastern European refugees and famously telling the police that he hoped the two hundred thousand pesetas stolen from his car once had helped a person in need.

"There are a lot of stories about Kubala. . . . [S]ome were true, but others were pure invention. . . . I think he was a great player but also a normal guy who liked to have fun, particularly after really big matches when we thought the whole world was our play area . . . like when we won a match against Real Madrid—that was well worth celebrating," recalled Ramallets, the Barca goalkeeper and Spanish international.

Kubala's inspiration helped Barca win the Generalissimo's Cup on May 27, 1951, beating Real Sociedad 3–0. In the 1951–1952 season that followed, Barca went on to win the Spanish double and the Copa Latina (played by the Spanish, Italian, French, and Portuguese champions), together with two summer tournaments, the Martino Rosso and the Eva Duarte. In one of several memorable performances in *La Liga*, Kubala scored seven goals of the nine against one that secured his team's victory over Sporting Gijon. The "season of the five cups" marked FC Barcelona's transformation into a major international club. It was a time when the club not only played great soccer, but also showed that it had survived the regime's repression to take its place in the emerging Spanish society as one of the country's most respected soccer institutions.

Many years later when a democratic Catalonia was rediscovering its political and cultural identity after the death of Franco, one of Spain's most talented musicians, Joan Manuel Serrat, wrote a song of tribute to Kubala, and his colleagues Basora Cesar, Moreno, and Machon, who made up the front five. A passionate Barca fan, Serrat felt as close to Kubala in spirit as the Argentinean tango singer Carlos Gardel had been to Pepe Samitier. As Serrat sang, "For me there was no one like Kubala. . . . I was happy to play with him, carry his portrait in my wallet." Born four years after the end of the Spanish Civil War, in 1943, in Poble Sec, a poor suburb of Barcelona, the son of an immigrant from the South, Serrat grew up among the shortages and diplomatic isolationism of the postwar years when Kubala's days of glory brought many afternoons of joy to soccer fans in Barcelona and beyond.

This was a time when live radio commentaries became increasing popular, soccer results were posted in bars, and when television, although as expensive as a first house, began to be bought for the sake of watching a big match. In 1959 there were five thousand registered television owners in Barcelona. Another six thousand sets were sold in that year in the days leading up to live coverage of a Barca–Real Madrid match.

No other players contributed to Spanish club soccer's transformation during these years as much as Di Stéfano and Kubala. But it was a different story when it came to the national squad, where the players did themselves and the team no favors and where management proved so conflictive as to nullify any positive contribution they might have otherwise made.

Helenio Herrera: "We are going to win"

CHAPTER 19

Herrera, the Magician

In a period of twelve years, between the World Cup of 1950 and the World Cup of 1962, Spain's national squad appointed sixteen coach-managers, none of whom had the talent, organization, or vision to draw on the best from club soccer and transform it into a competitive squad capable of winning titles. Perhaps the one who did, Helenio Herrera, who served as Spain's national coach between 1959 and 1962, proved too arrogant a personality and too divisive in his tactics to ensure a truly national enterprise. While individual clubs enriched the game they played with foreign imports and the lessons they learned from a variety of talented coaches, Spain as a soccer nation would grasp only belatedly the foreign tricks and spells with which it had been briefly dazzled during the tour of San Lorenzo de Almagro. Of Herrera's many claims to fame, few can be as negative as the fact that he alienated both Alfredo Di Stéfano and Ladislau Kubala, two of the greatest figures in the history of Spanish soccer.

Herrera was a nomad who, at his best, brought a magician's touch along with a strong personality to the profession of soccer manager-coach. He was born in Argentina to Spanish immigrants—his father was an exiled anarchist. When he was four he immigrated with his parents to Casablanca, where he adopted French citizenship. Herrera would later claim that he learnt what he needed to know about soccer—his school of life, as he called it—as a boy growing up in North Africa, mixing and playing with Arabs, Jews, French, and Spaniards.

During his two-year stint at FC Barcelona (1958–1960), he used his powers of psychology to motivate a team that all too often seemed overladen with its own self-conscious sense of history and an under-lying inferiority complex with respect to its rival Real Madrid. The way Barca emerged from its periodic doldrums and flourished under Herrera was so quick that it fueled conspiracy theories in Madrid of trickery, secret rituals, even illicit drugs, although much of the negative media coverage was fueled by the coach's unashamed mercantilism. Nonetheless, he won the respect of his players, with the exception of the aging Kubala, whom he judged surplus to requirements.

As one of the younger Barca players and a future Spanish international at the time, Fusté recalled, "Herrera was soccer's psychologist. . . . [H]e was very good at motivating his players. . . . [H]e would convince them they were better than the opponent. . . . He got me into play when I was seventeen. . . . I looked up to much older players like Kubala and Evaristo and Ramallets as if they were gods. Herrera knew how to make the best use of the resources at his command."

Herrera brought Spanish and Italian club soccer into the modern era of coaches stamping this style and worldview on their players and in the process becoming the first manager to collect credit for a team's performance. Up to that time managers were more marginal, with the exception perhaps of prewar examples of eccentric Englishmen such as Athletic's Mr. Pentland or fearless Irishmen such as FC Barcelona's Patrick O'Connell. During the 1950s teams were better known for their players, such as Di Stéfano's Real Madrid, than their managers. Yet Catalans remember the Herrera era, while Inter FC during the 1960s is still referred to as Herrera's Inter.

He came to be popularly known as "the Magician" on account of his innovative psychological motivating skills, which some of today's most successful coaches like Pep Guardiola and José Mourinho were destined to emulate. His pep talks would be punctuated with phrases like "He who doesn't give it all doesn't give anything." Herrera was disdainful of other managers in Spain for their failure to engage with players and to bring about a real change in their attitude. His prematch warm-ups, like his training sessions, were intense affairs, and his press conferences usually controversial, as were his prematch preparations. After providing his players with a cup of tea made up of spices and herbs only he knew the true identity of, Herrera would gather his players around him in a circle. Then, throwing the ball at each in turn, he would scream a question, looking each player directly in the eyes. "What do you think of the match? How are we going to play? Why are we going to win?" he would ask. The questions gathered in speed and intensity as he went around the circle. Then as a collective frenzy appeared to reach its climax, the circle would split and the players sprint before returning to the fold, at which point the team would shout, "We are going to win!"

Herrera encouraged superstition, which he believed complemented the traditional Virgin cults to which most Spanish clubs were linked because of the Catholicism of a majority of players and fans. He found a susceptible target of his own tricks in the case of the Galician-born Luis Suárez, the attacking midfielder nicknamed El Arquitecto (The Architect) for his visionary passing and explosive goal-scoring ability.

Galicia has never boasted as many soccer stars as other major regions of Spain. After Suárez, only Real Madrid's Amancio would lay claim to enduring fame, and they both chose at an early stage in their careers to emigrate to bigger non-Galician clubs. Other Spaniards say that the Gallegos lack the strength of Basques, the imagination of Catalans, the courage of Castilians, and the mischievous artfulness of Andalusians. So the popular soccer joke goes: "An Andalusian kicks the ball out of play and smiles. The Gallego takes twenty minutes to recover it."

But Suárez was different. He was not only a fine and creative inside-forward, the first Spanish-born player to be voted European Soccer Player of the Year in 1960, but he was also deeply superstitious. Thus, while looking on Suárez as Di Stéfano's "legitimate heir," Herrera played on his star player's belief that a glass of wine, accidentally spilled during a prematch meal, augured well for his goal-scoring chances. When Suárez wasn't looking, Herrera would give his wine glass a good tap and exclaim in a loud voice, "What a pity we've ruined the table-cloth!" Suárez would then immediately run up, dip his finger in the spilled wine, and then touch first his forehead and then the tip of his shoe.

Despite his tricks, Herrera had a genuine knowledge of the game and how it could be played best to entertain and secure victory. Herrera experimented with some innovative attacking soccer, using full-backs as wingbacks defensively supported by the *libero*, or center-half stopper, to launch faster counterattacks and turn some of the easier games into goal sprees. But he also knew how to close down opponents by having the sweeper stay behind the defense, with the rest of the team marking man-to-man and counterattacking on the break. Herrera claimed that his tactics were slightly different from the *catenaccio*, or cult of defense, that came to be identified with Italian teams with a reputation for negative play. He himself liked to use, among his options, a system whereby the center backs in front of the sweeper were markers, while the fullbacks had to be able to run with the ball and attack.

Herrera was full of praise for two foreign signings by Barca, the Hungarian Kocsis—the "Golden Head" who also had a sure touch and strength of foot, and Czibor, fast on and off the ball and similarly skilled in goal scoring. While Czibor liked to describe himself as the "engineer among the workers," Herrera insisted on a collective team effort. A competitive spirit, strength and speed, and technique were what constituted a winning formula. In an era of foreign imports, arguably Herrera's greatest contribution to the health of the Spanish league was in following the example of Athletic Bilbao and encouraging Barca's youth system—players like Olivella, Gensana, Gracia, Verges, and Tejada. "We owe them many of our victories; they played not just with class but with an absolute dedication to the club colours."

When some three years before he died in 1997 Herrera was visited at his Venice palazzo by author Simon Kuper and was asked to talk about his time in Spain, Herrera explained that he played his "tricky foreigners in attack"—Kocsis, Villaverde, Czibor, and so on—while basing his defense on homegrown talent, whom he referred to as "my big Catalans": Ramallets, Olivella, Rodro, Gracia, Segarra, Gensana. "To the Catalans, I talked 'Colours of Catalonia play for your nation,' and to the foreigners I talked 'money.'"

Herrera moved from FC Barcelona to Milan's Internazionale in 1960 where he continued to also coach the Spanish squad. As things turned out, it was Galician-born Luis Suárez, neither a Catalan nor a foreigner, who ended up following in Herrera's footsteps in the same year for 250 million Italian lire in the world's most expensive transfer deal.

Herrera's soccer career involved him in coaching six Spanish clubs, including Barca, and his spell as a coach of Spain that was to last from

1959 to 1962. He was in this post when in May 1960 Franco's personal intervention forced Spain's withdrawal from its quarterfinal matches against the Soviet Union in the first-ever European Nations Cup. The ties had been preceded by growing optimism in the Spanish camp after convincing victories in earlier qualifying matches against Poland and Yugoslavia and similar impressive victories in two friendlies, 3–1 against Italy at the Camp Nou and 3–0 against England at the Bernabéu, all under the management of Herrera. He had taken charge of the Spanish squad in 1959 and from the outset counted on such talent as Real Madrid stars Di Stéfano, Gento, Del Sol, Barça's Luis Suárez, Ramallets, and Segarra as well as Joaquin Peiro and "Txus" Pereda, the attacking midfielders then playing for Atletico de Madrid and Sevilla, respectively.

Herrera convinced his men they would beat the Russians and go and secure the title. Yet Franco quashed whatever dreams this fusion of the best of Spanish club soccer may have had of European soccer glory by not allowing the squad to play on Soviet territory and insisting that both legs be played on neutral territory—a request that Moscow declined. Franco was partly influenced by consideration for Spanish veterans of the World War II Blue Division who had fought and suffered with the Germans on the eastern front and some of whom were reportedly still detained in Soviet concentration camps. But he later claimed that what ultimately led to his decision were the detailed police reports he received warning that the Soviet media were predicting huge support not just in Moscow but also at the Bernabéu for the Russian team. Franco smelled a communist conspiracy: a Soviet-led propaganda exercise aimed at exposing the Spanish regime's unpopularity among exiles from the Civil War and surviving supporters of the Republic. This combined with a Russian request that the Soviet anthem be played and the Soviet flag be flown in the Real Madrid stadium proved altogether too much for Franco, and his appointees in the Spanish Soccer Federation—all Civil War comrades—did as they were ordered and withdrew the Spanish team from the competition.

The background to the controversy was never reported in Spain's highly censored media at the time other than to belatedly try to shift the blame to the Soviet Union for insisting on playing on neutral ground. The row was taken very badly by some of the players, who privately resented such a blatant intrusion of politics into their sporting activities. As the Spanish international Txus Pereda told me in an interview conducted in 2010 (he was to die of cancer a year later):

> We all returned home with a huge sense of sadness. I and the others had never been to Russia. We were genuinely interested in visiting a country that was a mystery to us and most Spaniards who had not gone into exile in the Civil War or fought there in World War II. It was also a great opportunity to play in a major competition final. I remember we are all gathered in the Spanish Federation offices in Madrid when they suddenly told us the match was off and we could all go home. It was all because of [political] pressure. Some ministers said yes, others said no, but it was Franco who was the boss, and he said no.

Herrera expressed his disappointment publicly on behalf of the team—without directly raising the issue of politics, still less blaming Franco. The official rumor mill suggested that this had little to do with any sense of patriotic opportunity or love of soccer but rather the loss of the financial bonuses Herrera had been promised by the Spanish Federation as an incentive to beat the Russians. Abroad it did little to improve Franco's image among his critics. The London *Times* condemned what it described as Franco's arbitrary and blatantly political coercive act that had violated the founding principles of the International Olympic Committee and FIFA. The newspaper suggested, not inaccurately, that Franco was making a point about Spain's credentials as an anticommunist Cold War warrior as a way of impressing his military and commercial ally, the United States. It certainly had very little to do with soccer.

Herrera survived for another two years as manager of the Spanish squad, but he made as many enemies as friends, and the former eventually caught up with him. The Argentine initially courted criticism for dropping Kubala from Barca first and then from the national squad, justifying the move on loss of form and lack of discipline linked to the Hungarian's heavy drinking.

Herrera forced out not only Kubala, but also another legend of Spanish soccer—Pepe Samitier, the former star player–turned–technical director of FC Barcelona. After a row with Herrera, Samitier moved to Real Madrid, where he had as many friends as in the Catalan capital, not least Franco himself, and where he harbored an enduring grudge against the Argentine. By the time Spain qualified for the World Cup in Chile in 1962, Herrera had become, as Alfredo Relaño puts it, the "baddy of the film . . . for many an innovator, for others a real anti-Christ of soccer."

On paper the Spanish squad that qualified for the World Cup in Chile in 1962, with Herrera as coach, could only impress, such was the talent and experience displayed. It included four nationalized foreigners—Di Stéfano, the Uruguayan-born Real Madrid central defender José Santamaría, Puskás, and *Barca*'s Paraguayan-born striker Eulogio Martínez—together with a coterie of homegrown stardom that included Gento, Collar, Peiro, Garay, Adelardo, and Del Sol. Yet Spain did not get past the first round where it was grouped together with Mexico and the two eventual finalist runners-up Czechoslovakia and Brazil, which won the championship.

As Brian Glanville has written, the component pieces of the Brazil team had "sprung apart, then strangely and steadily come together again." During the four years since they had last won the World Cup, two key Brazilian players had played at the club level in the Spanish *Liga* with contrasting fortunes. Vava, who scored twice in the 1958 final, went on to have two successful seasons with Atletico de Madrid. The other was Didi, one of the few foreign stars brought in by Bernabéu who did not prove a success at Real Madrid, partly because he never seemed to be quite up to the energy and speed of his teammates and partly because of personal problems involving his wife. She was a journalist who claimed that Di Stéfano was jealous of her husband and mistreated him. Di Stéfano blamed Didi for not fighting enough for the ball and losing it too easily. "The Bernabéu stadium likes quality, but it also values effort, work, commitment—it wants a battle. It's a public that is used to winning and to win you have to fight," Di Stéfano once said. In other words, Didi was a lesser being.

Arguably, bad luck rather than bad soccer conspired against Helenio Herrera's Spanish squad. It got off to a faltering start, losing 0–1 against the Czechs, their early pressure blocked by a solid defense, their flow of play increasingly interrupted by brutal tackles that crippled Herrera's stars and led one of them, Martínez, out of pure frustration, to lash out with a kick to an opponent's stomach. In the next game, against Mexico, the Spaniards rediscovered their rhythm. Again a strong defense resisted the Spanish pressure, but this time the gods were smiling, and Peiro scored the winner in the final minute.

In their final game in the group, Spain faced Brazil. The Spaniards needed a draw, if not a win, to qualify. It was a game in which Didi had planned to take his revenge on Di Stéfano, but Di Stéfano was left out of the Spanish team after pulling a muscle. Before the tournament got under way, Di Stéfano's father turned up with a "magic" liniment, but to no avail. A conflict of egos had led to an enduring rift between Di Stéfano and Herrera. As the then young Spanish international Fusté later recalled, "Di Stéfano was a guy who liked to lead, to be the boss, and he wanted to go on being the boss. The problem was that Herrera wanted to be boss as well, and there wasn't room for both of them."

For the game against Brazil, Herrera took a major gamble, which was also a questionable statement of self-belief, by making no fewer than nine changes from his original eleven. He dropped two star forwards, Del Sol and Suárez, his goalkeeper Carmelo, and his center-half Santamaría. Instead, he drew up a traditional attacking five with Puskás and Gento alongside three Atletico de Madrid players led by Peiro. In what some commentators regarded as one of the best games of the competition, Spain played with commitment and flair. Those watching the game included the seasoned English journalist Brian Glanville, who noted that for the first hour of the game, Spain played a defensive game that had Brazil at full stretch, before a swift counterattack led by the nationalized Puskás helped create the first Spanish goal. Spain kept its composure and their lead for another thirty-eight minutes, at which point Brazil equalized. Then with four minutes of normal time left, Brazil scored the winner. As Glanville himself concluded, it was a very near thing and arguably a "manifest injustice to Spain," which he judged the best-organized and most motivated team on the day. Nevertheless, Spain's resulting elimination from the 1962 World Cup reignited a national debate about the future of Spanish soccer, which brought with it some nasty prejudices from Spain's darker past.

Nationalist attacks focused on the foreign influence that had formed part of the Spanish expedition. The state-controlled Spanish sports daily *Marca* led the charge, claiming that Spain had underperformed as a result of not being sufficiently Spanish in selection and spirit. While conceding that nationalized foreign players like Di Stéfano, Puskás, and Kubala and managers like Daucik (Kubala's Hungarian father-in-law), the Paraguayan Manuel Fleitas, and Herrera himself had added "color and excitement" while also helping clubs like FC Barcelona, Real Madrid, and Atletico de Madrid win domestic and European competitions, the newspaper argued that the same foreigners were blocking the development of homegrown talent. "Even worse, the national team is now so full of foreigners and so conditioned by foreign tactics that it no longer plays like a team of real Spaniards, with passion, with aggression, with courage, with virility, and above all with fury," said *Marca*.

Not even Spain's star international Luis Suárez, a Spaniard born and bred, escaped criticism, the fact that he had chosen to leave his country to play in a foreign club held against him as antipatriotic—or so it seemed to his detractors. As for Herrera, he made so many enemies along the way during his time in Spain that he, above all others, became the target of unbridled criticism painting him as a mercenary with no loyalty but to himself.

José Villalonga and players celebrate Spain's European
Nations Cup victory over the Soviet Union, 1964

CHAPTER 20

An Officer in Charge

Herrera was replaced as Spanish coach by José Villalonga, a Spanish thoroughbred. Born in Cordoba in 1919, Villalonga during the Spanish Civil War had enlisted as a volunteer nationalist soldier, aged sixteen, before being promoted to subaltern. After the conflict was over, he entered the Military Academy and in 1947, with the rank of lieutenant, was named professor of physical education before doing a crash course in soccer coaching.

Villalonga was a soldier the regime could trust politically. But with a decent track record at the club level in the postwar *Liga*, he was also considered a safe pair of hands in soccer terms. As manager of Real Madrid during the mid-1950s, he coached both foreigners and Spaniards, winning *La Liga* and the Copa Latina in his first season before taking the club to its first European Cup victory. In 1959 he became coach at Atletico de Madrid. The club at the time shone with players like Enrique Collar and Adelardo—both internationals—and Miguel Jones, who was brought up in Bilbao, played in SD Indauxtu with Lezama but was eventually turned down for selection by Athletic on the grounds that his birth in Spanish Guinea disqualified him from the necessary status as a Basque. A similar fate befell two other Indauxtu players, José Garate and Jesus Pereda, Basque bred but born outside the region.

Villalonga took Atletico de Madrid to two successive victories over Real Madrid in the Copa del Generalissimo in 1961 and 1962 and over Fiorentino in the final of the European Cup Winners' Cup in 1962, so that it entered the history books as the first Spanish club to win a European championship with an unbeaten record during the tournament. These were glory days for Atletico—*los colchoneros*, the mattress men named because the old-style Spanish mattresses were covered in red and white stripes like the club colors. These were as good a times for the Spanish league's most erratic performers as that earlier period of success when—under Helenio Herrera—the club won the league championship in 1950 and 1951. Two players from Villalonga's period—Joaquin Peiro and Enrique Collar—came to be dubbed the "Infernal Wing" (Ala Infernal) because of the combined work ethos, speed, and skill they demonstrated down the left flank.

Villalonga's appointment as national coach was not without criticism. Diehard Real Madrid fans regarded him as a bit of a traitor for moving to Atletico. The Spanish soccer world generally saw him for what he was—a soldier turned PE teacher with limited technical knowledge of the game whose successes were due more to the individual talent of his players than to inspiration he might have given them. Yet political considerations appear to have prevailed, and Villalonga was given the opportunity to prove that he was not as bad as some people made him out to be.

He made a virtue of imposing the discipline and the physical training he had learned in the barracks on the national squad and showing some aptitude in the selection process. While retaining Luis Suárez as one of his star players, Villalonga drew ambitiously on an emerging generation of young Spanish club talent with Athletic Bilbao's Iribar in goal and players like Amancio, Marcelino, Fusté, and Pereda—the best crop from the two big clubs, Real Madrid and FC Barcelona—contributing to a team that was both robust defensively and capable of scoring goals. There were no nationalized Spaniards. In fact, a new decree made in 1963 banned foreign players from Spanish soccer, a policy enforced for the next ten years.

On June 21, 1964, Spain met the Soviet Union in the final at the Bernabéu stadium in Madrid at the European Nations Cup, an achievement in itself, given Spain's failure to make such progress in earlier tournaments. The fact that the final was to be played in the Spanish capital gave it an extra political edge. Unlike four years previously, both countries approached the event with a good dose of political pragmatism. The Spanish authorities had gone to considerable lengths to strengthen ties with international sporting bodies. Spain, a country that had to depend on its soccer clubs to break through its diplomatic isolation, was rewarded with the privilege of organizing a high-profile sporting event that was televised to fifteen European countries. For the Russians it was also an opportunity to engage with an ally of the United States, two years after the debacle of the Cuban missile crisis had brought the world close to nuclear destruction.

Politics played its part in other ways, too. An unnamed senior Falange official, a fanatical anticommunist from the Civil War, plotted to secretly drug the Russian players, a plan that was ultimately vetoed by Franco. Before making up his mind to let the event go ahead, let alone attend it personally, Franco consulted one of his more trusted allies, José Solís Ruiz, secretary-general of the regime's political movement. Solís Ruiz suggested that soccer, despite minimum state investment in it, could be used to divert an emerging postwar generation from any ideas of political dissidence. "Less Latin, more soccer," Solís

Ruiz told his leader. Franco, still worried about the possibility that he might be photographed or filmed handing a trophy to a communist, next talked to his personal doctor, Vicente Gil, who fancied himself as something of a soccer expert. "Don't you worry, Paco, we are going to win," Gil told him. Franco gave orders for preparations for the tournament to go ahead.

Villalonga acted as any loyal officer would. He prepared his players for the game as if it were a critical encounter of a protracted war on which the destiny of the nation rested. As one of his star players, Pereda, recalled:

> Two weeks before the match, Villalonga gathered us in a training camp in La Ventosa on the road from Madrid to Corunna where Franco used to go and shoot. One day he told us all to sit in a circle and watch him draw a miniature soccer field in the sand. He made one side up with stones and the other with pines and told us that we were the stones and the Russian were the pines, before crushing the pines with the rocks. He then said: "you see pines can't crush rocks; its rocks that crush pines and you are the rocks because you are stronger in mind and body." And that is how he psyched us up to beat them. When we played in Madrid, it was pure politics—any fool realized that. It was Franco against communism. For him it was not just a battle, it was war.

Franco needed little persuasion to milk the occasion as only he could. Entering the Bernabéu stadium with his wife, Doña Carmen, and a retinue of ministers and officials, the Generalissimo was greeted with prearranged cries of "Franco, Franco, Franco." They were initiated by groups of *Falangistas* but soon spread around the crowd of 125,000 that had packed into the Bernabéu stadium to support their national team in a kind of collective hysteria. Few relished the occasion as much as Villalonga, who looked at his team as his best regiment. As he declared in a pregame press conference, he had prepared a "young, impassioned, aggressive, virile team based on typical Hispanic values." Soccer and politics were in perfect synchronicity.

As things turned out, both teams—one representing a totalitarian fascist state, the other a totalitarian socialist one—were a fair match for each other. It was raining and the ground was muddy. It was a tough game, with the ball and the players slipping and sliding, although not without skill. Five minutes into the game, Suárez delivered one of his classic visionary crosses that landed at Pereda's feet and produced the opening goal. While elation broke out all over the stadium, Franco in the presidential box raised his arms slightly and smiled. The roar in the stadium had barely died down when the Russians counterattacked and scored. Franco's countenance momentarily darkened, as if news had just reached him of a major military reverse. The game from then on became a test of strength and endurance, with each side showing huge resilience in their back lines, as the downpour became heavier and muffled the enthusiasm of the drenched spectators. Seven minutes from the end, Rivilla intercepted a pass from Ivanov to Juasainov and embarked on a fast run down the right wing. He passed to Pereda, who crossed to Marcelino, who headed the goal just past the left post of the net, beating the Russian Lev Yashin, one of the greatest goal-keepers of all time. This time Franco almost got to his feet, and his arms moved farther and his smile was broader. The stadium erupted again, this time with a sense that it was all over—and it was. Amid euphoric scenes, Stanley Rous, the UEFA president, handed the cup to Olivella, the captain. Franco had gotten used to taking center stage at big soccer events, personally attending all the domestic finals and handing the Spanish Cup (renamed the Generalissimo's Cup) and the League Cup to the victors. But on this occasion he was happy to defer to international protocol, knowing that he would benefit politically anyway. By arrangement with Villalonga and the Spanish Soccer Federation, and in a well-publicized act, Olivella subsequently dedicated the Nations Cup to Franco on behalf of his team and his coach.

The Spanish militarist paper *Arriba* led the media reaction: "The Spanish fury has returned at last. The victory has demonstrated to the world that the Spanish Fury—*La Furia*—is invincible, when enjoyed with passion, aggression, courage and virility." Villalonga, meanwhile, spoke like a triumphant general dedicating the outcome of battle to his commander in chief: "I think quite frankly that we deserved to win and because it's been a just victory it is only right that we should offer it with all our respect to his Excellency the Head of State who has been a very special witness of how these boys have fought to achieve it. The eleven have been, without distinction, eleven lions who have marked a new milestone in the history of Spain's international soccer."

In a series of comments, one proved unconsciously prophetic: "We have always paid tribute to Spain's great achievement in the Olympics of 1920. Perhaps today's will endure as an example for the next forty-four years," said Villalonga. The year was 1964. Not till 2008 would Spanish national squads win another major competition.

Two years after winning the European Nations Cup, Villalonga kept the majority of his squad unchanged, with the hope of similar success in the World Cup in England. But it proved a typically Quixotic pipe dream. Not only was the squad getting old, but it had also run out of luck.

A second Group 2 match provided the great surprise of the first week of the series, when Spain lost 1–2 to a rough and efficient Argentine side in a game that saw Luis Suárez hacked down on two occasions. In Argentina's later quarterfinals encounter with the host, England, such brutal tactics led to a controversial sending off of their captain, Rattin—the man the English tabloids had dubbed "the Animal." After he was shown a red card, Rattin had defiantly traded insults with the Wembley crowd. By then Spain had been knocked out of the tournament. Narrowly beating Switzerland 2–1, Spain went on to lose to West Germany 1–2.

Like the regime that he so loyally personified, Villalonga's grip on the squad was no longer what it once had been. Some of the players had grown resentful of a coach who racketed up discipline but seemed lacking in creative ideas. This in turn conspired against the development of a team ethos, with some of the younger players mistrusting Villalonga's motivation. FC Barcelona's Fusté was one of them. He recalled:

> What failed for us in England was the fact that the military still wanted to rule the national squad; for reasons of international prestige they got Villalonga to bring in from Italy highly paid star players like Suarez and Del Sol, although they were already too old. The whole campaign was badly planned, and one of the goals was scored by Pirri after he had clearly handled it. It was as evident as Maradona's against England twenty years later, and, like Diego did then, he got away with it. The difference was that Argentina went on to become champions in Mexico 1986—and this time England emerged victorious.

This was one World Cup in which Spain's stars failed to shine, as Luis Suárez was later honest enough to admit. "We played very badly, myself in particular," he admitted when interviewed many years later for a documentary commemorating the centenary of the Spanish Soccer Federation.

Among the younger players on that team was the Basque Iribar. He was just twenty-three when he played in the England World Cup and was already fast becoming one of Spanish soccer's goalkeeper

legends on his club Athletic. But for him the experience of playing for
Spain proved a huge disappointment. As he told me:

> We had a league with some great soccer players, but we just didn't
> seem to hack it internationally. The truth is that after the 1966
> World Cup, there were some great national squads—like Brazil,
> Argentina, Italy, and Germany—with a huge potential. Along the
> way we had some bad luck, but the truth was that other teams were
> better than ours; they were better trained and had a fresher out-
> look. I know the regime liked to talk of *La Furia*, but it was a term
> that was invented by some journalist, not by the players. It wasn't
> fury that we were lacking; it was a clear style, a model—a system.

A Barca fan: "More than a club"

CHAPTER 21

Rivals

It is perhaps as good a point as any in the ongoing narrative to examine more closely the rivalry between the two giants FC Barcelona and Real Madrid and the one key phenomenon that has straddled much of the history of Spanish soccer and been fundamental to both its evolution and its popularity. The infamous game between the two clubs in the aftermath of the Spanish Civil War in Real Madrid's stadium in Chamartín during which an atmosphere of visceral hatred led to the visitors being thrashed 11–1 was the first of a series of postwar controversial encounters that would develop as part of world soccer's most intense and enduring club rivalries. It was a rivalry that, while having its roots in politics and culture, became driven by a momentum of mutual creation. It fed on itself, reflecting the growing popularity of soccer as a sport, while manifesting itself most violently at times of maximum political anxiety.

The bad blood that ran through every encounter remained a constant for more than a half century. There was rarely an encounter when both sides could claim a level playing field. It did not matter whether the game was played in Madrid or Barcelona; each match was intensely partisan. The occasion when fans set aside tribal loyalties and applauded a player because of how well he played, not because of the shirt he wore, was rare. I have witnessed this only twice—when FC Barcelona's Ronaldinho and later Messi received a standing ovation from the home fans at the Bernabéu in recognition of their outstanding play. By contrast, one of the most abusive incidents I can recall witnessing in any *gran clasico* was when Figo returned to the Camp Nou for the first time since November 2002 when he changed his club colors. While at FC Barcelona, Figo had made 172 appearances for the Catalans and won the league twice. But he had committed the ultimate sin of transferring from FC Barcelona to Real Madrid, setting a new record transfer fee of £37 million. The cacophony of jeers and expletives, together with the cans, lighters, and other loose missiles that accompanied the Portuguese international's every move, climaxed with a severed suckling pig's whole head being thrown at him by local fans as he prepared to take a corner kick.

Through much of the history of this rivalry the referee stood accused of being a fellow conspirator rather than an arbitrator, hated by one side as much as he was loved by the other. As a general rule the loser would always feel cheated, while FC Barcelona has tended to show itself as less magnanimous in victory and a worse loser. In the past this might reflect a certain inferiority complex FC Barcelona developed during Real Madrid's golden years of the 1950s, when its rival laid justifiable claim to playing the best club soccer in the world. In more recent times, roles were reversed when José Mourinho characterized his early days as manager of Real Madrid by blaming the supremacy of FC Barcelona on too much diving by the Catalans and too many unjustified decisions against the players in white.

Battle lines were first drawn in the Spanish capital in 1912, when twelve minutes from the end of one of their first competitive games against Real Madrid the whole FC Barcelona team abandoned the game, claiming that the referee was against them. During the 1960s, Real Madrid adopted a particular dislike for British referees, holding one of them in particular responsible for disallowing goals by Di Sté-fano and Gento and giving FC Barcelona a disputed penalty. On June 6, 1970, a young, inexperienced referee from San Sebastián, Emilio Guruceta, was in the eye of the storm when he gave a controversial penalty to Real Madrid during a second-leg quarterfinal tie in the Spanish Cup. The penalty was awarded after Real Madrid's Manolo Velázquez seemed to have been brought down well outside the box. The stadium erupted in protest. There was an unprecedented field invasion and running battles with riot police.

Although Franco would live and rule for another five years, this was a defining moment in Spanish soccer. The Guruceta case, named after the referee who made the wrong call in Real Madrid's favor, was the first time that Spanish soccer had gotten out of the dictator's control. Until that moment, by allowing FC Barcelona to function, he had divided and ruled, exploiting the political confusion of the Catalans, many of whom had fought for him in the Civil War. His intention was never to prevent Barca from winning titles, but to see Spanish soccer become an ever more popular sport thanks to the rivalries of its two great clubs.

It is a conflict that I have followed closely as long as I have been a soccer fan. It is a subject that has taken up much of my childhood, youth, and professional life, and my experience of it has been from the perspective of both camps, having been born and brought up in Madrid, while spending family vacation time in Catalonia and sharing much of my working life in Spain between Barcelona and the Spanish capital.

It was such a background that no doubt led me to cross paths with the Irish actor Ardal O'Hanlon in 2006, among the countless memorable encounters I have had along my journey into Spanish soccer. I had never met Ardal when I received a phone call from him out of the blue early that year. The comedy series *Father Ted* in which O'Hanlon plays a goofy young Irish priest called Father Doogall had long been a favorite of mine, so I felt honored, if surprised, to hear from him. It turned out Ardal was doing another television series—this time with a slightly more serious bent, on great soccer rivalries, and wanted me to help him out in Spain. It was an offer I didn't even consider refusing, and within hours I was sharing some tapas and vinos with Ardal and his production team in Barcelona's Old Quarter, near the cathedral.

Ardal has the disconcerting personality of all good comedians—an intensely private person offstage, both thoughtful and intelligent and far from brash or outspoken. While refusing to be tagged as political, both his father and his grandfather were deeply involved in the politics of the Irish state, which gave him a special insight into the divided politics of Spain and its soccer. Ardal was also a keen observer of the ordinary daily grind of life—as well as its peaks and troughs. His instinctive irreverence was underpinned by intelligence, laughter mixed in with occasional dark moods. Of his talents not just as a television actor but as one of Ireland's (and the UK's) most gifted stand-up comedians, I was aware. More of a discovery was his passion for Spanish soccer, and one club in particular. "I've been infatuated with soccer since the age of four," Ardal admitted. It dated his infatuation to 1969. "First it was Leeds, then in 1974 it was the Dutch, and then when Cruyff went to Barcelona it was Leeds, Holland, and Barca!" He went on: "The infatuation grew and then fell off for a while—when I discovered girls and 'other things'—but the dream of visiting the Camp Nou never quite disappeared. The first time I came here was about ten years ago on my honeymoon. It was my wife's first-ever soccer match, and she loved it."

He reminded me that my own infatuation with the stadium had begun when on a first visit as a young television researcher in 1976 I had watched Cruyff lead his team out to play in a game against Athletic Bilbao and the stadium filled with Catalan and Basque flags. It was the first time that such a blatant display of non-Spanish nationalist loyalties had happened in a soccer stadium since the Spanish Civil War. Franco had banned both flags throughout his dictatorship. Years later I ended up taking one of my daughters to the Camp Nou for the first time, and she loved it. It proved a happier experience than for her younger sister, who on another occasion had to put up with the racist abuse from Chelsea hooligans at Stamford Bridge because she supported Barca in a Champions League match.

But back to Ardal. I was struck by Ardal's familiarity with relevant Spanish history—or at least its mythification—which he commented on with his comedian's eye for the telling anecdote and knack for synthesis. "That's Columbus's statue over there," he observed while walking down by the harbor, "but you won't find him pointing toward the Americas—this being Barcelona, he is pointing toward the Mediterranean. The Catalans claim Columbus as one of their own, which is a bit of a surprise considering it was largely his fault that Catalonia went into a very long and steep decline. Columbus opened up the new trade routes to the West, but the king and queen of Spain forbade the Catalans from using them. Thus Barcelona was thwarted, nor for the last time, by the dastardly Spaniards. But they refuse to lie down."

Over the next days of filming we were both on a mutual learning curve and forged a strong friendship around soccer that belied our age difference—I was twelve years older than he was. Between us I think we tried to illuminate some truths as well as dispel some myths. The fact that neither of us had parents who were particular soccer fans and thus without a tribal loyalty helped us approach a divisive subject through a more or less objective lens.

So we began to share some unquestionable truths. Of all the regions that constituted Spain, it was the Catalans that historically had been the most forceful in asserting their identity. No matter that their version of history from medieval times onward exaggerates the extent to which Catalonia was once a nation as opposed to a region. History is perhaps nowhere more argued over and with such passion than in Catalonia, where it is a political weapon in the battle for identities. Two centuries ago the English chronicler of Spain Richard Ford commented, with some foresight : "No province of the unamalgamated bundle which forms the conventional monarchy of Spain hangs more loosely to the crown than Catalonia, this classical country of revolt, which is ever ready to fly off." The Catalans certainly had a legitimate grievance based on the belief that their history differed from that of the myth of a united nation-state ruled from Madrid, and this had fueled one of their enduring passions.

One cannot begin to understand Spanish soccer's greatest club rivalry outside the context of Catalonia's relationship with the rest of Spain. Or to put it another way, one cannot begin to understand FC Barcelona's perception of Real Madrid as the main enemy without taking in Catalan politics, culture, and history and the interrelationship of all three with soccer. Much of the history of Catalonia, as viewed by a majority of FC Barcelona fans, is a story of humiliation and frustration, the aspirations of this region curbed and stomped on by the centralizing tendencies of Madrid, the potential of Barcelona as one of the great capitals of the Mediterranean never fully realized, and the perceived close links between Real Madrid and the center of power in the Spanish capital.

Some of the facts of Catalan history are fairly straightforward even if seen through the mind of a comedian like Ardal O'Hanlon and hard to take too seriously. "You can feel the spirit of Wilfred the Hairy here," proclaimed Ardal later one afternoon in the Camp Nou as local fans began to converge for the latest Barca–Real Madrid encounter, with their Catalan and Barca flags and shouting in one uninterrupted cry *"Visca Barca Visca Catalunya"* (Catalan for Up with Catalonia, Up with Barca.). Somewhere in the stadium someone had lifted a large poster with the manifesto CATALONIA IS NOT SPAIN.

Catalonia was recovered from the Moorish occupation in the early eighth century, long before much of the rest of Spain, and had its various fiefdoms united under an inspired count called Wilfred the Hairy (he was indeed called that because he was a heavily bearded man, as he is remembered to this day in statue form and the history books of Catalan schoolkids). While considered by some the founder of Catalonia, this medieval warrior was still a vassal to Charles the Bald (who indeed lost his hair in early adulthood for reasons unknown). It was another Catalan warrior count, Borell the Second, who finally broke his vassalage from the intruding French king, Hugh Capet, in what Catalan nationalism would later claim was the birth of political Catalonia in 988. For then on the counts of Barcelona became, through a marriage in 1137, the kings of Aragon, who would later go on a conquering spree that extended south as far as Alicante and east to the Balearics and beyond to Sardinia, Sicily, Corsica, and southern Italy— Catalonia's very own days of imperial glory.

Fast-forward to the end of the Spanish Civil War: thousands of Catalans imprisoned or executed or forced into exile by Franco. At this point you may well ask what all this history has to do with the militancy that drives soccer's greatest rivalry. Rest assured that Barca fans take their history very seriously, however mythological. During the late 1990s I toured Spain in a bus filled with one of FC Barcelona's most radical group of fans. They called themselves the Almogavers. Their T-shirts and banners depicted medieval knights in full armor. So what was all this about, I asked Marc, the young secretary of the fan club. "The Almogavers were Catalan soldiers of the thirteenth century [actually they were mercenaries for the king of Greece] who conquered the Mediterranean. They'd go into battle on foot, holding their swords, and fight off whole armies on horseback."

Then Marc, together with some his mates, broke into the Barca anthem, "Tot el camp es un clam, som la gente blaugrana" (The whole stadium is a rallying cry, we are the people of red and blue)—the Barca colors, blue and red, the colors every club fanatic will insist are the colors of freedom. "We want Barca to conquer Europe just like the Almogavers," Marc will go on to tell me. He is holding a small banner bearing the words *Barca i Catalunya sempre al nostre cor* (Barca and Catalonia always in our hearts). "It's one and the same thing. That's what drives me. I've done so much for Barca, missed my exams, missed a whole year at college. You might say I'm fanatical. I like to consider myself someone who loves Barca with all my heart. If that's fanaticism, then I'm a fanatic."

That such loyalty is often mixed up with a visceral dislike of Real Madrid has to do with the fact that long after Wilfred the Hairy and Columbus had been buried, things got far worse for Catalonia before they got better, first with the united Kingdoms of Aragon and Castile moving the balance of political and economic power toward the center and then in 1714 the Bourbon regime of King Philip V depriving the Catalans of their local parliament and other rights, such as the power to raise their own taxes. Yet Catalonia was to prosper economically over the next two centuries, exporting wool and paper and embracing the Industrial Revolution before most of the rest of Spain, providing jobs for thousands of migrants from other regions and in effect subsidizing the more backward areas of Spain. Catalonia came to look at the rest of Spain, and Madrid in particular, not only as arrogant, and intolerant, but also ungrateful.

FC Barcelona drew its strength from troubled times, giving the region as a whole a necessary feeling of collective self-confidence. The collapse of the Spanish empire with the loss of Cuba in 1898 fueled Catalan nationalism. The birth of FC Barcelona at the start of the twentieth century made it early on a central focus of Catalan nationalism along with the reemergence of a Catalan nationalist party, parliament, and newspapers. "Barcelona became one of the most vibrant and wealthiest cities in Europe, home to the artists Gaudi, Picasso, Miró, and Dalí. Dalí entered a competition sponsored by FC Barcelona; Miró painted a poster for the club. FC Barcelona was a crucial part of Catalonia's newfound optimism and prosperity," enthused Ardal O'Hanlon.

It was all to change, though, after the Spanish Civil War. In 1942, for all this show of public self-confidence, Spain was a country politically divided within itself. Catalonia was once again denied its local parliament, Castilian was once again imposed as an official language, and the Catalan flag was banned. And although the management of FC Barcelona was handpicked by the regime, soccer provided an escape valve for suppressed emotions.

While a majority of Spanish soccer clubs were purged after the Spanish Civil War of political dissidents, and found themselves with little option but to recruit new members supportive of the new regime, FC Barcelona still managed to preserve an identity as a Catalan institution. The official postwar newsreels show the club's stadium, Les Corts, as a crowded theater of orderly entertainment, with no anti-regime flags or slogans or chants. But beneath the apparent conformity, a sense of resentment, revenge, and resistance persisted.

In 1947 Gregorio López Raimundo, the head of the Catalan Community Party, returned secretly from exile in France with a false passport and started going to Les Corts, both as a fan and as a political militant. He not only enjoyed the soccer, but also felt more protected from persecution in the stadium than he did on any street corner in Barcelona. As he told me many years later when I interviewed him about his years in clandestinity: "Out in the city, fascism was very visible—the names of the streets, the Falangist crests, the portraits of Franco, the flags. But in the stadium you were among the masses, and I felt—maybe I was imagining it, but I felt it all the same—that everyone around me was really antifascist deep down, at least in the stands. Maybe things were a little different where people were sitting; the club management was proregime, handpicked no doubt during the early Franco years but not the fans—they identified themselves with a democratic Catalonia."

It was not until 1968, a year marking revolution in large swaths of the world, that FC Barcelona's new president, Narcis de Carreras took it upon himself to give the club marketing department a dream motto: "Barca es mes que un club" (Barca is more than just a club). In other words, it could not be compared to any other soccer club, let alone Real Madrid, because it represented so much more in political, cultural, and social terms. Catalans might have been divided over exactly what Catalonia meant—was it a region or a nation—but from now on there could be no doubt about Barca. As Bobby Robson, one of its managers, would later tell me: "Barcelona is a nation without a state, and Barca is its army."

The politics of Real Madrid do not lend themselves so easily to mottoes or manifestos. One of Spanish soccer's most literate commentators, the Argentine-born former Real Madrid player and manager Jorge Valdano—no old Francoist he—once tried to explain this to me: "Real Madrid is a team that only thinks in soccer terms, not political or nationalistic ones. . . . I think that is a huge advantage it has over FC Barcelona, which thinks too much in political terms. The worst thing you can do to a soccer player is to give an excuse to justify his frustration."

Undoubtedly, the 1950s were Real Madrid's golden years, when everyone seemed happy, at least in the club. Barca fans console themselves to this day by claiming that one of the major stars, Alfredo Di Stéfano, was "robbed" by the rival in a questionable transfer deal that had a helping hand from the Spanish state. But the legend rests with Real Madrid as the first Spanish club not only to become champions of Europe but also to subsequently hang on to the titles over several seasons. To Real Madrid fans, old and young, it was Di Stéfano who gave them a sense of identity during a period of history when Spain remained relatively isolated in the world. He came to personify success on a global scale, something that during the 1950s could not be said of any Spanish company, let alone Franco. Di Stéfano, long retired, was asked once by Inocencio Arias, a former Real Madrid director and personal friend, what he thought defined the Real Madrid fan: "It wants the team to fight . . . it wants it to win . . . but it wants it to win first and then to play."

During our stay in Barcelona, Ardal and I were not short of Catalans prepared to simply dismiss Real Madrid as Franco's team. But Real Madrid fans who belonged to the first generation to be born after the Spanish Civil War and who did not share their parents' pro-Franco inclinations feel insulted by this, even more so now that Spain has been a democracy for a while.

In a short memoir published in the Spanish newspaper *El Pais* in 1994, novelist Javier Marias recalls becoming a Real Madrid fan, in 1957, at age six, despite belonging to a group of friends many of whose fathers, like his own, were all anti-Franco. "The enthusiasm I felt for Real Madrid was mainly provoked by one man and he was called Di Stéfano—no doubt. But there was something else—Madrid was a club that neither cheated nor had fear and was blessed with drama. These may seem trivial matters, but in the city of my childhood everything else seemed to lack any worth and only designed to make you fear and everything was sordid rather than dramatic. Real Madrid was like an oasis, like the cinema on Saturday."

But if Real Madrid provided a kind of sanctuary to those who did not consider themselves part of the Franco regime, it has tolerated long after Franco's demise among its supporters those of a more politically extreme bent. I remember arriving at Munich Airport some years back with a group of Real Madrid fans and seeing a section of them arrested by the police under German's anti-Nazi laws. On another occasion I decided to join a small group of Barca fans at the Bernabéu. As we arrived at the Real Madrid stadium, our small group of Barca fans had to run the gauntlet. The Utra Surs were waiting with their usual vocabulary of racist abuse against FC Barcelona black players and against Catalonia generally.

Nonetheless, it's no use pointing, as Marias and others do, to the fact that prior to Di Stéfano, Franco ruled the country and Real Madrid never won a domestic championship, let alone an international one, as evidence that this was not the regime's team—that there was no political fix.

The case for the prosecution against soccer "collaborators" even of Marias's "liberal" ilk collected enough evidence to confirm generations of Barca fans in their prejudice. Real Madrid's "black book," or its history, according to its Catalan nationalist detractors, notes just how trusted Real Madrid was as an ally by the Franco regime when it played in Venezuela representing Spain in an international club tournament in 1952. "The behaviour of Real Madrid from directors through to players has been irreproachable in all aspects and they have left us with an unsurpassable impression of impeccable sporting good manners and patriotism," commented the official state bulletin at the end of the tournament. No such assurance could be given to FC Barcelona, a club whose loyalty to the regime could never be taken for granted as long as there was a simmering undercurrent of Catalan nationalism that fed on feelings of injustice, resentment, and envy.

During the 1950s, years during which the Spanish national squad continued to underachieve and Spain remained relatively isolated internationally, Real Madrid, much to the chagrin of Barca supporters, helped promote an image of Spanish success overseas. Santiago Bernabéu's club in effect converted itself, together with emigration and oranges, into Franco's most important export. And because this was a period that saw the expansion of televised soccer across borders, it put Real Madrid firmly on the map as *the* representative of Spanish soccer at its best, with its mixture of foreign stars and homegrown talent playing creative, offensive soccer in a way no other club in the world could match.

The reputation that Real Madrid built up beyond Spain's borders was already apparent in the 1955–1956 season, which marked the inaugural of a European Cup tournament that would prove its potential not only to get around the diplomatic barriers of the Cold War but also to raise the international profile of major clubs and their revenue-raising capacity. On the eve of the tournament's first final in Paris, the Spanish embassy in the French capital hosted a reception that attracted an impressive guest list from the French sporting world as well as senior representatives from international bodies like FIFA and the International Olympic Committee. It was the best-attended reception the Francoist embassy had had since the days of the Spanish Republican government prior to the Spanish Civil War.

In the season before, FC Barcelona, with Kubala as its star, came to Paris and against Nice won the Copa Latina. But this tournament was restricted to southern Europe's clubs and lacked a pedigree in the wider soccer establishment. It was the European Cup, the dream child of Gabriel Hunot, a former French international and the editor of the widely respected sports daily *L'Equipe* that established itself as the most prized trophy in world club soccer, setting a marker for a new age in which soccer became a matter of celebrity as much as success. The legend of Real Madrid as the most successful sporting institution in the world is bound up with it because no other institution can claim to have won it so many times—six successive championship victories between 1954 and 1960.

Such a record has been absorbed by Barca fans over the years, nurturing their loyalty rather than diminishing it, and ensuring that the rivalry between FC Barcelona and Real Madrid becomes more intense as each new encounter approaches. In 2006, four days before *el gran clasico*, Ardal O'Hanlon signed up as a member of the Barca soccer club. He called it the proudest day of his life, as good, probably better, than the day he got his first Irish passport.

Johan Cruyff: Dutch international, Catalan icon

CHAPTER 22

The Death of Franco

O n Thursday, November 20, 1975, Spain's prime minister, Carlos Arias-Navarro, tearfully announced the death of General Francisco Franco, the man who had cast a long shadow over the nation's destiny for four decades and influenced every aspect of Spanish life, not least soccer.

Vicente Marco, a presenter with the then hugely popular radio program *Carrusel Deportivo* (Sport carousel), told his listeners that players in all *La Liga* matches would wear black armbands as a sign or mourning and respect. "They will pay tribute to the late head of state, Francisco Franco, and a landmark in our history who will be a point of reference from now onward. Fans and players will pray an Our Father together in his memory."

Before dying, Franco had decided to formalize the succession of the Bourbon dynasty—out of power since 1931—and decreed that his successor as head of state would be Prince Juan Carlos, the grandson of King Alfonso XIII. But the hopes of diehard Francoist loyalists that the young prince would meekly follow in Franco's footsteps proved remarkably shortsighted. As the new king of Spain, Juan Carlos would convert into a constitutional monarch and oversee a restoration of democracy for the first time since before the Spanish Civil War. While the expectation of reform of the Spanish state—with a restoration of autonomy to the regions—stirred enduring rivalries, Spanish soccer was now set to evolve within the context of profound political and social liberalization.

When Franco died, the season of *La Liga* was in its tenth week. Earlier in the month Real Madrid, coached by the Montenegrin Milijan Miljaniæ, had progressed into the quarterfinals of the European Cup after beating Derby County 6–5 on aggregate in the second round. Miljaniæ was not to every Real Madrid fan's taste because of his tendency to focus on defending rather than attacking. But as long as the team went on winning, he had a job. Madrid had secured its lead at the top of the table, ahead of Hercules, Athletic Bilbao, Atletico de Madrid, and FC Barcelona after a controversial away victory over newly promoted Sevilla at the Sánchez Pizjuán stadium. Real Madrid's German midfielder Paul Breitner scored a goal through a hole in the side of the Sevilla net. The referee claimed it was a straightforward goal. After a sports newspaper published a photograph showing the ball indeed entering through the net, the home crowd declared it the most scandalous phantom goal in history.

On the Sunday following the death of Franco, Real Madrid and Zaragoza players wore their armbands as they faced each other in the Bernabéu. In the Basque Country and Catalonia, not all players similarly mourned. While some Franco loyalists had wanted *La Liga* to be temporarily suspended as a further sign of respect toward the old dictator, King Juan Carlos decreed the games should go ahead. It was his way of infusing a sense of normality among the masses but also a sign that the young king was his own man.

Spanish soccer, meanwhile, adapted itself to the changing political environment with remarkable ease, not least in Real Madrid, the club whose enemies had always tarnished with the brush of collaboration with the Franco regime. One of the most respected Real Madrid players was Vicente del Bosque, who had joined the team five years earlier. He had earned a reputation as a playmaker in midfield. Del Bosque was also a discreet anti-Francoist. Born in 1950, he had grown up amid memories of his family suffering as a result of being on the losing side of the Civil War. Del Bosque's father was a Republican railway clerk who had served a prison sentence under Franco for his political beliefs. "Inside the club we all took the news of Franco's death pretty calmly. We were, after all, politically independent," del Bosque told me many years later, the first time we met. "I remember that in those days everyone in Spain was talking about whether there was going to be *rupture* or *reforma* [a total break from the past or just an orderly reform]; fortunately, we took a path of reform that allowed us to live our lives normally."

Del Bosque had willed himself to believe in soccer's potential to break through the barriers of politics. He always disapproved of the caricature of Real Madrid as "Franco's team." He believed that even in the Franco years, Real Madrid had fans of all political tendencies but with a common belief that the club, along with the Spanish national team, could and should play the best soccer in the world. When Santiago Bernabéu, the club's long-serving president and a Francoist Civil War veteran, died in June 1978, del Bosque was one of the players that honored his contribution to the game by carrying his coffin. Bernabéu outlived Franco by nearly three years. But whereas statues were torn down and streets renamed after Franco's death, the stadium Bernabéu built would remain named after him, an enduring monument to one of the great figures of Spanish soccer.

The death of Franco produced mixed emotions no more so that in Catalonia, a region that had grown economically during the regime while its political and cultural identity were repressed. At FC Barcelona, the club president, Agustin Montal, sent three telegrams to Madrid, one to Franco's private office, expressing "sadness at the irreplaceable loss of the Head of State"; the second to Franco's widow, Doña Carmen Polo de Franco, and her family, "with our most heartfelt condolence"; and the third to Franco's appointed successor, King Juan Carlos, declaring "the personal loyalty of our club, and the hope of a future of peaceful and democratic coexistence represented by your Royal Highness."

At FC Barcelona there was a touch of tragicomedy the day Franco died. "Gentlemen, the Caudillo is dead," the concierge announced solemnly after interrupting a meeting of the club president, Montal, with some of his senior officials. Among those present was Jaume Rosell, the club secretary and father of a future club president, Sandro, and he provided me with his eyewitness account. "There were two reactions: those who said, 'Let's open a bottle of *cava*,' and the others, who stayed silent and were evidently scared shitless [given their Francoist tendencies]. Among the latter was a director who said he didn't feel well and who went home. Poor guy, it seems the news gave him a stomach upset. Among the happier reactions was that of his brother— he was a communist!"

Later, after the main meeting had dispersed, Rosell stayed behind with the chief secretary of the club, Joan Granados. Alone in Montal's room, they found their eyes focusing on a bust of Franco that was perched high on a shelf. Instinctively, Granados got up on a chair, picked up the bust, and threw it across the room, at Rosell. By accident Franco nearly hit him on the head, before striking the ground and shattering into little bits. Rosell had feared it might be made of bronze. In fact, it was made of plaster. He exclaimed, "Fuck me, we thought this was so solid that it could never break, and now it turns out it's nothing but shitty plaster!" A few minutes later some Barca fans turned up. Rosell had an enduring memory of that moment:

They [the fans] were in a state of high excitement. We handed them some photographs of Franco that were hanging up in another room. Then we gave instructions for the removal of a sign that was in the stadium remembering the Francoist members of Barca who had fallen during the Civil war—"For Spain and for God," it stated. We put the sign in a box and took it down to the basement, where we put it well out of the way, hidden from view, for it seemed to me that such a sentiment did not belong to the history of Barca, although I didn't think we should destroy it as other things were destroyed.

By the time of Franco's death, the administration of FC Barcelona had come under the increasing influence of the Catalan nationalist movement, headed by Jordi Pujol. The two men who had toyed with Franco's bust before seeing it shatter—Rosell and Granados—were active members of Pujol's party, Convergencia Democratica de Catalunya. And it was the bank that Pujol controlled, Banca Catalana, that helped finance one of the most important transfers in Spanish soccer history—that of the Dutchman Johan Cruyff—after the Spanish Soccer Federation lifted the ban on foreign players, allowing two per team, on May 26, 1973.

Cruyff was already something of a legend, as a player with Ajax and the Dutch national team. It was under Ajax's coach, Rinus Michels, that Cruyff emerged as the star performer of what the Dutch called *total soccer*. The concept, which had seen earlier manifestations in South America, was one in which every player was supposed to have the technical and physical ability to interchange roles and positions at will. At its best, the system was supposed to have players in a seemingly effortless collective flow for most of the game: an exciting mixture of dribbling, first-touch passing, and creatively executed goals rather than long balls or kicks into touch.

The number-14 Cruyff was the personification of total soccer. Although he might play center-forward, he was often seen playing through the midfield or out on either wing, his ever-changing position on the field playing havoc with any conventional concept of defense or counterattack. A profile by a local Dutch journalist published in the 1970s noted, "Wherever he plays, with his radius of action, his ability to run past defenders at speed, his inimitable movement, his hard shot with both feet, his running for every ball, his stamina and his sense of positioning, he makes defences despair. . . . His greatest pleasure is playing beautiful soccer." Another chronicler of Dutch soccer, David Winner, notes how the idea took hold that what Cruyff and the other players at Ajax were doing was something more than soccer: "It was no longer men kicking a ball around a muddy field. It was something refined and intriguing. It was Art."

On August 18, 1973, Cruyff was bought by FC Barcelona in a record $1 million transfer—the highest price paid to that point by the Catalan club for any player. The club had as its coach Rinus Michels, the fellow Dutchman Cruyff would describe as his "first and only soccer master." The key deal maker was Armando Caraben, an economist and lawyer who was then serving as the FC Barcelona secretary. Married to a Dutchwoman, Marjolijn van der Meer, whom he had met one summer as a student in the Costa Brava, Caraben had gotten to know Holland and its soccer well and had established a friendship with Cruyff and his wife. A committed Catalan nationalist and opponent of the regime, Caraben saw a political opportunity. He gambled, correctly as it turned out, that the Dutchman's inspiration would increase Barca's popularity at a time of historic political change from dictatorship to democracy. Caraben had watched Cruyff play many times and was convinced not only of his goal-scoring abilities, but also of his capacity to organize a team around his talent.

Cruyff's arrival in Barcelona fueled a sense of huge expectation in Spanish soccer that mirrored the hopes that many Spaniards, not least Catalans, had of a better Spain post-Franco. An article in the magazine *Dicen* described Cruyff's coming as a key moment in the club's history, on a par with that of the arrival in the 1950s of the great Hungarian Kubala. It predicted a new period of glory. Whereas Kubala came as a vehicle of Franco's anticommunist propaganda, Cruyff came from a European country that had pioneered some of the social freedoms and cultural innovations of the 1960s.

Fans were not disappointed. Cruyff electrified the Spanish league in his first season. He was dubbed El Salvador (the Savior), lifting FC Barcelona from the bottom of the table to the top, thus making them *Liga* champions for the first time since 1960. After Barca had easily crushed Granada early on in the season, the club magazine reported, "Cruyff not only plays for the rest of the team, he makes the team play. His quality brings out the best in those other Barca players whose quality was never in doubt but who sometimes stumbled rather than show the true measure of their worth. The team has turned into a homogenous unit, full of ideas and at ease with itself. And what all this means is that soccer has begun being fun again, it's recovered that special grace which makes it the favorite sport of the masses."

Michels as coach had concerns that Cruyff's diva status might demoralize his teammates, and there were rumors that Marcial was among those who resented suddenly being projected as mere appendixes. But for every team colleague in whom Cruyff provoked envy, there were others who felt only admiration. As the Spanish international Charly Rexach told me, "We all had our sense of pride that made us feel that we were as good as the next one, and that meant that for a while Barca had a team that wanted to prove it could play soccer."

FC Barcelona played some wonderful soccer that season and delivered where it most mattered, beating Real Madrid 5–0 in the Bernabéu, with two goals by Asensi, and one each by Cruyff, Juan Carlos and Sotil. Cruyff's goal was, well, pure Cruyff. Picking up the ball from just inside Real's half, on the turn, the Dutchman dribbled first with the uncluttered, floating speed of a gazelle and then weaved in and out of the Real defense, his nimble frame turning at sharp angles, and then skipping effortlessly over a final desperate sliding tackle. Cruyff took the ball on his left foot and then struck home, easily beating the goalkeeper.

The *New York Times* correspondent later wrote that Cruyff had done more for the spirit of the Catalan nation in ninety minutes than any politicians had achieved in years of stifled struggle. A few days before the game Cruyff had gone to the Franco authorities and insisted that his newly born son be registered as Jordi, the Catalan word for George and the local patron saint, in defiance of an official ruling that only Spanish or Castilian names could be used in official documents. "It took me some time to understand what was happening politically in Spain, although I realized soon enough how important the club was in Catalan terms," Cruyff told me. Unwittingly, the birth of a son transformed itself into the Dutchman's first political act in Spain.

Following the death of Franco, there were other instances when Spanish soccer took on an even more blatant political symbolism. Cruyff and Iribar, as FC Barcelona and Athletic Bilbao captains, respectively, led their teams out to the Camp Nou. The stadium was bathed in the colors of the Catalan and Basque nationalist flags, as the stadium united in giving the players a standing ovation. It was the run-up to the 1977 free elections—the first to be held in more than forty years. Iribar, who had played as a Spanish international during the Franco years, had by then nailed his colors to the cause of the Basque people, actively campaigning for the release of political prisoners.

On December 5, 1975, less than a month after the death of Franco, the Athletic captain, Iribar, and the captain of Real Sociedad, Kortabarria, walked out into a packed Atocha stadium in San Sebastián holding the banned Basque flag, the Ikurrina. The flag had been smuggled into the stadium by Josean de la Hoz Uranga, one of the Real Sociedad players, hidden in his gear bag. It was publicly displayed only after each captain had consulted with their teams in the dressing room and obtained unanimous approval. Uranga recalled later:

> We were all in Real Sociedad at the time native players who had come up through the youth team, and we all had our concerns and feelings. The majority of us were Basque nationalists, with a few in favor of all-out independence from Spain. Democracy had yet to find a firm foundation, and we were in a transition period, with the Basque people demanding change. . . . When we came out into the stadium with the flag it was a very emotional moment. There were a lot of people who cried. There were about sixteen thousand spectators in Atocha, and the stadium erupted.

Such was the popular support for the Basque flag that the local police chief ordered his men not to intervene rather than provoke a riot of incalculable consequences. Times were changing anyway in Spain now that Franco was dead, and the old diehards of the regime were fighting a losing battle to keep the country under authoritarian rule.

In January 2001 I interviewed Iribar at Athletic's training ground of Lezama (named after the player who had been a boy refugee in the UK during the Civil War) in the highland outside Bilbao. Much water had flowed under the Spanish political bridge over the previous twenty-five years. The years of terrorism by ETA in post-Franco Spain had fueled deep divisions in the Basque Country. Iribar had long since retired from soccer and had been put in charge of "institutional relations" by Athletic after his potato merchandising business had fallen on bad times. It was rumored locally that a key contract to supply members of the security forces had been canceled by the client on political grounds. Iribar remained a popular figure in Bilbao, but in Madrid, he had made enemies because of his support for Basque nationalism

"I am writing a book about Spanish soccer and trying to put it into a political, sociological context . . . ," I began. Iribar interrupted, "Well, I am telling you that here we talk about soccer and nothing else, exclusively about sport." It was of course nonsense, and we both knew it. Three months later the Spanish newspaper *El Pais* published an extensive conversation between Iribar and another Basque soccer legend, Real Sociedad's Roberto López Ufarte, who played the day the banned Ikurrina flag was brought out in Atocha stadium. As the two veterans walked along the beach of Zarautz, they pondered the historical significance of that event. "I think it marked an important step that helped a great deal the process toward the legalization of the Ikurrina. . . . [T]he fact is that it was that derby between our two teams that had endured as my best soccer memory—and that is despite the fact that we [Athletic] lost 0–5!" Iribar recalled.

During our earlier encounter, Iribar remained cautious before opening up slightly when I told him that as a young journalist I had filmed that day in the Camp Nou when he and Cruyff had come out to a sea of Basque and Catalan flags. How had he felt? "Well, the dictatorship had ended, and we were in a transition toward democracy and there was a general expression of joy in the stadium that day, a real hunger for liberty on both sides so that the game became a mirror of what a reflection of all that was happening. You could feel a real sense of happiness of being part of a democratic process and of winning freedom—you could feel it in the stadium, in the streets."

Yet for all the political euphoria and expectation of change stimulated by the death of Franco, Spanish soccer struggled to dominate internationally. The loss of hegemony of Spanish clubs at the European level reached its most striking moment in April 1973 when Ajax, the reigning champions, thrashed Bayern Munich before destroying Real Madrid in the semifinals. Ajax won 2–1 in Amsterdam and faced a hostile crowd of 110,000 for the return leg at the Bernabéu. Gerrie Mühren scored in the first half to give Ajax a 1–0 lead. But it was Mühren's brilliant display in the second half that drew a rare tribute from the massed host fans.

Mühren later spoke of how as a child, like so many fans around the world, he had idolized the Real Madrid team of the golden years and how it had always been his dream to play good soccer against the Spanish champions. On that day in the Bernabéu, Ajax and Real Madrid changed positions. As he put it, "Before that it was always the big Real Madrid and the little Ajax—but when they saw me doing what I did, the balance changed. The Real Madrid players were looking. They nearly applauded. The stadium was standing up. It was the moment Ajax took over."

It was not just Real Madrid that bowed to greater opponents in this period. Having failed to qualify for the 1974 World Cup, the Spanish national team coached by Kubala reached the quarterfinals of the 1976 European Championship, before losing on aggregate 1–3 to a strong West Germany. Returning to the World Cup in Argentina in 1978, Spain failed to get beyond the first-round group stage although once again a certain bad luck was blamed for Spain's underachievement. Spain lost 1–2 in a tougher than expected opening game with Austria. Next, when facing Brazil, the Spaniards kept level at 0–0 before the midfielder Julio Cardeñosa, the Real Betis midfielder, was faced with an open goal and muffed it. In the next game Spain met Sweden in their last game in the group, needing a win to pressure Brazil. Cardeñosa this time partly made up for his earlier giveaway with a good second-half performance, while his teammate FC Barcelona's Asensi, another attacking midfielder, scored the winning goal. But it was not enough to go through to the next round. It the aftermath of the 1978 World Cup, the country's two biggest clubs, FC Barcelona and Real Madrid, competed for supremacy in an increasingly charged political environment. Of the two it was Real Madrid that had change forced on it from within its own organization rather sooner than it would have otherwise hoped. Change at Real Madrid tended to come slowly, with right-wing elements deeply entrenched in the club's administrative structure. The death of the long-ruling club president Santiago Bernabéu in June 1978, the year after Spain had celebrated its first post-Franco parliamentary elections, led to a carefully manipulated transfer of power to a "steady-as-you-go" candidate, Luis de Carlos, another Francoist war veteran who had served the club loyally as its treasurer. De Carlos's deliberate strategy of administrative continuity, while in effect disengaging Real Madrid from the evolving political process, was relatively risk-proof as long as the club could continue to be successful. The club's record during the seven years of his presidency was mixed and fell short of the high benchmark set by the gold years. The club won two successive league championships in de Carlos's first two seasons at the helm, but then lost its dominance in *La Liga* as Basque soccer staged a revival. Athletic Bilbao and Real Sociedad shared four league titles between them, with another going to FC Barcelona.

Nonetheless, de Carlos had pledged that Real Madrid would regain its European crown under his presidency, so it was in an atmosphere of huge expectation that thirty thousand of its fans descended on Paris's Parc des Princes stadium on May 27, 1981, to face Liverpool in the final of the European Cup. Real Madrid had not won the competition in fifteen years. Most fans dreamed of reliving that day, May 13, 1956, when the legendary Di Stéfano had led his team of superstars to victory in the European Cup, ushering in an extended period of unrivaled excellence in Spanish club soccer.

The 1981 final involved players of considerable stature on both sides. Liverpool had Graeme Souness, Alan Hansen, and Kenny Dalgish. Real Madrid fielded their own English "star," Laurie Cunningham, along with the German Uli Stielike and talented Spanish players such as Carlos Santillana, Vicente del Bosque, and José Antonio Camacho. The side also included one of Spanish soccer's legends—the fast, highly skillful winger from Malaga Juan Gómez González, popularly known as Juanito. The player's spirited temperament was always associated with leading heroic fight-backs by his team. During his ten years with the club (1977–1987) it won five league championships, two King's Cups, and two UEFA cups. He never recovered psychologically or professionally from the five-year ban he received from UEFA in April 1987 for famously stomping on the head of Bayern Munich's Lothar Matthäus in a European Cup. He retired the following year and was killed in a car crash in 1992, at age thirty-seven. Ever since then, in honor of the number 7 shirt Juanito wore, the seventh minute of every game Real Madrid plays at the Bernabéu is marked by the radical Ultra Surs with the commemorative cry "Illa, illa, illa, Juanito maravilla" (roughly translated as "Hey, hey, hey, Juanito is simply great").

The 1981 Real Madrid–Liverpool encounter proved anticlimactic, entering the collective memory of diehard *Madridistas* as the "final of fear," with each side more concerned with defending itself than scoring goals. Liverpool won 1–0 thanks to a goal by Alan Kennedy. "It was a pity that we lost, but to have got that far was quite an achievement for the team we had then," recalled del Bosque many years. In the aftermath of the 1981 European Cup final, the infamous neofascist hooligan brigade the Ultra Surs emerged as a distinct pressure group within Spanish soccer, named because they occupied the south stands of the Bernabéu while delivering provocative, often abusive chants against visitors, particularly against Basque teams and FC Barcelona, and their city rivals Atletico de Madrid, each of whom had their contingent of hard-core fans.

The genesis of the Ultra Surs is disputed to this day by even its own members. One told me that it was the assault that some Real Madrid fans, including their wives, had suffered at the hands of Liverpool thugs in the 1981 final. "There were a few among the younger Real Madrid supporters who saw what happened, and how the Spaniards reacted, and vowed from there on to never surrender again, and be prepared—if necessary to be as violent as the English." But other Ultra Sur veterans recall an earlier encounter with West Ham fans and other games against Italian clubs.

The imitation of foreign cultures along with a rebellion against the more orderly, traditional forms of club-support organizations imposed by old hierarchies—the fan clubs known as the *peñas*—was perhaps an inevitable consequence of Spain's transition from dictatorship to democracy. The Ultras Surs, based in the capital of Spain, associated as they were with Spain's most successful club, had the largest following among the Spanish radical fans yet represented a mishmash of political and social backgrounds. They included neo-Nazis and skinheads, many of them unemployed and united by a common attitude of generational rebellion and inherited prejudice against rival clubs in particular, although not exclusively. As Fernando Carreño, a Spanish journalist who has investigated the darker side of Real Madrid, points out: "The Ultra Surs are neo-fascist because although their space is theoretically open to anyone according to the basic requirement that he is a fervent Madrid supporter, in reality anyone who is not politically and socially to the right of Genghis Khan stands to have a bad time in their midst."

Other significant radicalized elements would grow in clubs like Rayo Vallecano, associated with postwar industrial neighborhoods (anarchists), and towns with a reputation for militant politics like Pamplona in Navarre (considered by some of its inhabitants as belonging to the Basque nation where Osasuna *ultras* picked up the flag of radical left-wing Basque separatism in response to the more conservative Basque nationalist supporters of Athletic Bilbao. Similarly, in the Catalan capital, FC Barcelona saw the emergence within its stadium of the *boixos nois*, who came to be associated with a violent expression of Catalan nationalism in contrast to what they perceived as the right-wing Spanish followers of Espanyol, the Brigadas Blanquiazules.

These radical fans together with fan clubs across Spain developed in post-Franco Spain around long-standing rivalries between clubs and the resurgent regional standard-bearers. By contrast, the relative lack of popular support for Spain's national team reflected the absence of an agreed-upon national identity given the continuing and unresolved political tensions between Madrid and the regions. It was also the inevitable consequence of the poor performance of the national squad.

One of the consequences of the Franco period—its cultural insularity and socioeconomic backwardness, including poor communications and infrastructure—meant the absence of a critical mass of fans prepared and able to travel to away games. Although this was common to both club soccer and national soccer, it was particularly pronounced in the few numbers that traditionally accompanied the national squad, in striking contrast to other European countries.

Spanish club-soccer rivalries intensified as Spanish's nascent democracy swam in troubled waters. In February 1981 the country survived an attempted extreme right-wing military coup. Spain was being governed by a caretaker prime minister, the center-right Leopoldo Calvo-Sotelo, in the lead-up to fresh elections when it hosted the 1982 World Cup. The tournament, played as it was across stadia in different regions of Spain, should have proved a showcase for the still relatively young democratic state and might have galvanized a larger measure of support had not it turned into a national embarrassment, on and off the field. The gods seemed set against Spain from the moment the draw held in Madrid turned to farce. Scarcely had FIFA president Joana Havelange praised the hosts for taking on the challenge of organizing the biggest soccer tournament "in the heroic spirit of Don Quixote" when the revolving drums from which the teams, each represented by a ball, were supposed to be drawn stuck. Widespread complaints about tickets and hotel arrangements followed, as did allegations—in the opening games—that the cards, including refereeing, might be stacked so as to ensure that Spain progressed toward the final.

Questions about the probity of referees were not new in the world of soccer. But in Spain it had developed almost into a national pastime. The advent of democracy—and the lifting of censorship—fueled an acrimonious debate about the extent to which Real Madrid's success during the Franco years and beyond could be partly explained by biased refereeing. It was Sporting Gijon fans that in 1979 had responded to the expulsion of one of its players in a game against Real Madrid with cries of "Asi, Asi gana el Madrid" (That is how Madrid wins); it was a cry that would echo across the stands of other stadiums in subsequent seasons. In fact, Real Madrid's success was generally achieved by good teams, not corrupt referees, and it never enjoyed a monopoly of championship titles, which might have been the case had they been able to count on friendly referees. In fact, there were numerous examples of critical decisions that had gone against the club. Unquestionably during the years of the dictatorship, anger against referees was an escape valve, a diversion, a necessary counterpoint within the stadium to the political suppression outside it. Even after Franco died, the referee remained a convenient target for abuse, as old soccer rivalries were kept alive and the hopes Spaniards had for their democracy gave way on occasion to disillusionment, on and off the field.

In the 1982 World Cup held in Spain, the host nation's squad was of such poor quality in soccer terms that it had to seek the help of referees simply to survive. This became evident in the opening game Spain played against Honduras in Valencia, a town with a club named after it that, although never achieving anywhere near the international respect of Real Madrid and FC Barcelona, had during the 1950s and 1970s drawn on the talents of foreign stars like the Argentine Mario Kempes, the Dutchmen Faas Wilkes and Johnny Rep, and the Austrian Kurt Jara to produce some exciting soccer. Four-time *La Liga* champions by 1971, Valencia went on to win the Copa del Rey in the 1978–1979 season and then to win its second international trophy the following year, beating Arsenal in the final of the European Cup Winners' Cup.

The people of Valencia were used to watching world-class soccer. But what they got instead from the Spanish squad was a performance worthy of a village scrap from a team always rumored to be in a state of permanent disfunctionality from the moment they entered the locker room. Conceding a seventh-minute goal, the Spaniards struggled against the unrated Hondurians and ended up resorting to diving and appealing for penalties, eventually getting a disputed one, which allowed them to secure a draw without any honor. In the next game, it was again mainly thanks to a referee that Spain prevailed, this time with another controversial penalty (awarded for a cynical foul committed by Juanito, but outside the box), helping them to an unimpressive 2–1 victory against Yugoslavia.

Spain next returned to Valencia, only to be beaten by Northern Ireland, thanks to a goal by Gerry Armstrong. The Irish won considerable plaudits from the international media, overcoming all the odds—the sweltering Mediterranean heat, a hostile crowd, rough tackling by the Spanish, and a referee who did them no favors. As for Armstrong, he was nicknamed "Don Quick Quote" for the ease with which he dealt with the press requests for comments. He was destined to eventually become a Spanish soccer pundit with Sky TV after a career that included playing with Real Mallorca.

Spain managed to progress through to the next round, second in its group, behind Northern Ireland but just ahead of Yugoslavia on goals scored. But they ended up at the bottom of their next group after losing 1–2 to Germany and drawing 0–0 with England, in the Santiago Bernabéu, of all places. The former Real Madrid player who had coached the team, José Santamaría, was fired after shouldering the blame for the lackluster performance by his players. The debacle sparked a national debate about the nature and future direction of Spanish soccer, nowhere more so than in Real Madrid, a club that had belatedly acclimated to the new democracy.

Raúl: A very traditional Spanish kid

CHAPTER 23

The Vulture Squad and Raúl

In late October 2010, some two thousand fans gathered in the Salto de Caballo, a municipal stadium (capacity five thousand) on the outskirts of the once-imperial Spanish city of Toledo to watch a charity match between a team of Real Madrid veterans and the local soccer club. Some well-known Madrid stars who had long since retired from the game muscled in, more for fun than hard work, but with a hint of strutting arrogance, like privileged, overgrown schoolboys. Their opponents were a ragtag collective of physically rather less healthy and underpaid individuals, downtrodden representatives of CD Toledo, a club that had never gotten beyond the Third Division since joining the Spanish league after the Civil War. Amid the beer paunches and ruddy faces, Real Madrid's Emilio Butragueño, a small, trim figure with the chiseled handsomeness of a middle-aged Robert Redford, directed play from midfield with distinction, his quick and accurate passing and positioning of the ball as well as killer instinct near the goal a constant threat to the ragtag defense of the amateur hosts and an inspiration to the veterans and onlookers alike.

Soccer fans in Toledo, like much of the country, were still basking in the memory of Spain's recent World Cup win, and the crowd had come in no mood to see a simple kick-around. Thanks to Butragueño's enduring skills and work ethos, they were treated to an entertaining spectacle well worth the money they had given to the Catholic charity Caritas. Butragueño's grace on the field, his deft touch with the ball, and his intelligent positioning off it, was watched by a predominantly young crowd of reverential fans. Butragueño's gentle artistry contrasted with the imposing architectural severity of the nearby Alcazar, the military museum—a former barracks—that during the 1930s had been the setting for one of the bloodiest encounters of the Civil War. Spain, like its soccer, had entered the modern era. The veterans beat Toledo 9–0.

My friend Inocencio "Chencho" Arias, a Spanish diplomat and Real Madrid fanatic, even in his busiest periods as a government official based in Madrid during Butragueño's heyday in the 1980s, tried to see every game in which he played. "It was like following a famous matador—you had to hurry and see Butragueño for fear that an injury like a bull's goring might deprive you of relishing his art forever," said Chencho. "He played four and a half good years, but he had something few players in the world have—an ability to play with the ball in a very reduced area that electrified the fans. In my case, he'd make me cry with sheer emotion."

The Dutch international Leo Beenhakker, who managed the great Real Madrid team of the late 1980s, once praised what he called the ruthless winning streak he encountered in Spanish soccer compared to the creative yet underachieving school of Dutch soccer favored by Cruyff and others. As he told David Winner:

Every Dutchman has an opinion about everything. When you go to a hotel with the Dutch, one player says "Hey, it's too big," and the other says it's too small. "It's too hot," "It's too cold," "It's too. . . ." We are busy with everything, ev-er-y-thing! But when I went to a hotel with a Spanish team—and they're all big stars, Hugo Sanchez, Butragueño, Gordillo, Michel, Camacho, Santillana, Juanito, great players—they come and it's: "Ok, this is fine. Where's my room? OK. Bye." They sit quietly and they don't talk about the bus, and about the driver and the driver's wife. No! Come on! They think: "We are here to play a soccer match. We play and we kill them. And then we go home." That's the difference.

Beenhakker was speaking ten years before La Roja may have suggested a different thesis. He was right at the time—up to a point. That generation of Real Madrid players expressed the spirit of *La Furia* at its most effective. But to watch El Buitre (The Vulture) play for Real Madrid at his peak was to experience the excitement of a new generation of players full of creative ideas. They were a mirror image of the outpouring of new cinema, theater, art, and media during Spain's transition to democracy—the so-called cultural *movida*, or movement—which represented a liberation of mind and body from many of the taboos imposed by the Franco regime. Was there a connection between the soccer and the cultural "revolution"? Yes, in soccer terms, it meant style and spirit, as well as success. Leo Beenhakker may have believed in aggressive, attacking soccer, but he was no Captain Villalonga clutching a military manual. *La Furia* had entered the modern era.

To watch El Buitre, nicknamed thus because of his predatory instinct, was to follow his swerves and acceleration through defenders, his explosive speed inside the penalty box, an ability to reach, in a split second or two, a place where you least expected him, and to create a goal out of nothing. He forged the core of an inspirational soccer quintet, named after him as the Quinta del Buitre, literally translated as the Vulture Squad. The five others were Manuel Sanchis, Rafael Martin Sanchez, Miguel "Michel" Gonzalez, Pardeza, and Martín Vázquez. As Sanchis told me, "We were young guys from Madrid who shared a similar view on how soccer should be played—we wanted it to be bold and attacking—and we saw ourselves as part of what was happening in Spain, more widely at the time, part of a generation that wanted change, that was prepared to take risks."

It was the mid-1980s. The first socialist government in Spain in more than a half century was reaching the end of its first term and was about to be reelected on a manifesto of deepening democratic and social reform based around the country's protracted admission into the European Community. During the late 1970s the arrival of Johan Cruyff as a player had raised FC Barcelona's profile and popularity, making it *the* cool club, soccer at its most creative and bold when Barcelona itself was enjoying a major cultural revival. In May 1979 FC Barcelona won the European Cup Winners' Cup, beating Fortuna of Dusseldorf 4–3. By contrast, Real Madrid had dragged its feet culturally and socially, with the Bernabéu stadium for a while turning as gray in spirit as the concrete slabs that supported its structures. Worse, between 1982 and 1984, with the Bernabéu stadium still tainted as the stadium where Spain lost the World Cup, Real Madrid was in danger of making its reputation for invincibility look like a bad joke. The old player and legend Di Stéfano survived just two seasons before being sacked as Real Madrid coach when the club finished as runner-up in the league championship but failed to win any trophies.

A new postwar generation of Real Madrid fans, who had watched Di Stéfano play as young boys, had grown up disillusioned with the club's inability to repeat those glory days. They suffered instead the humiliation of seeing Barca lay claim to being more in step with the country's overwhelming desire for change. Then in May 1985 Real Madrid caught up with Spanish society and appointed as president of the Spanish "White House" Ramón Mendoza, three years after his candidacy had been rejected by the club's old guard.

Mendoza, a controversial businessman, blamed his earlier defeat on dubious tactics employed by a self-serving conservative clique within the club and their right-wing political allies. They included leaks to the media, emanating from Spanish intelligence sources, suggesting that he had been employed as a Russian spy by the KGB while trading with the Soviet Union during the latter years of the Franco regime and alleged to at one point have helped finance the Spanish Communist Party. Britain's secret service, MI6, and the CIA shared suspicions about Mendoza's political links at a time when Spain was settling in as a relatively young member of NATO. What is certainly true is that Mendoza shared a drink with the legendary communist, veteran firebrand of the Spanish Civil War La Pasionaria, while she was in exile in Moscow and helped publish the Spanish translation of Soviet president Leonid Brezhnev's memoirs.

Yet Mendoza's buffoonery was perhaps best epitomized by his self-description as a "political independent with a full belly." Certainly, his reputation as a political opportunist may provide an explanation as to how he managed eventually to take power at Real Madrid. Once in the hot seat he continued to make some questionable allies. For example, he openly courted Madrid's hooligan pack—the Ultra Surs— finding in FC Barcelona president Núñez a willing sparring partner who was only too happy to stir up the antagonism between the two clubs. On one occasion Mendoza accompanied a group of Ultra Surs to the Barajas airport in Madrid, to greet a Real Madrid team after a game against Barca. President and fans together chanted abuse at Catalonia.

Mendoza never quite fulfilled his dream of enjoying the international high profile of two of his greatest friends, the Italians Silvio Berlusconi and Gianni Agnelli, who so skillfully exploited their political, business, media, and soccer interests to forge, for many years, an unrivaled power base, at least in their own country. Mendoza's silvery gray hair was on the long side, he dressed in flashy jackets without a tie, he liked fast cars, intelligent women, and partying, and he was, for a while, a most suitable and influential addition to a new cult of dazzling celebrity spawned by the power-bloated socialist government. More important, he was appointed on a pledge to reverse the declining fortunes of Real Madrid.

Mendoza's most positive legacy is that under his presidency the Quinta del Buitre—the Vulture Squad of young Spanish players led by Butragueño—was allowed to flourish from its early beginnings in the club's youth teams, even if Mendoza may have been motivated by a need to save money on expensive foreign players. La Quinta became hugely popular for a while and connected not only within itself but also with other players of different personality and background, as well as undoubted talent. Such was the case of the agile Mexican-born Hugo Sánchez who coined the phrase Quinta de los Machos—the Virile Squad—just to remind the fans that Spanish soccer had not abandoned *La Furia*. Sánchez relished provoking opposition defenders and goalkeepers as well as their fans—an attitude that won him the fervent support of the Ultra Surs.

For years Real Madrid had lacked what its rival FC Barcelona seemed to have built from early times into its DNA: a sense of itself, its history, its place in society, its style of soccer that could puncture the myth perpetuated by its enemies that it was a club who owed its claim to greatness and its popularity to Franco. Only after Franco died did the club begin to develop a counternarrative capable of reaching out to a broader fan base that not only took pride in the soccer achievements of the past in a way that depoliticized them but also laid claim to an enduring and privileged presence in the heart and soul of Spanish soccer.

Emilio Butragueño had passed his peak when another Spanish star, Raúl González—popularly known as simply Raúl—rose in his footsteps. Raúl was born in Madrid in 1977, three years after David Beckham was born in Leytonstone and seven years before Fernando Torres was born. Raúl played as a junior with Atletico de Madrid before moving to Real Madrid in 1992 at age fifteen. At the time, Cruyff's FC Barcelona was the team everyone wanted to watch in Spain.

Raúl contributed to Real Madrid's greatness and became a pivotal figure in the national squad, just as El Buitre had been. What separated the two stars were temperament and circumstances. Of the many tributes that have been made to Butragueño over the years, few have been as eloquent as that made by his teammate Michel, part of a group of Spanish players that in their heyday were as loyally supportive as a band of brothers. "His talent lay in intuition, in the always intelligent spark of his play. . . . His time was perfectly structured. The ball didn't surround him day and night. He found it quite easy to disconnect from the sound of soccer, he was untroubled by the media. . . . Perhaps there were people who would have liked to have seen him more involved in his profession, but Emilio was genuine and unique. He had his own personal vision of what soccer should be."

Whereas El Buitre was infused with zen, Raúl sweated through his shirt like a fundamentalist. Whereas El Buitre felt himself to be one more on a team, Raúl took his role of captaincy very seriously—in the eyes of some of his teammates too seriously. They found him *pesado* (hard work). He provoked confrontations and simmering resentments in the locker room. These became more acute at Real Madrid, with the imposition by club president Florentino Pérez of his *galactico* model, yearly superstar foreign signings, and endless managerial changes that led to clashes of egos and fueled resentment among the aspiring homegrown talent. Part of Raúl's problem was that he was a very traditional Spanish kid who at Real Madrid ended in the deep end of soccer as a global money-spinning enterprise with its sponsorship deals and endless media events.

It takes a thick skin and a steady mind to survive in a soccer environment where Spain's two biggest clubs each have two sports mass-circulation dailies print up to ten or more pages on each every day. Add to that the coverage in television, radio, and other broadsheets, and it's constant Judgment Day. Raúl functioned but in a way that denied him El Buitre's popularity.

In June 2002 Raúl's record at the club level among the players attending the World Cup in Japan and Korea marked him out as a special case. Turning twenty-six years old, Raúl had won three European Cups, two Spanish Championships, and scored more goals than any other player in the Champions League and for the Spanish national side. A profile of him at the time by author and journalist Simon Kuper asserted, now that El Buitre had long retired, that at the highest level of the game there was no more proven game winner than Raúl, who "may confidently be expected to keep performing the way he is now, or better, for another five or six years." Kuper wrote, "If there is any love or loyalty behind those eyes [of Raúl] it is only his inner circle of family and one or two friends who know about it. Otherwise he is humorless, pitiless, calculating and ferociously single-minded. Think Al Pacino in *The Godfather*. The one who systematically annihilates his enemies as his child is being baptized. That's Raúl." My fanatical Real Madrid friend Chencho Arias put it somewhat differently. "He had balls. He played his heart out and surprised people with his devil's trickery."

Raúl scored his first goal for Real Madrid on November 5, 1994, one week after making his debut on the team, in a 4–2 derby win over

Atletico. Over the next fifteen years he would go from promising youngster to Real Madrid's joint top scorer of all time, along with Di Stéfano. Having played alongside and outlasted the likes of Zidane, Ronaldo, Figo, and Roberto Carlos at the Bernabéu, the number 7's status as a *los merengues* legend seemed beyond doubt.

Certainly, there were moments destined to live long in the collective memory of Real Madrid fans: his part in May 1998 in ending the club's thirty-two-year wait for another European Champions' Club title in the renamed Champion League as part of team that beat Juventus in the final 1–0; the moment, celebrated to this day in the club's more militant fan clubs, when following a crucial equalizer against FC Barcelona he celebrated by lifting his finger to his lips and quite literally reducing the Camp Nou to a stunned silence; that same season when despite his club missing out on the *La Liga* title, he was crowned his country's Pichichi, or top scorer; and the final goal he scored in his club's 3–0 Champions League victory in the all-Spain Champions League final against Valencia in May 2000, when after receiving a long pass from Savio well inside his own half he ran the length of the field before dribbling around the goalkeeper—not just any goalkeeper but Canizares, a Spanish international and among Europe's best—and stroked the ball into the net. Five weeks earlier, in the second leg of the quarterfinal against Manchester United, Raúl, still aged only twenty-three, had lit up the night at Old Trafford with a brace of brilliant goals, earning from Alex Ferguson the rare accolade of "the best player in the world." Two seasons later, in 2002, Raúl was one of the goal scorers in Real Madrid's 2–1 victory over Bayer Leverkusen, the club's ninth European Cup success and a new record. Raúl's reputation had grown as a proven game winner. He had the ability to turn a game around, thanks to his rock-hard single-mindedness and what Jorge Valdano called his "insolent self-belief," qualities he employed for the sole purpose of winning.

To his most loyal fans—who saw the true native Spanish Real Madrid player as the personification of the traditional values of Spanish nationhood, Raúl was totemic and thus untouchable. When the player celebrated sweet moments of conquest like in the victory over Valencia in the Champions League in Paris, he did so by taking a bullfighter's cape and showing that he was both a matador and a torero, a killer and fighter.

Yet in October 2007, in a season during which he captained Real Madrid to a league title, thus ending a three-year major trophy drought, he was dropped from the national squad just before a game that could make or break Spain's qualification for the European Championship.

In a thirteen-year career, Raúl had won five league titles, three European Cups, and two Pichichi awards, but he was no different from any other Spanish player in that during this time he had never won anything with Spain. This fact divided Spanish fans between pro- and anti-*Raúlistas*, a debate that for a while seemed as irreconcilable and destructive as that which had led the country to civil war. The fact that Raúl's form had markedly deteriorated just as his identity as a player had been lost in a Madrid put in the hands of foreign superstars mattered little to those who had mythologized him as the latest version of their knight in shining armor.

Chencho Arias claimed to have cried only three times in his life: at the funeral of the Spanish Jesuit priests murdered by a death squad in El Salvador, the final scene of some movie he'd seen in New York, and the goal Raúl scored during the 1998 Intercontinental Club Cup against Vasco de Gama of Brazil in Japan. Clarence Seedorf had struck a long pass from midfield, from right to left. Raúl received the ball, controlled it perfectly with the left foot, beat one defender, next another, before pushing it to his right and striking it home to clinch the trophy. "Proust's exquisite cake was cattle shit compared to what I relished in that moment—Real Madrid in all its glory," recalled Chencho.

But such memories had faded fast among those who instead of looking back were looking toward the future to see if Spain's reputation as Europe's great underachiever could be corrected. Luis Aragonés became the first Spanish coach to act on the basis that if La Roja was to succeed, he could do without a player that in addition to no longer being able to hit the target had a reputation for alienating teammates and celebrating too often his own personal achievements. At his prime Raúl proved himself an instinctive lock picker and could be trusted to take up his own position anywhere in the forward area. But he lacked El Buitre's good grace and selfless artistry. Spain had to move on without Raúl. To that extent Raúl's rise and fall marked a period of transition for Spanish soccer: when a new generation of players took over from the old and the best lessons learned at the youth and club levels were transferred to the national team.

Jesus Gil: Property magnate and Soccer Chief

CHAPTER 24

Of God, Mammon, and Philosophy

When the former Real Madrid president Ramón Mendoza died on April 4, 2001, it was widely reported that he expired while enjoying a massage on a Caribbean island. He was seventy-three years old and vacationing with his latest lover, an attractive female lawyer forty-two years his junior. He was buried three days later in Madrid's Almudena cemetery, named after the capital's favorite Virgin to whom generations of Real Madrid players have paid homage. His coffin was covered in the flags of the club and Spain. The many dignitaries and celebrities who personally gave their condolences to his family included King Juan Carlos.

At the time, the Spanish people had fallen out of love with the socialist government of Felipe González whose third term in office had fallen apart amid mounting allegations of corruption and incompetence.

The center-right led by José Maria Aznar was about to take power. Spain had clearly moved a long way in matters of public morality, not least in the soccer world.

But for the presence of priests and bishops at the Almudena, one could have been forgiven that the Real Madrid of Mendoza's time was from another social planet that had existed in the days of Franco and in the aftermath of his death. In 1969 when the democracies of the Western world were immersed in sex, drugs, protest, and rock and roll, Real Madrid's long-serving president, Santiago Bernabéu, reflected on his duty as a servant of the Francoist state: "What we want is to keep people happy. People like soccer a lot, and with soccer Spaniards can deal better with their everyday problems. We are living in a time of such misunderstanding and such horrible confusion that what people want is calm."

A highly moral man, Bernabéu's own success predated the get-rich boom years of the 1960s. While a visionary of global soccer, he shared none of its material obsessions. His enduring popularity stemmed from his apparent ability to remain uncorrupted by the power that his position gave him. Bernabéu was never accused of personally enriching himself on Real Madrid's account. He paid his players what he thought they deserved and no more and kept a tight hold on their expenses—something that some of them found difficult to swallow amid the increasing conspicuous consumption that characterized the 1960s.

He was at heart a traditionalist. While delegating the day-to-day administration of the club, he liked to run his players like members of a family and was helped in that by his inseparable wife, Maria. She used to recite the rosary each morning for her husband and his team. She would also give prayer cards of Saint Teresa and jerseys to the newborn children of the players.

One of the Real Madrid veterans from the 1960s, Ignacio Zoco, told me once that Bernabéu found it increasingly difficult to come to terms with the changes that began to impact his country. Zoco recalled, "He didn't like long hair, beards, players who played with their shirt hanging out of their shorts or their socks halfway down their ankles. . . . He liked to see a team play in its uniform and wanted to see us all keep on the straight and narrow."

Bernabéu was not pleased when Pirri, one of his star players during the 1960s, became the first at Real Madrid to marry an actress. Until then, any show woman—whether actress or flamenco artist—involved in the life of a Spanish soccer player was seen as a negative influence, better kept on the sidelines, and certainly not legitimized. Some ten years earlier, Spanish soccer had been rocked by the very public and controversial affairs that one of the most famous singers of the Franco era, the sultry and outspoken Gypsy Lola Flores, had with at least two leading players, FC Barcelona's Gustavo Biosca and Atletico de Madrid's Gerardo Coque. As a result, Flores was demonized by the traditionalists in the world of Spanish soccer as an unprincipled whore who not only undermined family life but also impacted negatively the field performance of the players concerned.

The memory of Lola Flores played heavily on Bernabéu's mind, so he tried to control his players' sex lives. When it came to Zoco's choice of lover and wife, Bernabéu approved. She was Maria Ostiz, a soft-spoken and modest folksinger who represented Spain at its most morally disciplined. The childless Bernabéu treated her like a daughter-in-law after adopting Zoco as one of his favorite players. Zoco shared with me a telling anecdote of Maria's first encounter with Bernabéu, soon after the player's marriage to the singer. She and Zoco were walking in the Real Madrid training facility when he spotted Bernabéu and decided to introduce her to him. The president's first words to

Maria, whom he had never spoken to until then, were these: "Maria, the day Ignacio retires, you will have to leave him with me as a breeding bull." Unsurprisingly, Maria was speechless.

I remember many years later interviewing Butragueño, El Buitre, about his time during the 1980s when Spanish players became seriously rich for the first time and certain foreign imports drew them to the wild side and into the flashbulbs of the paparazzi. "At first I used to get followed all over the place by pressmen to see if they could catch me with anybody, but when they always saw me with the same girl I think they got bored," he recalled. He had a long-term girlfriend who later became his wife, Sonia.

While Real Madrid took a while to shake off its traditionalist image, FC Barcelona had long been anticipating the death of Franco. On November 17, 1974, almost exactly a year to the day before Franco's death, Barca fans took part in a political demonstration in the Benedictine monastery at Montserrat, in the mountains outside the Catalan capital. The monastery during the Spanish Civil War had lost some of its monks to anarchist execution squads but during the years of the Franco regime had become increasingly involved in the campaign for democratic rights.

On that autumn day some six thousand people gathered at the monastery as part of a series of events organized to celebrate the seventy-fifth anniversary of FC Barcelona's foundation. Among those present was the future president of post-Franco Spain's first democratically elected Catalan government, Jordi Pujol, then a forty-two-year-old banker and former political prisoner of the Franco regime. Pujol was taken to his first Barca game, in the old Les Corts stadium, at age six, in the spring of 1936, just days before the outbreak of the Civil War. Pujol would later write, "Barca is like other folkloric manifestations of our people—Montserrat is another example—a reserve we can draw on when other sources dry up, when the doors of normality are closed to us."

After the Spanish Civil War, Franco came to Montserrat on a number of occasions to pray before the Virgin there. It was his way of telling the Catalans that the Virgin was Spanish first and foremost. But FC Barcelona's devotion to the Virgin of Montserrat long outlived Franco, as did its tradition of dedicating every cup won to the Virgin of La Merce, the "Mother" of Barcelona, the Catalan capital, and for players—if they wished to—to pray in the Camp Nou chapel prior to a big game.

No Spanish club worth its name has abandoned its holy icons over the years. Even Real Madrid, whose fans celebrate victory before the goddess Cibeles, do so only out of convenience rather than any deference to any pre-Christian pantheon. The square surrounding the eighteenth-century statue depicting the goddess of nature on her chariot stands firmly in the center of one of the capital's busiest commercial, administrative, and residential neighborhoods. The club's patron still remains the Virgin of Almudena, and to this each major victory is marked by floral offerings as well as the fountain of Cibeles covered in Real Madrid fans and embraced by players and fans alike.

Spanish soccer's enduring propensity to mix sport with religion suggests that the Catholic faith has remained deeply embedded in the collective subconscious, however much Spanish society becomes laicized and the Catholic Church loses its traditional powers. But it is money more than religious faith that has arguably shaped some of the key developments of Spanish soccer in the modern era.

In May 1978 the club elected a construction magnate, a non-Catalan native named José Lluis Núñez, as its new president. Núñez had made his first millions during the Franco era. He ran a rather nasty election campaign in which he mixed black propaganda against his opponents while boasting of his own ambition to break with tradition and move full square into the modern era: *Romper con el porron* (Break with the wine jar). Previously, the running of FC Barcelona had been passed from one textile boss to another, just as peasants pass their wine from one to the other.

The winning candidate owned the biggest construction company in Catalonia and was especially well known in Barcelona for his involvement in more than two decades of redevelopment. He had made a fortune out of the unconstrained and unplanned urban growth that had taken place in Catalonia in response to an influx of migrants from other parts of Spain.

Núñez was a migrant himself from the Basque Country, the son of a customs officer working for the Spanish state. He managed to get his hands on Catalonia's great sporting institution by playing the Left against the Right and marketing himself, with the aid of a group of influential local journalists, as the only candidate who represented a real break with the past, the new rich taking on the old bourgeoisie.

Núñez was being somewhat economical with the truth. He had made his first fortune under Franco. Nevertheless, during his campaign Núñez promised he would find the money not just to buy some of the best players in the world, but also for the expansion of the Camp Nou, in effect making FC Barcelona as big if not bigger than its archrival, Real Madrid. Another election slogan promised a "triumphant" Barca. One of the architects of his campaign, journalist Domingo Garcia, told me:

> Núñez was a product of a rebellion by a small sector of Barca against the establishment, against those families who had between them maintained control over the presidency for decades. The club had become a political instrument [for Catalan nationalism] but

had been a disaster in soccer terms for most of the time. It was true that a lot of people felt sentimentally attached to the club as an expression of their nationalism, but there were also people who were fed up to the back teeth of seeing Real Madrid win the league too often and calling itself the best team in Spain.

If Núñez had pledged a triumphant Barca, he had done so anticipating what was to become one of the guiding principles of most wealthy clubs in Europe: success is possible only with star players, and star players cannot be bought without money. So a search began for a player who could fill the Camp Nou's increased capacity—from 90,000 to 120,000—and win titles in a way that Cruyff the player had failed to do while at FC Barcelona.

In 1982 the club signed Diego Maradona. The Argentine, like the rest of his squad, had had a lackluster World Cup campaign, distracted by his country's doomed war with Britain over the Falklands, and finally humiliated when he was shown a red card in the closing minutes of his team's group-stage game against Brazil. But FC Barcelona's talent scouts had done their homework and had identified Maradona's huge potential. In Madrid the cautious men of soccer, and a few conservative politicians, accused FC Barcelona of mindless extravagance when they paid $7.3 million for the twenty-one-year-old who had not played club soccer outside Argentina. Núñez boldly proclaimed, "Maradona is going to revitalize soccer and thanks to him we've going to avoid a financial crisis. We deserve a monument to be built in our honor over this."

On July 28, 1982, three weeks after Argentina was knocked out of the World Cup, Maradona took to the field of the Camp Nou for the traditional start-of-the-season presentation ceremony. There were 50,000 fans present to honor him along with Bernhard Schuster, the

star of West Germany's 1980 European Nations Cup victory. Once
the season was under way, Maradona's impact was immediate, inspiring his colleagues and bringing many afternoons of palpable enjoy-
ment to Spanish fans generally as they marveled at a player of such
unique talent. One of his teammates, "Lobo" Carrasco, told me: "He
was like a chameleon. On the soccer field he was transformed. He was
so sure of himself. He seemed to have total control of the ball. When
he ran with it and dribbled through the defense, it seemed he had it
tied to his boots. In training sessions the rest of the team would just
stop and watch him. No one seemed to generate such interest. We all
felt it was a real pleasure just to be able to witness what he could do."

Maradona not only brought a new excitement on the field, but also
ushered in a period of unprecedented personal wealth and power in
Spanish soccer. During the early 1980s FC Barcelona benefited not
only from increased ticket sales and merchandising and sponsorship
receipts but also from the creation of new Catalan media groups, led by
the regional television channel TV3. Across Spain the evolution of a
new style of newspaper freed from official censorship and appealing to
a politically diverse readership encouraged the development of a sports
journalism of analysis, criticism, and debate, alongside game reportage.
Styles of play, team systems, and management were put under closer
scrutiny. Meanwhile, a distinct whiff of scandal began to be smelled in
Spanish soccer.

Few figures in Spanish soccer were to prove as controversial as
Jesús Gil, the property magnate who took over the presidency of
Atletico de Madrid in 1987. Gil was elected on a populist pledge to
transform the club of also-rans into a serious challenger to the *Liga*
crown and a competitor in Europe. His initial investment in new
players such as the Portuguese international Paulo Futre, López
Ufarte from Real Sociedad, and Goicochea from Athletic Bilbao

raised Atletico's quality as a team. However, the club's organization and reputation were destined to be severely damaged by Gil's volatile character and dubious business practices. During his time as president, Gil erratically dealt with a selection of managers such as Ron Atkinson, César Menotti, and Javier Clemente—and none seeing out his original contract. In one season alone Gil went through a record five managers!

In soccer terms Gil produced mixed results. Atletico improved its competitiveness in *La Liga* in the first two seasons under his presidency, only to end up relegated to the Second Division in the third, on the fiftieth anniversary of its earlier reincarnation as the Atletico Aviacion, when in the first period of the Franco dictatorship the club had become Spanish champions. It was a reminder that whatever political influences the club might have once had, Gil no longer had it all his own way in a democracy. On the contrary, beyond Atletico's Calderon stadium, the construction magnate who tried to create his own political fiefdom as mayor of the luxury resort of Marbella increasingly became a judicial outcast, pursued by tax inspectors and the courts. In the late 1990s Atletico de Madrid's headquarters were raided by police acting on orders from Spain's special anticorruption prosecutor investigating alleged diversion of municipal funds. Other prosecutions would follow, drawing an array of public personalities, from bullfighters' wives to soccer players and actors, into a complex web of opaque property deals, alleged bribes, and personal favors. In the midst of ongoing prosecutions, Gil was banned for two years from traveling to European games with his club after calling a French referee a homosexual.

In 1991 Gil's many detractors in the press and the political establishment lost no time in labeling him a fascist. Gil preached noncorruption, although his own style and his criminal record reduced the credibility of this message. His insults attracted a stream of libel writs from Spain's great and good. The one memory he was unable to flick away with a curse was of the fifty-eight people who died in 1969 when the roof of a restaurant he was building near Madrid collapsed on a party of three hundred. Gil was sent to prison for five years for being responsible for the structural "economies" that caused the collapse. He served eighteen months before paying a fine of 400 million Spanish pesetas and being pardoned by General Franco.

Gil died before he was ever imprisoned in democratic Spain. His funeral on May 17, 2004, provoked a mass outpouring of collective mourning from forty thousand followers, many of them Atletico fans who remained grateful for the fleeting and unexpected triumphs he helped secure for them and the way he seemed to make a virtue of taking on Real Madrid and FC Barcelona against the odds. But the cast of characters—drawn from the higher echelons of Spanish politics and soccer—that joined his more identifiable fans to pay their last respects at his funeral suggested a darker narrative in which there was no clear separation between saints and sinners in the evolving democracy of post-Franco Spain. They included Atletico, Real Madrid, and Athletic Bilbao players—among them Spanish internationals, foreign players, and managers who had played in *La Liga*; past and present presidents of Real Madrid, FC Barcelona, and Real Betis; senior officials of the Spanish Soccer Federation; and elected politicians of Spain's center-right Partido Popular and PSOE socialist parties.

While Gil came under intense media scrutiny, Spain's two biggest clubs remained answerable, according to their statutes, to the fans. In practice both clubs became powerful fiefdoms within Spanish soccer, a duopoly backed by the country's leading banks and businesses as they secured sponsorship and marketing deals, television contracts, and star players at a value that left the majority of Spanish clubs behind and unable to compete.

In Madrid a broader debate about how Spanish soccer was played—its lost potential and enduring prejudices and the need to overcome them—began to emerge in the sports pages of *El Pais*, a newspaper published for the first time in 1978, three years after Franco's death. It had as its specific mission helping the nascent democracy affirm itself while banishing the old demons that had cast a shadow over all aspects of society, including club and national soccer. It would take time before Real Madrid and Spanish soccer more generally found in Jorge Valdano, a philosopher as well as a player, a new voice capable of articulating a vision of Spanish soccer less as a test of virility than an art form.

Valdano emigrated to Spain in 1975, months before the bloody military coup. He played first for Alaves and then for Zaragoza before joining Real Madrid in 1984. Three years later he retired as a player after being felled by hepatitis. But by then Valdano had played with two of the most talented players in the history of soccer. He had played alongside Butragueño in the Quinta del Buitre and with Maradona in the 1986 World Cup. In formulating his views about how soccer could best be played, Valdano was also influenced by his compatriot César Menotti, the manager of the Argentine squad that won the 1978 World Cup and failed to retain it in 1982 before signing up with FC Barcelona.

Menotti had grown up in his native Argentina in Rosario, a town with a tradition of radical politics and stylish soccer. In the 1960s he had developed a reputation as an antiestablishment figure. Tall, long-haired, and with sleepy good looks, El Flaco (The Thin One), as he was popularly known, developed a creative style of soccer based on a slow tempo and elegant touches. He did not fit in easily with the heavy marking and kick-and-run tactics that characterized the two Argentine teams he played for during those years: Racing and Boca Juniors. In 1967 he opted for temporary exile, playing first for the Generals in

New York and then in 1969 with Santos, the Brazilian team Pelé had put on the world map. After a brief time as a journalist he returned to soccer in 1973, when he was appointed coach at Huracán. His year there coincided with a period of growing political upheaval in Argentina. Menotti become widely known in Argentina as an articulate defender of a style he claimed was an original native creation responsible for improving the quality of soccer in Europe, not least Spain, where such talents as Real Madrid's Di Stéfano played with a mixture of carefully choreographed technique and instinctive daring.

One of Menotti's philosophical tracts, *Football Without Tricks*, sold well in Latin America and Spain during the early 1980s. In it he contrasted his admiration for a free and creative style of soccer with the "tyranny" of the defensive, destructive play favored by authoritarian managers. Within days of his arrival as the new coach of FC Barcelona in 1982, Menotti engaged in a widely publicized verbal slanging match with Javier Clemente, then manager of Athletic Bilbao. Basque born and bred and politically conservative, Clemente was distrusted by the Left, but regarded as something of a legend by many Athletic fans because of his three years as a player during which he had heroically struggled against injuries with the kind of resilience and spirit of self-sacrifice the club had traditionally made its trademark.

In the year after Spain failed to win the World Cup it had hosted, Clemente set about creating one of the most successful teams in Athletic's history, drawing from the club's trailblazing youth academy players such as Santiago Urkiaga, Miguel de Andrés, Ismael Urtubi, Estanislao Argote, and Andoni Zubizarreta to play alongside respected veterans like Dani and Andoni Goikoetxea. The Basque was in no mood to be given soccer lessons by the Argentine. Clemente regarded Menotti as a womanizer and chain-smoking hippie who had been on a downward professional curve since winning the World Cup. But Menotti was focused on his target, blaming Clemente for personifying all that had gone wrong with Spanish soccer in the past. "The day Spain as represented by Clemente decides to be a bull-fighter rather than a bull on the pitch it will play better soccer," Menotti declared.

The row between the two men intensified after a league game in the Camp Nou on September 24, 1983, in which the Athletic defender Goikoetxea tackled Maradona from behind, breaking a run that could easily have ended in a goal. The tackle, one of the most brutal ever seen in Spanish club soccer, so shocked Edward Owen, a Spanish-based tabloid English journalist, that he dreamed up the memorable description of Goikoetxea as "the butcher of Bilbao." Barca won the match 4–0 and a second league encounter at San Mames by 2–1. This was no consolation to Maradona, who spent three months recovering from a severe injury to his left ankle. And what particularly angered Menotti was that Athletic went on to win *La Liga* in 1983. This was a huge achievement for a club that had in previous years suffered one of its periodic dips with an enduring and painful memory of the 1976–1977 season when it had lost the King's Cup final against a resurgent Betis and weeks later suffered a further blow, losing to Juventus in the UEFA Cup final.

By the following season, relations between FC Barcelona and Athletic had fallen to an all-time low, the mutual acrimony banishing to a distant past the political and social synergies Catalans and Basques had in their opposition to Franco and mutual respect for each other's national identities. "The shooting season was declared open and two clubs with a huge sense of history and who for years had shown exemplary mutual respect, threw everything they had at each other," wrote the Bilbao-based journalist Jon Agiriano, one of Athletic's most incisive chroniclers.

FC Barcelona in those days fell well short of a "dream team." For all its individual talent, it was a hardened contingent, less beautiful than vengeful, and determined to destroy Athletic by fair means or foul. For all his musings about the beautiful game, Menotti could and did draw on the brutal tactics he had learned in his early days as a player with Racing and Boca Juniors. "Barcelona is prepared to respond to a determined violence with the same violence," Menotti declared on the eve of his team's King's Cup final encounter with Athletic. "Clemente hasn't the balls to look me in the eye and call me stupid," Maradona threw in for good measure. Clemente hit back: "Maradona is both stupid and castrated. It's a shame that a player like him who earns so much money has no human qualities whatsoever."

On May 5, 1984, the two sides met at the Bernabéu. Nearly one hundred thousand fans divided between followers of each team turned the stadium into a cauldron. While Menotti chain-smoked and Maradona rallied the troops, in the Bilbao locker room, one of the players, Natxo Biritxinaga, tried to break the unbearable tension by dressing in drag. A few minutes before the start of the game, he disappeared, only to return dressed as Eva Nasarre, a popular television star. The team broke into fits of laugher. Then they fell silent again and prepared themselves for battle.

It was a dirty match from the outset. Bilbao took an early lead and then held on to it with an uncompromising defense that frustrated Barca's flow of play. Menotti's players, led by Maradona, became increasingly angry, with their few shots at goal easily dealt with by Andoni Zubizarreta, Spain's international goalkeeper. By the time the referee blew the final whistle, the fuse had been lit for an explosion. Maradona was in the thick of it, hitting out at Sola after the Athletic player gave him a "fuck off" sign. Then several players from each side joined in, with kung-fu kicks and Wild West punches.

The brawl, viewed by millions on television, was eventually brought to a stop by club officials. But the enduring image was to be that of the total horror on the face of democratic Spain's constitutional monarch,

King Juan Carlos, as if his country was disintegrating before his eyes, just over three years since he had successfully shrugged off an attempted military coup. It was certainly the worst act of violence to involve players ever in the history of Spanish soccer. It precipitated Menotti's and Maradona's exit from FC Barcelona and the Spanish league while elevating Clemente to hero status among Athletic fans for winning the double. Both trophies were dedicated—as tradition demanded—to Bilbao's patron saint, the Virgin of Begoña.

FC Barcelona: European Cup Champions, Wembley, 1992

CHAPTER 25

The Cruyff Factor and Venables

With a history made up of more disappointments than victories and the humiliation of the 1982 World Cup a recent memory, Spain had much to prove in the subsequent European Nations Cup. Given the bitter rivalries in Spanish club soccer, it was no small miracle that in 1984 Spain's underachieving national squad enjoyed something of a revival. The credit was largely due to the management of Miguel Muñoz, who had come to the job with an impressive track record as a player and coach with Real Madrid. As a player, Muñoz had been part of the golden Di Stéfano years of the 1950s, scoring the club's first-ever goal in the European Cup against Servette FC and subsequently serving as captain in two consecutive competition wins.

His time in charge of Real Madrid as coach (1960–1974) was one of the club's most successful eras in *La Liga*; under his guidance they won the league nine times, while winning the European Cup twice. After leaving Real Madrid in 1974 he worked seven more seasons at the club level (Granada, Hercules, Las Palmas, and Sevilla) before taking on the challenge of molding Spanish soccer's disparate talent base into a national unit.

His initial squad managed to reconcile Barca (Julio Alberto, Victor Muñoz, Carrasco) and Athletic players Urkiaga and Goikoetxea alongside key Real Madrid figures such as Gallego, Camacho, and Santillana. It also counted on the talent of Zaragoza's Juan Senor, Sporting de Gijon's Maceda, and Betis's Rafael Gordillo. Under Muñoz the Spanish side relied on a tradition of spirited rather than elaborate play, a collective work ethos rather than any individual skill.

In the European Nations Cup of 1984, the Spanish side started well, finishing at the top of its group, above Portugal and West Germany, before beating the Danes in the semifinals. Then they lost 0–2 to France in the final. Two years later, Spain got off to a good start in the 1986 World Cup in Mexico and proceeded well thanks to the technical brilliance of Emilio Butragueño and Michel, stars of Real Madrid's Vulture Squad.

The Spaniards qualified from a group that included the bookies' favorite, Brazil, and went on to thrash the Danes 5–1 in the second round, with an entertaining and lethal display of offensive soccer that overwhelmed the opposition. Then Spain was knocked out in a quarterfinal penalty shoot-out against Belgium. The defeat was blamed by the team on bad luck. As one of their number, Michel, would reflect in its aftermath: "Did we do something bad to create that penalty shoot-out and end eliminated from the tournament? Well, no. But in that combination of detail that separates success from sadness, we always lacked good fortune."

Yet after the 1986 World Cup, whatever self-confidence Muñoz had instilled in Spain as a competitive national squad disappeared. It not only underachieved but also underperformed in the 1988 European Championship in West Germany, outplayed and beaten in matches against Italy and the hosts. In the World Cup in Italy in 1990, hopes were raised with Luis Suárez as the new coach. Suárez was widely remembered as one of the great Spanish players. The Golden Galician, as he was nicknamed, had enthused fans with his amazing talent for moving the ball, great vision, and explosive shot. He had also developed a reputation for his elegant style. It was often said that he was such a graceful sportsman that he could have played soccer just as well in a dinner jacket.

Yet despite Suárez's proven track record as a player, Spain's experience of Italia in 1990 under his tutelage was not a happy one. As Michel later recalled, "The World Cup in Italy in 1990 was one of those experiences that you don't want even your worst enemy to have to go through." Relations between the squad and the media were fraught. As the pressure mounted, the chemistry between coach and players became equally touchy. Suárez gambled by including players whose stars had shone in the past but who were now approaching the sell-back date in competitive soccer and whom journalists viewed as spoiled and overpaid. Any appeal to Spaniards' sense of patriotism was handicapped by the growing unpopularity of Spain's socialist government amid revelations of alleged financial impropriety and suggestions (later proved) that sectors of the Spanish security forces had been involved in a shoot-to-kill scenario against ETA sympathizers in the Basque Country.

Michel, the number 8 of the legendary Quinta del Buitre with a great skill for crosses, personified the disaster that hounded the national squad when he let slip through his place in the wall the Yugoslav free kick that booted Spain out of the tournament in the quarterfinals. As the player later recalled, "I came under attack from all sides. I emerged from that World Cup as if from an acute emergency ward, battered and bruised, publicly beaten to a pulp. I tried to keep face, for the sake of the other team members—but inside I felt destroyed."

Yet brighter days were ahead. Preplanning for the staging of the Olympics in Barcelona in 1992 had involved the biggest state investment in Spanish competitive sports ever, with a new, much improved nationwide structure for training soccer players from primary school to *La Liga*. With Spain's nascent democracy flush with EU funds, new stadia popped up in almost in every municipality in the country. Major clubs like Real Madrid and FC Barcelona followed the example set years previously by Athletic Bilbao and Sporting Gijon and began to strengthen their formation of teenagers with the potential to become first-team players.

The 1992 Olympics were memorable for many things—the physical transformation of Barcelona as a city, the duo sung by Montserrat Caballe and Freddie Mercury, the brilliance of the US basketball team led by Michael Jordan, Cuba's participation after years of exclusion, the dignity shown by the athletes from Ethiopia and the new postapartheid South Africa, but perhaps most of all by the way that the tournament generally showed off the potential of democratic Spain. While the Olympics were a showcase for the organizational skills of Catalonia's autonomous government, they were exported to the world as a Spanish event, very much framed by the high-profile presence of the Spanish royal family. This was no celebration of fascism as in the days of Franco but confirmation of a pluralist society held together, however tentatively, by a constitutional monarch who claimed to represent the rights of all Spaniards. At the Games' opening, the Spanish team was led out by the young heir to the Bourbon throne, Prince Felipe, while his father and mother—King Juan Carlos and Queen Sofia—took center stage in the VIP box with government ministers and local politicians. In a show of genuine enthusiasm, they all celebrated Spain's impressive clutch of medals. One of the memorable triumphs of those Olympics was the Spanish athlete Fermin Cacho winning the final of the 1,500 meters. But it was the gold won by Spain's young soccer team that proved most symbolic, marking a new era full of potential. The defining moment came in the final minute of Spain's bruising encounter with Poland in the soccer finals when Francisco Miguel Narváez Machón, better known as Kiko, picked up a deflection from the goalkeeper and struck it home to secure Spain the gold medal.

Among the other players on the winning Spanish team that day was a twenty-year-old called Pep Guardiola. Two years earlier Guardiola had been promoted from the youth to the first team of FC Barcelona by Johan Cruyff to fill the "number 4," the Dutchman's version of a quarterback—one with the capacity to buzz around midfield distributing passes, a pivotal figure in the Dutchman's updating of the 1970s' "total soccer." The promotion would prove providential, setting Guardiola on a career path that would lead him one day to coaching one of the best teams in the history of soccer, at FC Barcelona.

But before Guardiola, there was Johan Cruyff, whose playing days formed only half of the legend. Cruyff says of himself that it took him until he was thirty to understand why he did the things he did with the ball. He has since spent much of his life inspiring others with his philosophy of how soccer should be played. As a coach at FC Barcelona and as Guardiola's mentor, Cruyff can rightly claim ownership over the club's golden years and to infusing Spanish soccer generally with an example worth following.

The first time I met Johan Cruyff, he was relaxing in his family home up in the hills outside Barcelona. Somewhat in awe of the "Flying Dutchman" I had first seen leading out his Barca team at the

Camp Nou circa 1976, I had been brought to my first personal encounter by a Catalan friend, Armand Caraben, an economist and lawyer who during the 1970s had been instrumental in negotiating the Dutchman's transfer from Ajax to Catalonia. The meeting, towards the end of the twentieth century, was several years after Cruyff had retired from the front line. But if there was a style of Spanish soccer that took shape and achieved glory in the new millennium, it was Cruyff who planted some important seeds.

Over cold beer and a selection of Dutch cheeses and Spanish ham, Cruyff settled into our interview with his rapid-fire accented and curiously constructed English punctuated often by insightful musings on a sport not overwhelmed with literacy. "I like positioning of the ball, I like attack, I like to see the team dominating the situation. . . . The 'other' game was basically: play the long ball, close it down, and take it from there. It's a different approach, but I think my way brings out individual skill."

Before the Cruyff era, Barca had had three (foreign) managers in five consecutive years, each importing a star player or two who tended to dominate the team's overall strategy and performance—Schuster under Lattek, Maradona under Menotti, Archibald and Lineker under Venables. Cruyff thought that such a system undermined the club's sense of collective identity and ill-fitted the social and cultural context of Catalonia. He had learned enough from his own experience as a player to want to put it right. He came after all from Holland, a soccer country that had long stimulated young talent. So he focused on encouraging a new generation of Barca players who were coming through the club's youth training program and mixing them into teams with quality Basque players and a sprinkling of foreign stars. Such an initiative helped to bring about a general resurgence of Spanish soccer.

Cruyff explained how he spotted local talent that he knew he had to build on so as to give the team a sense of identity:

It just happened that when I arrived, there was a new crop of players who had come through the *cantera* [the youth team] and were ready to join the first team. There was the kind of availability that comes at the end of a cycle, every five or six years. But there was another situation that I understood. Fans the world over like to see good players who share their mentality, and preferably come from their country, and if a coach has to choose between a foreign and a local with equal qualities, he should go for the local. That way the fans are less likely to whistle him if things go wrong. In Barca, people like seeing players from the *cantera* in the first team; it makes them feel that the coach somehow is more a part of Barcelona that way. So I tried to do it the way they liked, to produce a game that they could claim as Catalan. Because I'd been here as a player I think I knew what they wanted.

Fellow Dutchman Rinus Michels influenced Cruyff, during their time together, as coach and player, respectively, at Ajax. Cruyff was impressed by the rigidity with which Michels stuck to his system. In Barcelona such rigidity brought Cruyff success but not without some internal dissent. For example, tension was provoked by Cruyff's determination to play Gary Lineker out of the position he had played most of his playing life. "I knew that Lineker was a goal scorer, and that is good for any team. But I also knew that with a more attacking system, and more players moving forward, the field was smaller up front. That is why I moved him from the center to the right side, to give him more space in which to use his spring," Cruyff told me.

Lineker saw it rather differently:

It became pretty apparent to me relatively quickly that Cruyff basically wanted his own people in and me out. But instead of coming along and saying to me, "You're not my type of player," he tried to mess me about by making me play on the wing. . . . I was just one of two wide players. I wasn't an individual; I was just a number, just like number 4—the center-back—was part of the system too. You wouldn't have thought in a million years that Gary Lineker could play on the wing, but I know why he did it—he did it so I would kick up a fuss, then the crowd would turn against me and he'd get rid of me that way.

Lineker was not without sympathizers. According to his agent, John Holmes, he was much admired on a personal and professional level by the "Brian Clough of Spanish soccer," Javier Clemente (more on him later), who during his passage through a succession of Spanish clubs prior to being put in charge of the Spanish squad tried, without success, to poach the English "matador." "Clemente always told Gary that Cruyff didn't really understand how soccer should be played and didn't value him as he should," Holmes told me. While he shared a mutual personal and professional respect, Lineker spurned Clemente's advances as he similarly turned away from an approach from Alex Ferguson, who wanted to have Lineker play alongside another former Barca player, Mark Hughes.

The Welshman Hughes had transferred to Man United via a loan to Bayern Munich after finding it hard to adapt to life in Barcelona (where he lasted no more than a season), unlike Lineker, who loved the climate and food and learned Catalan as well as Spanish while earning the nickname El Matador for his goal-scoring abilities. In bullfighting, *El Matador* describes the bullfighter at the point of killing the bull rather than involved in the elaborate process of bullfighting itself. It is the torero who uses his skill with the cape to confront the bull and gradually overwhelm him. Lineker was viewed as a classic striker, with a killer instinct up front but lacking the multitasking Cruyff demanded from his players. In the end the Englishman's disagreements with Cruyff proved irreconcilable, and Lineker left Barca for Tottenham Hotspur in a deal negotiated with the Spurs coach Terry Venables.

It was Venables who had brought Lineker to FC Barcelona—along with Steve Archibald—when he was appointed coach in 1985 in succession to César Menotti. Venables had played for and coached several English clubs before coming to Catalonia, where he had the most rewarding time of his career, taking FC Barcelona to its first league title in more than ten years in the 1984–1985 season and the European Cup final and Spanish league cup victory in the following season. Venables provided me with a valuable insight into the differences between English and Spanish soccer thanks to an interview he gave me at the FA headquarters in 1995 during his time as manager of the England, ten years after he quit FC Barcelona. He recalled:

When I was at Barcelona we would travel to San Sebastián by coach, a journey of seven or eight hours, and the players would just drink water, all the way there and back. In England, the players would drink water and Coca-Cola on the way to a match, but on the way back they would be swilling beer. In Spain, I did not see a single player smoke or drink until we won the league, and then they all got absolutely smashed. They were professional and the job was done. In England we do it every Saturday, after the match.

Venables went on, "The Spanish soccer players care about their condition, their fitness, and their behavior. They enjoy showing off their skills. The British are more functional; they get the job done and are professionals from that point of view, and if they lack the technical ability of the Spanish players, they do have resilience. . . . We both have our strengths and weaknesses, but the sight of a squad of highly skilled, motivated, and disciplined soccer players waiting for me at my first training session with Barcelona was a very welcome one."

The exception was Maradona who was already negotiating a transfer to Napoli, having already fallen out with FC Barcelona president Núñez over pay and conditions. Núñez, who had exploited Maradona's early years at FC Barcelona to make the club a lot of money, could not wait to see the back of him after the Argentine lost form and private detectives discovered mounting evidence of his debauched private life.

El Tel, as Venables was nicknamed in his native UK because of his ease before the cameras, became a popular figure in Barcelona, earning a respectful place in the list of English managers who have graced Spanish soccer with their presence. But it was Cruyff who within a year of Venables's departure had initiated one of the most exciting and entertaining periods in Spanish club history, taking FC Barcelona to its first-ever European Cup victory against Sampdoria at Wembley in 1992 and winning with the club a further ten domestic and international titles between 1988 and 1996. At a time when Spanish clubs were limited by UEFA rules as to the number of foreign players they could sign, Cruyff built up his team around a small number of key star signings—the Brits were replaced by the likes of Koeman, Laudrup, and Stoickhov, while young Spanish players such as Luis Milla and Pep Guardiola were promoted after being developed through the club's youth system.

In Guardiola Cruyff tapped a soccer-playing talent that not only fitted seamlessly into Barcelona's cultural and political mystique but was also destined to personify its periods of greatest success, as player and coach. Years would have to pass before Guardiola came to be respected more generally by Spaniards regardless of their political leanings and their divergent views as to which nation they owed their ultimate allegiance to.

Javier Clemente: A tough Basque

CHAPTER 26

The Bruiser from
Barakaldo

The year of Cruyff's dream team's apotheosis was also the year when Javier Clemente, a very different character than the Dutchman, was appointed as the new manager of the Spanish national team. Clemente was born among the steel mills of Barakaldo, the industrial suburb of Bilbao, the same neighborhood where José Lluis Núñez, the president of FC Barcelona, had once lived. But while the Núñez family abandoned the Basque Country for Catalonia, the Clementes were part of its social, political, and religious fabric. Javier's father worked as a foreman in the metallurgical conglomerate Altos Hornos de Vizcaya in a region that during the late 1970s was hit by the onset of recession—with factory closures fueling a tense political and social situation provoked by the violence of the Basque terrorist group ETA.

Clemente began playing for Athletic Bilbao at the age of sixteen, when he earned a reputation as a dedicated workhorse whose fighting spirit, passing skills, and vision off the ball defied his small five-foot-six stature. As a player, he came to personify Basque soccer at its best—a mixture of guts and gift, aggression and talent with the ball. He was a member of the Athletic team that won the Copa del Generalissimo in 1969, but his playing career was subsequently cut short at the age of nineteen by a crippling tackle from behind by a Sabadell player called Maranon, which he accepted with seemingly disarming stoicism. "I don't blame Maranon for anything," he would tell Alfredo Relaño of *El Pais* in 1977. "It was a very tough tackle, but there are many like that. It had been a tough match, and we were all a bit *picados* [stirred up like fighting bulls who have been lanced by the picador]. We were a minute away from the final whistle and I had the ball at my feet; he came in and broke my leg." His determination to try to recover from his injury turned into a personal odyssey, with his repeated attempts to recover frustrated by a series of botched operations and compulsory military service over an agonizing three-year period before he finally threw in the towel.

He retrained as a coach, despite being scarred physically, and some would argue mentally, for life. He would continue to show interested journalists the four inches of discolored and hacked skin on his leg for many years later, like a veteran showing off his war wound or a bull-fighter his worst goring. It fueled the myth of another icon of the Spanish fury—with Clemente, while at Athletic, making much of his distinctive Basque credentials.

In an extensive interview with a Bilbao journalist in 1985, Clemente proudly told the story of how as a schoolboy during the Franco years he had painted a picture of the banned Basque national flag, a gesture for which he was punished by his teacher with a black mark against his exam sheet. Nevertheless, he claimed not to bear an enduring grudge against the nuns and Salesian brothers who ran the school. His enduring loyalty—next to soccer—was to the Catholic faith.

After serving his apprenticeship with Arenas Club de Getxo, CD Baskonia, and Athletic's youth training academy in Lezama, he was promoted to the first team in 1981, and he set about putting together one of the most successful Athletic teams in the club's history. For the next five years he took the club into its last golden period, winning two league championships (1982–1983 and 1983–1984) and a Copa del Rey and SuperCopa in 1984. The celebrations of the triumphant two seasons coincided with a particularly nasty period of political violence involving the Basque terrorist separatist group ETA and the Spanish security forces. As has occurred for much of Spanish history, soccer was celebrated by those who genuinely enjoyed the game and those who sought to strengthen their political identity through their team. Add to this tribal loyalties based on family affiliation, and you had a combustible mix where soccer could as easily become a demonstration as a party.

Athletic's triumphs in the early 1980s were marked by the ringing of church bells, nuns applauding from the windows of their convents, and factory workers and militant students joining in the collective party as the team was transported along Bilbao's Nervión river on a barge. For a very short time the guns fell silent, at least in Bilbao. It was with Clemente that Athletic won its last league championship of the twentieth century, in 1984. From the balcony of the palace of Bilbao's mayor's office, Clemente declared that it was a victory for the people and not just the team. Just who the people were was kept deliberately vague. After all, Athletic fans ranged from old Franco diehards to ETA sympathizers. If there was something that united them, it was the myth of some imagined racial purity that could be found only in the region of Spain. A popular song at the time held up the club's Basque-only selection process as an example that other clubs were condemned not to follow. "We always fight with our own weapons, because we do not like imports" went its defining verse.

Clemente had a bust of Sabino Arana, the father of Basque nationalism, in a place of pride in his Bilbao home. Lest we forget, Arana was a controversial figure in Spanish history, claiming that the only true homeland, or *patria*, was Vizcaya, the province based around Bilbao, before proclaiming that his *patria* extended across several northern provinces and even across the French border. Arana claimed that the basic principles of Basque nationalism—as he saw them—were revealed to him on Whitsunday, a key date in the Catholic liturgical year commemorating the descent of the Holy Spirit on the disciples of Christ following his resurrection. Arana called his nation Euzkadi, one in which some Basques were clearly more equal than others. Before he died he penned some racist articles against the *maketos*—an offensive slang term used to identify the immigrants from other parts of Spain to include those in Barakaldo, where Clemente's dad lived and worked. Arana was not to every freethinking liberal's taste, but then Clemente was, well, Clemente.

The rest of Spain continued to look at most Basques as terrorists and remained distinctly unimpressed by Athletic, which it was claimed had won more by the mistakes of its betters than any superior skill of its own. But in Bilbao, frustrating the big clubs at that time—the Real Madrid of Martín Vázquez, Sanchis, Santillana, and Juanito, the FC Barcelona of Maradona and Schuster and the then powerful Valencia led by the aging Argentine world champion Mario Kempes—was seen as a noble achievement for a club with only modest resources based on homegrown talent.

During this period, Clemente was courted by the Basque Nationalist Party that Arana had founded, his professed cultural identity ("Us Basques are a race apart," he declared in a controversial interview with Spanish state television), no-nonsense work ethos, and religious convictions seemingly epitomizing the best traditional values of the Basque nation. In 1985, the then president of the PNV, the former Jesuit Xavier Arzallus, said of Clemente, "For me he is an example. Not because he is a coach of Athletic. Not because he is famous. Simply because he is a whole man, of the kind that Diagones looked for with a candle in the agora of Athens in daylight. And he is a complete Basque."

Later a friendly journalist asked Clemente to imagine the team he would most like to have in his life. Clemente volunteered just three "players" he would like to have with him in his version of a quasi-political and spiritual "dream team." Clemente named as two of his key players the Basque nationalist leader Arzallus and the auxiliary bishop of Bilbao. Only one other person was "selected" by Clemente, and that was Pope John Paul II, in the position of goalkeeper. Why? "Because he can save everything," said Clemente—such was his religious conviction and his loyalty to one of the most charismatic figures in papal history.

Clemente, the son of poor immigrants who grew up speaking Spanish and not Euskara, the Basque language, was distrusted as a reactionary by the left-wing sympathizers of ETA, the Basque separatist terrorist organization, and became a controversial and divisive figure in Spanish soccer, hated as much as he was loved, generating particular resentment among the Cruyff-inspired stylists of FC Barcelona. During Athletic's glory period, Clemente would make a habit of ensuring that the San Mames stadium was conditioned to undermine any visitor whose game was predicated on swift passing and rapid movement off the ball. He made famous the *manguerazo* (the sprinkler), even when it rained—as it often does in that part of Spain. The method involved soaking the field prior to the game to ensure that the turf covered at least half the boot and turned muddy within minutes of the game getting under way.

One of his favorite players was Andoni Goikoetxea, whose devastating tackle on Maradona's left ankle on September 23, 1983, had an eerie resemblance to the injury suffered by Clemente fourteen years earlier, as if the coach's tactics had been motivated by some psychological need for revenge. Goikoetxea was banned for eighteen games, later commuted to ten, after which Clemente brought him back into the team for Athletic's European Cup tie against Joe Fagan's Liverpool. With Liceranzu and Txema Noriega, the "Butcher of Bilbao" formed part of an uncompromising defense that with a great deal of cynical time wasting held the "reds" star attacking lineup of Dalgish, Souness, Ian Rush, Craig Johnston, and Michael Robinson to a frustrating goalless draw at Anfield. But Athletic lost 0–1 on the return leg at San Mames, thanks to a sixty-sixth-minute header from Rush.

Clemente thus failed to repeat the success of fifteen years earlier when he played on a team that eliminated one of the greatest Liverpool teams ever from the European Fair's Cup. During the 1968–1969 season, the two teams played each other in the first round of the tournament, a forerunner of the UEFA Cup. Both legs were 2–1 for the home side, which meant that the tie had to be settled by the toss of a coin at Anfield. The toss was successfully gambled by Athletic captain Koldo Aguirre.

Even in defeat Clemente, who in his best playing days was compared by his faithful admirers to "the blond Englishman" Bobby Charlton, showed little remorse, sticking obsessively with a style of play he claimed to have learned from his other English heroes, Bobby Robson (when at Ipswich) and Ronnie Allen, his coach at Athletic. He never apologized for his side's brutal treatment of Maradona in the King's Cup final against Barca on May 5, 1984. In 2010 he told journalist and author Orfeo Suarez, "We fought like dogs in that final of 1984, because with Maradona and Schuster we had to do some dirty work so they couldn't play against us. If we allowed them to play, we wouldn't have had a chance. As a result neither of them could get a touch on the ball, and we scored a goal and won."

The philosophy of the ends justifying the means evidently brought Clemente the results his fans wanted—but once Athletic's performance began to decline in *La Liga* and failed to deliver any major international trophy, the coach's arrogance and authoritarianism began to be viewed as a liability. In January 1986 Clemente squandered the collective good faith generated by Athletic's championship victories by relegating to the subs' bench one of the team's most successful and best-loved players, striker Manu Sarabia. The move was justified by Clemente on the questionable grounds that it was best to keep even the better players for the decisive minutes of the game. It proved hugely divisive among the fans and became widely criticized in the local media. Clemente was fired and became coach at Espanyol.

His move to a club that had traditionally been viewed as Barcelona's non-Catalan club, with many of its members drawn from the central government's civil service, may have seemed somewhat at odds with his Basque credentials, but they did no harm to Clemente's career, however controversial it remained. After getting Espanyol qualified for the UEFA Cup, the team beat Milan and Internazionale before losing to Bayer Leverkusen in a second-leg final penalty shoot-out. The defeat followed another of Clemente's cantankerous and unthinkable decisions—this time leaving out two of the team's best players, John Lauridsen and Ernesto Valverde.

Yet Clemente's reputation was such that he lived to fight another day. After a further successful spell at Atletico de Madrid and a brief return to Espanyol in the 1990–1991 season, Clemente was appointed coach of Spain's national team in a move celebrated by his diehard loyalists in the working-class districts of Bilbao, Barcelona, and Madrid but greeted with trepidation by a new generation of wise soccer commentators—among them Johan Cruyff and the then coach of Real Madrid, Argentine philosopher of soccer Jorge Valdano. They wanted the beautiful game of flowing, attacking soccer with the emphasis on quick passing and interchangeable positions to take dominance over Spanish soccer and feared the unpredictable consequences of his impulsive character on the development of a winning team.

Clemente's trademark was to pick players for his squad best known for their toughness and "efficiency" in defense. He had great faith, for example, in the Real Madrid powerhouse Fernando Hierro, a player who was equally at ease as a central defender or defensive midfielder with a talent focused on his range of passing skills and use of his height to score goals. At the same time, Clemente wasted little time in excluding from his squad all five components of the legendary Vulture Squad, a move that soured his relations with large swaths of Real Madrid fans. It was almost as if he saw star players as a challenge to his authority.

Clemente initially defied the pessimists by taking Spain on a relatively smooth run—eight wins and one loss in twelve matches—into the 1994 World Cup in the United States before losing to Italy in the quarterfinal when Roberto Baggio scored a late goal. In England in the Euro championships two years later, Spain fell at a similar stage.

In the World Cup in France in 1998, Clemente's strategy of remaining loyal to a select group of trusted players regardless if their form proved costly, with the aging Zubizarreta no longer able to protect the Spanish goal with the brilliance of his earlier years. Clemente did bring into the squad the twenty-year-old Raúl, a rising star in *La Liga*, but his inclusion failed to lift the team's spirits. Clemente was widely criticized as having lost his own killer instinct, as Spain failed to even reach the second round. He was eventually fired during the qualification for the 2000 European Championship in Belgium and Switzerland. In its time of need, the Spanish Federation recalled former Real Madrid player José Antonio Camacho as his replacement, but he too was destined to fail.

Fernando Torres: European Championship, 2008

CHAPTER 27

The Wise Man from Hortaleza

By the time of the World Cup in Germany in 2006, Spain had a new coach, Luis Aragonés. Spain had underperformed and underachieved under Clemente's successors, Camacho and Iñaki Sáenz. But with Aragonés, expectations once again rose that the Spanish Federation had finally picked someone who could motivate an emerging generation of players to combine in a team worthy of seriously challenging the best in the world, casting off the demons of the past that had condemned Spain to the status of soccer's great underachiever.

Aragonés was born three years into the Spanish Civil War in Hortaleza, a small rural Castilian community northeast of Madrid in an area held by the Republican forces. During the postwar years, the area was developed into one of the satellite towns that surrounded the capital. Aragonés, a heavily built youth with a reputation for speaking his mind and showing leadership in games, began playing with Getafe before joining Real Madrid. However, it was at the unpredictable if always entertaining Atletico de Madrid that he spent the longest time (1964–1974), sharing a Pichichi in 1970 as one of *La Liga*'s top scorers and reaching the European Cup final in 1974 before losing the championship to Bayern Munich.

Aragonés came to the job of national coach with a track record as one of the best-known names in Spanish soccer, thanks to his involvement, often successful, as a player and later coach in a variety of Spanish clubs, including FC Barcelona. The sheer scope of his experience meant that Aragonés over the years came to acquire a rich knowledge of the full potential of Spanish soccer and the varying styles and strategies of individual clubs, identifying what he thought worked best and keeping a keen eye on emerging talent.

Those who appreciated Aragonés came to see him as a major soccer "mind" and dubbed him El Sabio de Hortaleza (The Wise Man from Hortaleza). There was talk of him becoming coach in the 1980s. That the Spanish Federation delayed his appointment was partly due to Aragonés's unpredictable mood swings and a tendency to buckle under pressure. In 1988, while serving as a coach for one season at FC Barcelona, Aragonés had shown his weakness when the club was confronted with an unprecedented players' rebellion during which the seamier side of Spanish soccer had surfaced. The prelude to the rebellion was a rare investigation by Spain's tax inspectors into the complex arrangements Barca had conspired to keep its foreign players in particular well remunerated.

The investigation, which surfaced after Aragonés's predecessor at Barca, Terry Venables, had left for Tottenham, initially found that the German international Bernhard Schuster had signed two contracts with the Catalan club, although only one had been declared to the tax authorities. Further probes uncovered similar tax avoidance deals involving other players, including elaborate payments to offshore companies, designed to minimize the amount of tax they had to pay on their earnings. When the club was ordered to pay to the Spanish Inland Revenue what was owed, the club's president, José Lluis Núñez, passed the bill onto the players.

The reaction of the players was swift and very public. They called a press conference in Barcelona's Hotel Heredia, pointing out that the double contracts had been drawn with the club's full approval and encouragement and that it was therefore the club's responsibility to make provisions for the loss. In what came to be known as the "Mutiny of Heredia," the players issued a joint statement. "Núñez has deceived us as individuals and humiliated us as professionals," the statement declared. One of the Barca players absent on the day was Gary Lineker, who was away on call-up duty for the England squad and felt he had nothing to gain from being associated with the row. "You just couldn't imagine such a mutiny taking place in England. The fans just wouldn't buy it," Lineker told me when we discussed the incident.

Aragonés decided to get involved and suffered as a result. During a pregame strategy meeting with the players, Aragonés broke down in tears, the stress of managing one of the biggest clubs in the world exacerbated by the strained relationship between the team and the president. The mutiny eventually fizzled out, with the players failing to secure the support of the fans and the club engaging in some imaginative accounting. Then Núñez delivered a master stroke by bringing back to Barca, as Aragonés's replacement, the one person who seemed to be able to guarantee the success and spectacle that so many Barca fans pined for: Johan Cruyff.

As he grew older—and Aragonés was one of the oldest characters in modern Spanish soccer—his love of the game came to sustain him as he struggled with his weakness for drinking and gambling and dark moods and saying exactly what he felt in public. In October 2004, Aragonés was embroiled in a public controversy of a distasteful kind when a Spanish television crew filmed him coaching José Antonio Reyes and making a reference to the Spanish wing forward's Arsenal teammate Thierry Henry. Aragonés was heard telling Reyes, "Tell that *negro de mierda* [black shit] that you are better than him. Don't hold back. Tell him. Tell him from me. You have to believe in yourself. You're better than that *negro de mierda*."

The comments caused a wave of protest in the British media and caused some consternation elsewhere in the soccer world, although within Spain the media's reaction was generally muted. Aragonés himself was unapologetic for an offense he claimed not to have committed, insisting he had a "very easy conscience." In comments that echoed the less diplomatic period of the Clemente period, Aragonés stated, "I'm obliged to motivate my players to get the best results. As part of that job, I use colloquial language, with which we can all understand each other within the framework of the soccer world."

A month later black English players Ashley Cole and Shaun Wright-Phillips were subjected to racist abuse from the crowd at the Bernabéu during an England-Spain "friendly." The Spanish Soccer Federation was initially fined £44,650. But it took the federation another five months to take any further action of its own, and when it came it horrified antiracism campaigners by its levity. Aragonés was fined 3,000 euros, equivalent to his estimated day's wages. The director general of Spain's Sports Council, Rafael Blanco, dismissed any link between the reaction of isolated groups of fans and Aragonés's comments.

Immigration was still a relevantly recent topic on democratic Spain's social and political agenda. At the beginning of the 1990s the population was made up almost entirely of Spaniards, with immigrants accounting for less than 1 percent of residents. But the past decade has seen an influx from around the globe, mostly from other European countries, South America, and North Africa. With a buoyant economy and historically low birthrate, Spain had in the early years of the twenty-first century become the main destination for immigrants into Europe.

Aragonés unwittingly put Spanish soccer's attitudes toward race under international scrutiny, exposing a culture at best of ambivalence, at worst of collective denial within Spain itself at a time when its politicians were struggling to formulate a national consensus around how best to deal with the issue. Henry himself described the ineffectiveness of the fines as "absolutely ridiculous." "You really have to look at the Spanish authorities and they must take a long look at themselves. They obviously don't care about racism. It is laughable. They fined Aragonés for the sake of it, not because they felt he did something wrong," he declared.

By contrast, Henry's other Spanish Arsenal colleague Manuel Almunia, along with players from *La Liga*, black and white, including the Brazilian-born Spanish international midfielder Marcos Senna, followed the line adopted by Spanish officials, insisting that Aragonés was really a decent guy but a victim of overreaction and misunderstanding. He had been lost in translation, in other words.

Aragonés was not fired, after the Spanish media further excused the monkey chants. Writing in *El Mundo*, Spanish journalist Carlos Carbajosa claimed the British reaction was part of a conspiracy typical of the deceiving, perfidious Albion. "Because the Spanish coach had been attacked as a racist by the English press, the counter-attack had to be jeering at the blacks because, if the blacks did not exist, none of this would have happened," he wrote. Thus, the problem, according to Carbajosa, was not the Spanish racism but the aggressive imposition of a "politically correct" agenda by the hypocritical English tabloid press.

While a minority of Spanish commentators were critical of Aragonés, the episode, as the seasoned Irish Hispanist Paddy Woodworth pointed out, revealed "deeply contradictory attitudes to race in the Spanish psyche, which go back a long, long way." However, perhaps the most surprising thing about the British media's response to the antiblack racism displayed by elements of the Spanish soccer world was that they should have been so shocked.

As any British journalist, player, or coach who has been closely involved in Spanish soccer over many years has witnessed, Spain has been no more immune to racism than any other country. Long after the Franco dictatorship had given way to parliamentary democracy in Spain, it was not uncommon to hear monkey chants and other racial abuse greet black players in Spanish stadia. In 2006, the FC Barcelona player Eto'o walked off the field after suffering continual racist abuse from Zaragoza fans. Three years later Barcelona fans were shown on national television repeatedly abusing Espanyol's Cameroon international goalkeeper Carlos Kameni, with the club's stewards doing nothing to deal with the situation.

Modern Spain has struggled to come to terms with itself as a multicultural society when faced with the huge rise in immigration in recent years. Nevertheless, a growing number of Spanish-born sons of immigrants were making their way through the youth academies to the first teams of major clubs and competing for places on the national squad. Perhaps one of the most interesting recent examples was the promotion in December 2009 of Jonás Ramalho—the son of an Angolan father and a Basque mother—to the first team of Athletic, the last remaining major Spanish club to incorporate a black player, because of its long-standing policy of having only totally Basque-blood players.

Three years earlier, Spain, under Aragonés, came to the World Cup in Germany with few friends among the British press certainly.

The "racism" issue was not so easily dismissed. FIFA used the tournament to make much of its own impeccable credentials as world soccer's moral arbitrator by promoting a somewhat superficial initiative to "kick out racism." Despite the campaign, FIFA was criticized by some commentators not just for turning a convenient blind eye to the presence of the Ukrainian manager Oleg Blokhin, who had escaped any sanction after making an unashamedly racist attack on black soccer players in his country, but also for providing similar immunity to Aragonés.

Yet Aragonés had come to the world stage with an impressive unbeaten record and a different narrative with which to win hearts and minds. It was Aragonés in an early encounter with the Spanish media that referred to his squad as La Roja. Ever since most Spaniards could remember—and that dated back to the Franco years—the squad had been called *la seleccion nacional* (the national team). But the definition of nationhood became a complicated business in post-Franco Spain, with various regions claiming increasing autonomy if not independence from Madrid. Only a minority of Spanish fans of an extreme-Right persuasion objected to the national team being branded and marketed with the color red that for them conjured memories of communists in the Civil War. There were others—again, a minority—who took a cynical view that Aragonés wanted to ingratiate himself with the incumbent socialist government of José Luis Zapatero, which was still amid its precrisis honeymoon period.

But Aragonés played down any deeper significance than the fact that the Spanish team had played in red shirts (and blue trousers) even during the latter years of the Franco regime, and no one could accuse him of political correctness. Spain was simply following in the steps of other successful soccer nations that had made a trademark of their shirt colors—Italy (Azure), France (Les Bleus), the Dutch (Brilliant Orange). For those with marketing ambitions, or of a more philosophical bent, La Roja transformed the somewhat destructive and negative *La Furia* of old into something as vital but more life-giving as wine or even blood, transfused rather than spilled. From such synchronicity, the best Spanish tourist posters had been made. Spain was not only different; it was now potentially better by far.

Spain got off to an impressive start, beating Ukraine 4–0, and ending up unbeaten at the top of their group after defeating Saudi Arabia and Tunis. With Marcos Senna, a bedrock in midfield, supported by two of the most versatile and hardworking defenders in *La Liga*—Barca's Carles Pujol and Real Madrid's Sergio Ramos—the squad's strike capability was beefed up with the inclusion of three young "turks," two from the Valencia stable: David Villa (a future Barca player) and David Silva and Atletico de Madrid's Fernando Torres, who would subsequently join another Spanish international, Xabi Alonso, and Spanish coach Rafa Benítez at Liverpool, before moving to Chelsea. Silva would later move to Manchester City.

But predictions in the Spanish media that La Roja, which had had an unbeaten run of twenty-five matches, would go on and beat France in the next round—*Marca* headlined "WE ARE GOING TO SEND ZIDANE INTO RETIREMENT!"—proved overoptimistic. Spain lost and exited the tournament. That autumn, following a defeat by Northern Ireland and by Sweden—seemingly making qualification for Euro 2008 difficult—Aragonés struggled to hang on to his job. The fickle Spanish media turned and called for his resignation, forcing the Spanish Federation's president, Ángel María Villar, belatedly to come to his defense in public.

Behind the scenes the federation had contacted other managers about taking over, but the plan was shelved after Spain beat Argentina 2–1 in a friendly and the players united behind Aragonés. "When one loses, everything is a disaster, there is a lot of criticism, and most of it at the *'Mister'* [the coach]. That is unfair and that is how we all saw it. We became stronger and more united around him," recalled Pujol.

In the coming months it became clear that far from contributing to another Spanish soccer disaster, Aragonés had laid the foundations of a predominately youth-based and dynamic project that deserved time to mature. Aragonés moved from being lampooned as an eccentric geriatric to living up to his legendary reputation for wisdom. At Euro 2008, he took Spain to its first major international trophy (outside the gold of the Olympics) in forty-four years, a Torres goal securing a precious 1–0 victory over Germany in Vienna.

Spain was finally the champion. And it had done it in a way that seemed to encompass all the best currents of style that had hitherto developed in a dysfunctional manner and mainly at club level. Spain played with the high-tempo virility that had been the badge of the English since they first arrived in Rio Tinto, but with the technique and inspired creativity that had shown itself over many years, crisscrossing the Atlantic. With players like Iniesta, Xavi, Cesc Fàbregas, Ramos, Torres, Villa, Silva, and Iker Casillas, Spain had a vibrant and harmonious organization, with movement, speed, offensive intent, and collective self-belief that made them hugely exciting to watch.

So what had brought about this transformative fusion? The answer lay partly in Aragonés's pragmatism and partly in the nature of the players themselves. Perhaps Aragonés's most defining moment was when, in the run-up to Euro 2008, he decided to exclude Raúl from his squad and brought in Tamudo Montero, the captain of Espanyol. With Torres and Villa injured, Aragonés gambled on another newcomer, Raúl Albiol, in defense along with Xavi as the backbone of his team. Spain played sensationally in a key qualifying match against Denmark, beating them 3–1, with the victory rounded off thanks to a superb debut international goal by Albert Riera after Aragonés had substituted Joaquin in the sixty-ninth minute. The game proved a huge morale boost for the Spanish squad, as it ensured their qualification for a tournament they believed they could win. As Xabi Alonso later recalled, "After Denmark, the squad's spirit, optimism, and confidence markedly improved. That victory helped us to believe in ourselves and to boost our sense of self-worth."

Drawing on the legacy, among others, of Cruyff, Aragonés had finally embraced *tiqui-taca*, the style that prioritized passing, patience, and possession above all else, and for this he drew on players for whom such beauty in motion came naturally. For years, Spanish commentators had tried to excuse their country's failure with talk of bad luck, without ever quite admitting that the country just did not have a collective unit of native players capable of delivering the successes they achieved at club level. But now the talk was of an exciting, unprecedented talent pool that transferred seamlessly from club to national squad and could coalesce to play soccer that was both aesthetic and effective.

A mixture of bad luck and bad play had combined to deny the Spanish national squad (with the exception of the Olympic gold in 1992) any major tournament victory since Marcelino's winning goal against Russia in the European Nations Cup final at the Bernabéu on June 21, 1964. Now the gods smiled on a team that felt it deserved to win, and could. A synchronicity between coach and team translated into a powerful force.

Minutes before the start of Spain's game against Germany in the finals of Euro 2008, Aragonés took Torres to one side in the dressing room and repeated a ritual he had once performed when the coach and the rising young star were both at Atletico de Madrid. "You are going to score two goals," Aragonés told Torres and then drew the sign of the cross on his forehead.

As things turned out, Torres scored only one goal, but it was the goal Spanish soccer had been waiting forty-four years for. Inside the German half, Xavi picked up a pass from Senna, faced Ballack and Schweinsteiger, turned, and with his back to them, and with eyes in the back of his head, twisted and passed the ball through forward on his right to Torres, who with a burst of acceleration ran on to it, switched direction to beat Lahm, then leaped, gazellelike, over Jens Lehmann, and stumbling, but without falling, struck it home. As Torres would later recall:

The ground was very wet and that new Adidas ball was very fast. I miscalculated its arrival and it seemed to get away ahead of me a little. Perhaps Lahm was too confident or just surprised by the ball's trajectory because it was going fast, very fast, and he gave me space on the right. I drew him out towards the left, he blocked me and then didn't look back. I decided to change direction and went to his right. At that moment I saw that Lehmann was coming out late and I realised there was a gap there. I thought the goalkeeper would reach the ball first, but on seeing the space, I lifted the ball and it turned in. I thought it might be going out because the ball was spinning, and because in the direction it was going, it looked as if it was going to go on the outside of the post. But the ground was so wet that the ball skidded and went in.

The Torres goal in the thirty-third minute of the Euro 2008 final at the Ernst Happel Stadium in Vienna was a defining moment in a tournament in which La Roja had finally proved themselves worthy champions of Europe, with their formidable attacking soccer. The creation of the goal epitomized the artistry Spain had stood for from the outset of the tournament. It was the moment when the Spanish squad's brightest young matador dispatched an aging bull that had lost its fire and nobility. The Germans tried to resist a team that passed the ball like gods. But this was a plodding veterans' Germany well past its sell-by date that in the end conceded the winning goal to a much better team, full of promise.

In an important sense this was an emblematic parting of the ways for Spanish soccer. Torres saw his star rise just as another legend of Spanish soccer, Raúl, saw his fall. But the new Spanish soccer of La Roja, however, was only partly built on Raúl's demise and Torres's maturity. It also came into being thanks to a generation of young and extremely talented Spanish players suited to a *tiqui-taca* style in which passing, patience, and possession were never taken to a slow, directionless extreme, but formed part of a rich choreography of at-tacking, winning soccer, built up in midfield by the likes of Iniesta and Xavi and in which players such as Villa and Torres provided the cutting edge.

As Xavi explained on being asked by the *Guardian*'s Sid Lowe to explain the secret of success, "Think quickly, look for spaces. That's what I do: look for spaces. All day. I'm always looking. All day, all day. [Xavi starts gesturing as if he is looking around, swinging his head.] Here? No. There? No. People who haven't played don't always realise how hard that is. Space, space, space. It's like being on the PlaySta-tion. I think shit, the defender's here, play it there. I see the space and pass. That's what I do."

High-tempo virility had long been the badge English soccer liked to flash, and Torres in particular had learned something of this after moving to play in the Premier League at Liverpool. To the extent that his goal against the Germans owed as much to pace, faith, and strength as much as touch and class, it was quintessentially Spanish, drawing in the best of the past and throwing it into the future as a vi-brant, creative hybrid.

Statistically, the margin of Spain's victory in Vienna was the same as Greece's victory in Euro 2004, with the two tournaments' goal tally equal at seventy-seven. But it was widely accepted that this was an infinitely better tournament. It wasn't about statistics, but the sheer flair and panache of the buildup and the beauty of the goals scored. It was also about a team's spirit, how players connected with each other, making the whole even better than its constituent parts, and rewarding a manager's faith in Spain's ability to perform and achieve. La Roja had come into its own.

Capello and Beckham at Real Madrid, 2007

CHAPTER 28

From Beckham
to Guardiola

Spain's impressive performance at Euro 2008 rekindled a sense of optimism about the future of international soccer, which had been eclipsed since the beginning of the millennium by the inexorable rise of clubs like Manchester United, Real Madrid, A. C. Milan, and Barcelona as global superbrands. There was a fear that this new club superiority had come at the expense of national, cultural identity. Globalization had raised the attraction to talented players, their agents, and their clubs to sell or be sold to the highest bidder. Everything seemed to have a price—even loyalty to one's roots. Cultural identity appeared to increasingly matter less than the business of winning the most lucrative deals, whether they be sponsorship or television.

A watershed moment was the European Court of Justice's ruling in 1995 in favor of the Belgium player Jean-Marc Bosman, who challenged the restrictions placed on foreign EU members playing within the national leagues of Europe. The ruling allowed a professional soccer player in the EU to move freely to another club at the end of his contract, in accordance with the new competition rules established by the EU single market in 1992. While destined to have a far-reaching impact on the business of international soccer, the extent to which globalization, and the freeing up of the market post-Bosman, shaped Spanish soccer was most evident in the Real Madrid that the construction magnate Florentino Pérez created after winning the presidency in 2000.

Real Madrid at the time was not short of trophies, but it was short of cash. Pérez believed that the club's weak financial situation reflected fundamentally a glaring imbalance between its spending on players and the underdeveloped exploitation of its image as one of the most successful clubs in the world. Modern soccer is littered with examples of clubs brandishing checkbooks only to end with headaches. Pérez seemed to work even bigger miracles with Real Madrid's balance sheet than with its team sheet. Over four seasons, Pérez took advantage of the speculative and overheated Spanish economy to sell off high-value real estate at huge profit and build up Real Madrid's marketing strategy around the purchase of a major new international star per year with the ability to appeal to consumers across frontiers.

Over three years Real Madrid developed its "brand" as a global club of *galacticos*—superstars—with record transfer deals led by Figo, Zidane, and Ronaldo. Not only were millions of new shirts sold, but the club negotiated upward its television and sponsorship contracts. It also became a formidable force on the field—less a team than a group of individual high-quality, hugely talented performers capable of putting on a fantastically entertaining show and also winning. With Figo, Real Madrid won the league championship, with Zidane the European Champions League and the World Club championship, and with Ronaldo the league again and the European Super Cup. Then it was time for David Beckham to come to Spain.

The Manchester United star's falling out with manager Alex Ferguson had become the club's worst-kept secret, so that it was no longer a question of if Beckham would leave but when. From early on in the saga Manchester United had no doubt that Beckham wanted to go to Real Madrid and that the club was determined to buy him. But that summer Joan Laporta, an ambitious young Catalan lawyer, spun the rumor that Beckham would transfer to FC Barcelona as soon as Laporta was elected president. Laporta was elected after boosting his poll ratings with a news item on the Manchester United official website that appeared to give the story some credibility. As one of Laporta's top aides told me, "We knew that Beckham was going to Real Madrid, but we wanted to win the presidency, and the Beckham 'story' was helpful." Manchester U's complicity was in using Laporta's political ambition to help raise the price Real Madrid was willing to pay.

As things turned out, Beckham's transfer from Manchester United to Real Madrid was officially announced with a masterly sense of timing just hours before he and his pop star–model wife, the ex-Spice Girl Victoria "Posh" Beckham, flew to Japan on a promotional tour for their sponsors. Thus, at a stroke Beckham's red-shirted Asian fans from Tokyo to Bangkok rushed into buying up the white merchandising of his new club. Back in Madrid, the latest modernization of the Bernabéu stadium was given the green light. A key element in the planning was the expansion of the number of high-value corporate VIP seats, with multinational companies based in Madrid lining up to write off the costs, in tax terms, as client entertainment. That August of 2003, Beckham emerged from the Bernabéu locker room and into a building site and there among the dust, like a proverbial phoenix rising from the ashes, calmly ran the gauntlet of the world's media.

Outside, along the ramp that leads up to the adjoining street from the club's private garage, hundreds of young, mostly female fans screamed with excitement and shouted "Guapo!" repeatedly as Beckham and Posh emerged from his car. Spanish newspapers carried photographs of the couple on their front pages. Lengthy reports focused on Beckham's glittering celebrity lifestyle and marketing power. Beckham came to Spain with the support of an army of legal advisers, agents, and PR men—a streamlined commercial operation the likes of which Spanish soccer had never witnessed.

At his official signing ceremony, Beckham held up his new Madrid shirt to a packed gathering of the world soccer media. At his side was Real Madrid's most admired veteran, Alfredo Di Stéfano, the player who fifty years earlier had helped transform Real Madrid into the most successful club in the world. It looked as if Di Stéfano's smile would disintegrate like wax any minute, such did the old man struggle with the sense that his beloved soccer had become a circus.

All everyone knew was that it had never been like this in Di Stéfano's time. Beckham—a master of the photo op and the ingratiating marketing phrase—uttered his only words so far learned in Spanish—*gracia*s and the club's traditional *Hala, Madrid.* The cry had been first uttered many decades previously by a young member of the Spanish royal household. Beckham later allowed himself to be photographed with a small Spanish boy named Alfonso, allegedly the son of a long-term Madrid fan. But all this had very little to do with preserving the identity of one of Spain's oldest and greatest clubs. It was instead part of a carefully managed choreography suited to the ambitions of the club's twenty-first-century money spinners.

That December 2003 I went to see Real Madrid's head of marketing, José Ángel Sánchez, to talk about Beckham in Spain. A smooth, dynamic salesman who operated in plush offices off Madrid's Castellana Avenue, Sanchez showed me spreadsheets of his marketing projections around the world in which territories beyond Spain were disputed with Manchester United and FC Barcelona. This was soccer played out like a game of Risk. He then told me about Beckham: "Buying Beckham is like buying into a business. He brings with him a whole range of customers, not just because of his value as a soccer player but also as a celebrity, he is an icon of modern society. . . . Real Madrid is not going to abandon its Spanish roots, but right now it's a club with many followers around the world, and this is a source of pride."

Looking at the global context of the Beckham phenomenon, and having watched, not least in the UK, "playing fields, pitches and open spaces consumed by the voracious property booms of the 1990's," David Goldblatt gloomily predicted youth soccer retreating "to teenagers' bedrooms and the pixiled images of soccer played out on a video game console."

Wanting to check out further the impact of Beckham on Spanish soccer, I visited one of Real Madrid's youth training schools, not in Madrid but in Barcelona. Funding the school in a territory historically monopolized by Real Madrid's archrival was a bold move by Florentino Pérez. It reflected the ruthless streak of an entrepreneur that relished hostile bids. But this was not so much a dawn raid as a calculated subversion from within. Ignacio Marquez, the school's director—no bearded academic but a slick young lawyer who read the *Financial Times*—was my host when I visited the school halfway through Beckham's first season in Spain. He talked about his academy as if it were a part social network site, part business school. He told me, "It is run according to the administrative and financial arrangements between Real Madrid and an educational foundation dedicated to the investigation and development of the teaching of soccer. It is state-of-the-art stuff—the development of spectacular individual skills with the tactics and strategies of play of an international standard."

The Real Madrid academy was conceived as a template for similar schools in Asia, South America, the United States, and the Middle East. It clearly served a particular social and political motive in Catalonia. Many of the schoolkids I saw that day were the sons of Spain's growing population of immigrants—Asians, South Americans, Africans, Arabs, eastern Europeans. I watched some of them in action. Kids, some not much older than seven, played with disarming skill and speed. Their part-time teachers included first-team players from the other Barcelona team, Espanyol. Soccer at the school was in addition to a normal curriculum, I was told—although I soon discovered that the word *normal* had to be qualified. While in Catalonia's state schools Catalan was taught as an obligatory first language, but here in this small enclave of Real Madrid, different rules prevailed: pupils not only dressed in white but were taught as a priority in Spanish, along with English and French.

Marquez strongly rejected my suggestion that, faced with a majority of Catalan nationalists in the region, this might be seen as a recipe for social division and alienation. "What we are doing here is helping the process of belonging to Spain, which an immigrant needs, by not only showing them how to play soccer but to be good in human terms—values like sacrifice, generosity, companionship," he insisted.

He wanted converts of the cause of Real Madrid. But I don't think the concept of nationhood really bothered him, and he wasn't in the business of being provocative for provocation's sake. Marquez was no Ultra Sur. The pupils were encouraged, for their own safety's sake, not to walk onto the streets of Barcelona dressed in Real Madrid's white shirts and pants. "To be honest, it's not recommended to go around Madrid sporting the colors of FC Barcelona either," he added for good measure. "There are extremes on both sides, and we don't want to play into their hands."

But just how much and what kind of a role model was Beckham turning out to be here in this conquered territory of Spain? Marquez replied, "I think Beckham is a difficult example. His image is not an easy one to replicate. You could say that to be like Beckham is impossible in reality, and that can make kids here feel as if they are under-achieving, depressed even."

Outside the school, Beckham did have an impact on Spanish soccer in the three seasons he played at Real Madrid, but most of it had to do with money. Spanish soccer journalists like the hugely knowledgeable Santiago Segurola tended to view Beckham as a pop celebrity first and foremost whose skills as a soccer player fell well short of those of several Spanish players past and present. Another Spanish journalist friend of mine, *Marca*'s long-serving Real Madrid specialist Ulises Sánchez-Flor, while admiring Beckham for his talent with a dead ball, felt he fell well short as a playmaker. His ability in one-touch play and dribbling was less apparent than his tendency to chase balls unnecessarily around the field, and to occasionally tackle in a way that in the theatrical Spanish league was destined to end in grief.

Marca dubbed Beckham Forrest Gump on account of his perceived lack of genuine creativity or intelligence, even if Beckham's attempt to reincarnate the *La Furia* of such Real Madrid legends as Juanito earned him some support from the Ultra Surs. The club's most fanatical fan base had warmly applauded him in January 2004 when he was awarded his first red card in Spain midway through Real Madrid's King Cup quarterfinal first-leg victory over Valencia at the Bernabéu.

In Spain, taking on the referee—a symbol of officialdom in a country ruled for large chunks of its history by dictatorships, but also prone to rebellion—was often seen as a badge of honor, and on that occasion Beckham's antireferee *hijo de puta* (another Spanish phrase he had learned) was applauded by thousands of supporters, watching in the stadium and on television. His second dismissal of 2004 proved less popular at a time when Real Madrid's performance as a team was floundering, not least because he took the opportunity of his suspension to turn out for Martin Keown's testimonial in London. Beckham played for three minutes at the Arsenal stadium and then was forced to dash back to Madrid after receiving an angry phone call from Pérez, who was not pleased with the temporarily, allegedly unauthorized absence of his star *galactico*.

When at the end of Beckham's first season in Spain Real Madrid lost 2–3 to Mallorca at the Bernabéu, their third successive home defeat, paving the way for Valencia's *La Liga* title win, Mallorca's then coach and future creator of La Roja, Luis Aragonés, made this disparaging remark about one of the most expensive players in the world: "Beckham is finding it difficult to play in the middle. He passes acceptably and works hard, but he doesn't think quickly. In the centre of midfield it's very important to know where you are going to place the ball before it comes to you. He doesn't think in a hurry." In other words, Beckham was still Forrest Gump.

In fairness Beckham was too easily a whipping boy for a deeper malaise affecting the *galactico* project. Real Madrid as a team, far from representing an exciting constellation, seemed dysfunctional and nearly burned out. Beckham was failing to click, while causing some friction in the locker room. Some Spanish players appeared to resent the media circus built up around him in the run-up to and in the aftermath of every game. But other superstars were failing, too. The great Frenchman and onetime World Cup hero of Les Bleus Zidane had ceased to live up to his earlier status as the crown jewel of the *galactico* project. He could not remember having ever played as badly as he did in the last game of the season.

Some Spanish commentators blamed Real Madrid's Portuguese Carlos Queiroz for not rotating enough and making little use of native-born players, including those who had come up through the club's youth academy. Queiroz had succumbed to pressure from President Pérez to make full use of his investment by playing the *galacticos* as often as possible, even if they were out of form. The show had to go on. The global audience demanded nothing less, the marketing men believed. Controversy also lingered over the circumstances of the former assistant Manchester United manager Queiroz's appointment, which had coincided with Beckham's arrival.

Queiroz had replaced an unceremoniously fired Vicente del Bosque, a mild-mannered and popular former Real Madrid player, as Beckham arrived in Madrid. In his four seasons in charge del Bosque had led Real Madrid through its most successful period in modern history: two Champions League titles in 2000 and 2002, two La Liga titles in 2001 and 2003, a Spanish Super Cup in 2001, a UEFA Super Cup in 2002, and an Intercontinental Cup in 2002 as well as finishing in the semifinals of the Champions League in every year he was in charge. Not since the golden years of the 1950s had the club had such a consistent record of success.

Del Bosque had patiently overseen the first intake of *los galacticos* over whose transfer he had no say and merged them into a coherent team. But he was fired in a shake-up of the club that also involved the exit of eleven players, among them Spanish internationals Fernando Hierro and Fernando Morientes, Englishman Steve McManaman, and Frenchman Claude Makélélé. "Del Bosque was showing signs of exhaustion. I want to be sincere about this—our belief was that he was not the right coach for the future," Pérez told the BBC.

Queiroz survived one season in the job before he too was sacrificed. Beckham's second season in Spain began with new head coach José Antonio Camacho, another former Real Madrid player who had been in charge of Spain's national squad. His tenure lasted only three matches, as Real Madrid slipped to the eighth spot in *La Liga*. A succession of lackluster and luckless coaches followed over the season, and Pérez resigned on February 27, 2006. (He would later be reelected as president.) Under his successor, Ramón Calderón, the new coach at Real Madrid was the Italian Fabio Capello, with a track record of trophy success in Serie A and a former stint at the Spanish club.

Capello's return to Spain was not universally welcomed by local fans. The two last trophies he had won, at Juventus, had been declared null and void after several players at the club had been embroiled in a game-fixing scandal of which Capello denied any involvement. Molded in the tradition of uncompromising defensive play and opportunistic goal scoring, Capello declared that the days of "beautiful soccer" were over, and what mattered were results.

While researching those days at Real Madrid, I discovered the roots of a common love that Capello and Beckham came to share. I was told by a Real Madrid veteran that when Capello began his first stint as coach at Real Madrid in 1996, he told his players that Spanish ham was unhealthy and ordered them to cut it from their diet. Only later did he come around to admiring its medicinal properties, judging Spain's *pata negra* ham of better quality than Italy's Parma prosciutto. In an earlier interview with *Marca*, memorable only for its total lack of substance, when Beckham was asked by a young workplacement British graduate what he liked best about Spanish culture, the superstar replied that he had discovered a liking for Spanish cured ham, *jamon Serrano*.

Whatever their common interests, Capello and Beckham did not have an easy run of their shared time in Spain. In January 2007, just five months into his new contract, Capello sensationally vowed that Beckham would never play for Real Madrid again after the player agreed to a deal to join LA Galaxy the following summer. Already the newly selected England manager, Steve McClaren, had made it clear that his future team had no place for Beckham, either. It looked as if Beckham's career in the top flight of soccer was effectively over. Beckham bounced back, his continued efforts in training and proven work rate convincing Capello to recall Beckham within a month, much to the delight of the club's marketing department. Beckham went on to help Real Madrid in a dramatic late-season surge to win *La Liga* in the final day of the season.

Following his departure to the United States, Beckham's celebrity in Spain proved ephemeral. He disappeared from the attention of the local sports media and the marketing world generally almost as quickly as he had once taken dominance over it, much in the manner of a shooting star. However, there were a growing crop of Spanish players who had learned a thing or two from him about marketing themselves. Advised by agents, they attempted to increase their net worth by posing for fashion photographs, appearing in style magazines and on advertising billboards and generally branding themselves on and off the field.

From Beckham's early days in Spain, Fernando Torres provided an early native response to the celebrity status of the expat Brit. While still playing for Atletico de Madrid, Torres's seemingly innocent charm and youthful good looks (he was eight years younger than Beckham) ensured him a popular following among Spanish fans. But *El Niño* (The Kid), as he was affectionately called, was much more than just a pretty face. Torres was a key element in Atletico's fight to return to *La Liga* after their humiliating demotion and became a growing presence on the Spanish national squad. Torres by the start of the season of 2004–2005 had emerged as one of the most attractive goal-scoring talents among a new generation of Spanish players who had the skills, energy, and projection to rival the superstar imports.

That autumn of 2005 fame landed in Torres's mailbox in the form of a letter informing him that the Madrid waxwork museum was going to make a model of him, as they had of other sporting greats. When Christmas came he was asked to inaugurate Madrid's Christmas celebrations from the balcony of the town hall. In 2007 he joined former Valencia coach Rafa Benítez and a group of Spanish players at Liverpool, where he became the fastest player in Liverpool history to score fifty goals for the club. In January 2011 Torres joined Chelsea for a record British transfer fee of £50 million, which also made him the most expensive Spanish player in history.

For Torres, a defining moment in his career came in May 2007, when during his last season with Atletico de Madrid his club was beaten 6–0 at home by FC Barcelona. "I reflected on the match and could not avoid the conclusion that Barcelona was a big club and Atletico were not yet," he later recalled. "The thought went round my head and I reached the conclusion that to compete with Barcelona— to really compete, as equals—we'd need five to eight years." It proved an overoptimistic forecast.

By 2007 FC Barcelona was on its way to affirming its status as the world's top club. It was also drawing together a generation of players who were to have a profound impact on the character and fortunes of Spanish national soccer. The seeds for this transformation were planted during the dream-team years of Johan Cruyff, when special emphasis was placed on developing the club's production of home-grown talent at its youth academy. The school was founded in 1978 and until just after the 2010 World Cup housed next to the Camp Nou in a converted traditional stone farmhouse, named La Masia— Catalan for *home*—in recognition of the club's identification with local culture, before moving to more modern premises more in keeping with its global marketing scheme.

To visit and talk with those involved in the project was to be reminded not just why FC Barcelona prided itself in being *mes que un club* (more than just a club) and to engage with soccer as much more than a sport. In La Masia it was a whole way of existence—and of course about how to play beautiful soccer.

La Masia was the icing on the cake of Barca's version of *futbol base*, Spain's well-financed and impeccably organized national soccer training program. The learning curve began to take shape in early kickarounds on beaches, neighborhood streets, and wastelands, but then became more focused as kids evolved through highly competitive soccer games in grade school and beyond and teachers were contacted by club scouts, looking for those with real potential to be top-flight professionals in their late teens.

In any one year some one hundred teenage kids—the youngest is eleven, but a majority are teenagers between the ages of fifteen and seventeen—were attached to La Masia either as boarders or as daytime attendees after being selected, with their parents' agreement, for an education that includes the curriculum followed by the region's state school system but places a special emphasis on a philosophy of excellence, both sporting and human.

During one of FC Barcelona's most recent golden periods, its director, Carles Folguera, was a quiet-spoken if intense former hockey player–turned–sports teacher specializing in child and youth psychology. In early 2011 he received me in a spartan office that could have otherwise been occupied by an abbot. The whole building was inauspicious, in stark contrast to the looming presence of the nearby stadium. La Masia, prior to its current plusher headquarters, had the air of a modern monastery about it, simply decorated and furnished, with touches of functionality such as computer screens but an underlying air of austere discipline. It reminded me of the quarters inhabited by the Benedictines of Montserrat, the mountain shrine outside Barcelona, where the Catalan virgin—her face darkened by the flames of votive candles, remains a key place of pilgrimage for Barca fans.

Catalonia would not have produced artists like Gaudí, Dalí, and Miró if it didn't appreciate the creative force of the extrovert, and Catalans have popularized the word *rauxa* to describe the irrational or crazy. But as central to the Catalan psyche—perhaps as a necessary counterbalance—was the equally popular term *seny*, which translates into "an air of sense and reliability." Folguera was a definite advocate of *seny*. The tiny and nimble-framed Andrés Iniesta, the monklike midfielder who, despite his humility on and off the field, came to display extraordinary touch, pace, and vision with FC Barcelona and La Roja, was La Masia's Spanish role model, while Lionel Messi was its most famous non-Spanish old boy, looked on as probably the best player of his generation.

Brought here as a young teenager from his native Argentina, Messi had turned into one of the greatest soccer players of all time, finding in the team ethos and style of FC Barcelona and the personal security and support offered to him by the club the perfect context for his talent to flourish. Undoubtedly, one of La Masia's greatest achievements was in ensuring that Messi was protected from any demons that might have threatened him from within or without at a critical point in his evolution as a human being. The club had a history of brilliant South Americans—Maradona, Romário, and Ronaldinho among them—who had buckled under the pressure of fame and allowed their personal lives to jeopardize their professional careers and knew it had to continue to be particularly mindful of ensuring that Messi's private life was safe and secure and that he was content with his treatment within the team. But it had the advantage of having brought Messi over to Barcelona when he was relatively unknown and at a young, impressionable age and of having paid for the hormonal boosting treatment without which his talent for the game would have been physically handicapped and uncompetitive. His best support staff included first-team players who had grown up with him and the principles and conduct that La Masia had instilled in him.

Folguera explained La Masia's mission:

I and the teaching staff try to engage with the pupils as much as possible to instill in them a set of fundamental values that have to do with respect for others, regardless of whether he is the cook or the director of the school. We then get them to realize that not everyone who comes here makes it, so they don't take their stay here for granted. It's important that a pupil knows that his talent is worth nothing unless it is accompanied by values such as commitment, discipline, solidarity, comradeship.

Discipline extended to a zero-tolerance policy on class absenteeism, drugs, alcohol, and uncontrolled website surfing, although Folguera swore that these problems never arose, thanks to effectively enforced rules and regulations combined with an enlightened program of workshops, consultative assemblies, brainstorms, and lectures by outside specialists on subjects ranging from the destructive qualities of cocaine to the security risks inherent in social networking. "We try to get our kids to understand that simply because you have eight hundred 'friends' on Facebook, this is not a guarantee of support and loyalty. Trust is knowing that a friend is not going to take a picture of you in the bathroom and then distribute it around the world. It's a question of privacy and respect," Folguera told me.

So, was this a religious education? I asked. Folguera replied, "No, religion doesn't play a part here. This is a lay education. It's about respecting the rules of the game, about leadership, about team building. . . . At the end of the day the kids who come here tend to take care of themselves because they don't want to squander the opportunity of fulfilling their dream, that of playing for Barca's first team one day."

It was that vision that also influenced the way La Masia went about choosing its pupils. The selection was divided into equal parts of three territories: Catalonia, the rest of Spain, and the rest of the world. It was thus less racially exclusive than Athletic Bilbao's Lezama School, which insisted that its pupils have Basque blood. Far from diluting Barca's identity, Folguera argued, the mix was a faithful reflection of the society in which the club played, enriching it with talent and molding it in the club colors. Moreover, Folguera claimed that this one-stop in-house education was La Masia's strength as an institution, compared, for example, to Real Madrid, which contracted out many of its courses to state schools.

So what about soccer? Well, I didn't need to be shown the carefully protected and secret lessons in skills, tactics, and strategy to realize that perhaps this well-financed no-visitors area was precisely the one that gave La Masia the edge over other reputable training schools such as Athletic Bilbao, Villarreal, and Sporting Gijon, although it continued to face tough competition for young hearts and minds from Real Madrid given the club's huge exposure on television and the web.

When I visited La Masia, the list of some of its former "star" pupils was the most striking testimony to its success. In addition to the Argentine national Messi, the Castilian-born Iniesta, and Pedro from the Canary Islands, they included its most famous Catalans—Pujol, Xavi, Busquets, Fàbregas, and Piqué. But of the old boys of La Masia one more than any other had earned a special place in the history of Spanish soccer—Pep Guardiola.

Guardiola's Catalan identity and soccer skills were defined at an early age. He was born in the small rural village of Santpedor, some thirty miles north of Barcelona, where locals spoke the Catalan language during the Franco years and poor local kids like him learned to kick a ball around in the narrow streets, playing off the stone walls. Guardiola was thirteen years old when in 1984 he arrived at La Masia. "*Mare meva* [Mamma mia]," he marveled in Catalan on his first day. "Every morning when I open the window, I will see the Camp Nou," he said on his first day as a boarder. He was there for the next five years. There were four bedrooms and ten talented youngsters in each of them. Guardiola shared a bunk with another village kid from a similar poor background. His name was Tito Vilanova. He was two years older than Guardiola and became a kind of mentor.

Tito never really made it as a player. He stayed in the lower divisions, where the grounds were not so good, the "playing fields of poverty," they called them in Spain, even if some of their facilities put many sports grounds elsewhere in Europe to shame. Guardiola was promoted through the ranks, but he never turned his back on his old friend Tito. When it came to managing the first team he called on Tito, just as he had when he was at the B team, to be his assistant and to remain one of his trusted friends. Both Guardiola and Tito shared an unflagging faith in La Masia's contribution to a soccer of style and grace. They also believed that its youngsters had an indestructible Barca strain in their DNA, which could be passed on to others, whatever their background or nationality.

While at the Masia, Guardiola learned Catalan poetry and listened to the songs of Lluís Llach, whose protest songs had become popular in the final years of the Franco regime. But much of his time was spent getting as close as he could to the Camp Nou, developing his own skills while spying as much as he could on the first-team players. He would in time look up to the Basque Andoni Zubizarreta and the Dane Michael Laudrup as his role models—examples of noble characters on and off the field. But the earlier and clearest image a lot of older Barca fans have of Guardiola is of a skinny, unshaven water boy running out from the touch line and embracing Pichi Alonso the day Terry Venables's team qualified for the European Cup.

Guardiola was promoted by Cruyff to the first team. Jorge Valdano, who would become one of many huge admirers of Guardiola, would famously remark that in the Catalan's game one noticed the pride of the neighborhood kid. Guardiola remained forever conscious of his Catalan village roots but also had luck on his side. At the time, Koeman was injured, Guillermo Amor was suspended because he had collected too many red cards, and Milla had left the club, leaving a gap that needed filling in midfield. In the end Guardiola got his big break because Cruyff had faith in him. "Cruyff believed I could do it and gave me the opportunity. I think there are a lot of people who sometimes miss out simply because they are not given the chance. I owe it to Cruyff," Guardiola said.

Cruyff certainly would not have picked Guardiola if he hadn't believed in him. As the Dutchman told me, "Guardiola could control the ball quickly and pass it quickly. He could deliver the ball in good condition so that another player could do something with it." On the legendary "dream team" that won both the League Cup and the European Cup in the 1991–1992 season, Guardiola formed part of an array of talent and skill that would for a while have even hard-core *Madridistas* watching in awe. It was arguably the best Spanish club since the golden years of Real Madrid in the 1950s. Its triumph at Wembley brought more than a million people out onto the streets of Barcelona. Pep Guardiola waved the Catalan flag from city hall and the offices of the *Genelaritat*. "Visca Barca, Visca Catalunya!" cried Jordi Pujol, the regional government's president. He was neither the first nor the last local politician to transform a soccer event into an act of political affirmation, the rallying cry for the club uttered in the same linguistic breath as the declaration of Catalan nationhood. But it was Guardiola who struck the most passionate and emotional note that day, declaring, "Ciutadans de Catalunya, ya la tenim aqui!" (Citizens of Catalonia, you have it here) as he raised the European Cup. Everyone there knew he had paraphrased the historic words of the former Catalan president Josep Tarradellas on his return, after Franco's death, from post–Civil War exile, and many Catalans loved him for it.

Guardiola's close involvement with Barca from his days as a young pupil, through to playing with Cruyff's "dream team," and later, as a young coach, leading the B team to promotion from the Third to the Second Division, turned into a major asset. As well as experiencing, as a Spanish international, the peaks and troughs of an underachieving national squad pre-Aragonés, Guardiola had also learned a lot about emerging talent, tactics, and strategy in one of the world's most successful soccer clubs. Barca was in Guardiola's DNA. "Okay," he told club president Joan Laporta on being offered his new job as manager of FC Barcelona in the spring of 2008, "but only if I can do it my way and with my people."

Iniesta celebrates the World Cup winner, 2010

CHAPTER 29

Champions of
the World

When Guardiola took over at FC Barcelona, the club had gone two seasons without winning trophies under the tutelage of Dutch international Frank Rijkaard, in striking contrast to an earlier record of two successive *Liga* championships (2004–2006) and a Champions League victory (2006). A sense of crisis had begun to infect the club. The team's Brazilian star, Ronaldinho, who had been instrumental in reviving Barca's fortunes, had lost form. He was suspected by senior club executives of drawing other players, including the young Argentine international Lionel Messi, into his wild nightlife and Rijkaard of running out of ideas and losing control.

In picking Guardiola, Laporta was taking a gamble. A former Spanish international and FC Barcelona captain, Guardiola had also played in Italy and for a short period in Qatar, but his management experience was limited to Barca's B team. However, Guardiola was one of soccer's great thinkers and, although reticent about giving interviews, was disarmingly articulate whenever he spoke in public. He published his equivalent of a book of proverbs—*Escoltant Guardiola* (Listening to Guardiola), which was subtitled *150 Lessons in Soccer and Life*. It showed that for him soccer was much more than just about Barca; it infused his sense of how soccer should be played by any team. As the Catalonia-based Dutch writer Edwin Winkels put it, "This book was unlike anything Cruyff, in dreadful Spanish, had ever written. Guardiola's Catalan was far superior to Cruyff's Dutch (or indeed to most English players' English). It was flawless, perfectly crafted, incisive, often very serious, and occasionally lighthearted. Guardiola was intelligent."

With his tall, thin frame and dark, brooding biblical looks, Guardiola cut an almost mystical figure—a perfect model for one of El Greco's religious pictures. Guardiola confessed that of all the teams he learned the most from, it was the Dutch Ajax—the three-time European champions of the early 1970s—that had an enduring influence with their creative "total soccer." As he recalled, "They played great soccer collectively. They built up a line of attack from the rear with great ease. . . . [A]ll players were fully aware of their role on the pitch and exercised discipline. Ball possession was their mantra. They were ready at all times to assist. They are capable of touch and movement with simplicity and brilliance."

Hardly anything escaped Guardiola about his players. He believed the face was the mirror of the soul. In other words, he put the person before the soccer player and was constantly on the lookout to ensure his well-being off the field as well as on. He was to show himself to be ruthless with those he lost faith in, such as Ronaldinho, Eto'o, and Bojan, all of whom he encouraged to transfer to another club. But with others he felt were essential to his mission, like the majority of La

Masia–educated stars, not least Messi, he was prepared to go that extra mile in terms of encouragement.

Hours after Messi's latest night out with Ronaldinho, when the Argentine's form had clearly dipped, Guardiola confronted him with a life-defining choice: either he went on following the Brazilian's hedonistic lifestyle and risked ending up like Maradona, a huge talent destroyed physically and mentally before realizing his full potential, or he remembered the values and discipline he had learned at La Masia and continued at Barca on his way to being one of the best players in the world. Messi agreed to resubmit himself to a disciplined regime of early nights, a healthy and low-alcohol diet, and training.

Later in May 2009, just before Guardiola's players walked out onto Rome's Olympic Stadium to play Manchester United in the final of the Champions League, he gathered them one last time in the locker room and there, to their surprise, got them to watch a video he had had specially made by a television journalist friend. The video showed the Barca players intercut with scenes from the film *Gladiator*, with Russell Crowe substituting for Guardiola as the team cheerleader. The message to the players was that they should face the imminent contest with courage and without fear and knowing that their best chance of survival and victory lay in unity and playing the soccer they had mastered. And so it was. Manchester United was systematically outplayed, as they struggled against the effectiveness and elaboration of Barca's shifting geometry, of players constantly swapping positions, while linking with each other and passing the ball from one to the other, one touch at a time, in a flowing and ever-changing display of creativity. Among them Messi was the linchpin of Barca's attacking trio, scoring the first goal after only ten minutes. But it was in the seventieth minute that the little big man educated by La Masia showed his true genius. Having sneaked into space between Ferdinand and O'Shea, Messi received a perfect cross from

Xavi and, lifting himself to the skies, delivered a header into the top corner with effortless accuracy. No "Hand of God" here, just sheer determination and brilliance. Messi offered the goal up to God anyway, having first embraced his players. Barca won 2–0 and was crowned the European club champion.

Eighteen years had gone by since Cruyff, in his third season as FC Barcelona coach, had brought Guardiola for the first time onto his first team. Under Cruyff's regime, Guardiola became a "number 4," Barcelona's equivalent of a quarterback, and was encouraged to control and pass the ball quickly and to fight to get it back. Guardiola would later keep a copy of a book by Cruyff, like a Bible, always by his bedside. His better-known sayings came to echo those of his guru—and had to do with attacking, owning the ball, collective effort, and the importance of passing the ball. "Without a pass, there is no ball control. Without ball control, there is no Barca," Guardiola stated. It was a philosophy that was destined not only to bring to Barca further success as one of the best club sides in history, but also to help transform the Spanish national squad for the first time into a worthy and widely admired world champion.

Another contributor to Spain's success, Luis Aragonés, had quit as national coach at the end of the European championships. Despite his achievement, the controversial coach's gruff and uncompromising manner had made him as many enemies as friends when he was on the job. He had people gunning for him in the media and within the Spanish Soccer Federation. Even in the immediate euphoria of victory, Aragonés told friends he didn't relish the continuing stress linked to the job and felt it was worth quitting while his reputation was up.

He was to miss Spanish players more than they missed him. His subsequent season working as coach for the Turkish club Fenerbahce went from bad to worse. Turkish fans nicknamed Aragonés *dede* (granddad), at first to convey the respect they wanted to show a wise and experienced elder, but with time to express their fury at a man they viewed as an incompetent geriatric.

Calls for his resignation increased after Fenerbahce lost the Turkish Cup to Istanbul rivals Beşiktaş. Then Fenerbahce, Champions League quarterfinalists in 2008, failed to reach the knockout stages of the competition and finished at the bottom of their group, with just two points. The club then headed for their lowest league finish in years, at which point Aragonés's days in Turkey were over. The Wise Man from Hortaleza was suddenly transformed into a dejected Don Quixote figure, humiliated and misunderstood, whereas his Spanish players had once looked up to him like a warlord.

But Spain's soccer authorities had made a wise choice for his succession in Vicente del Bosque, a less controversial figure with a reputation in Spanish club soccer for winning the loyalty of his players with his patient and unassuming style. Del Bosque was born in 1950 in Salamanca, in Castile, the same region as Madrid. I asked him once if a sense of geography was important to him. "I think the climate, the society in which you're born into, defines much of your life—in that sense I've considered myself a classic Castilian all my life," he answered. What did he mean? I thought of what the legendary Real Madrid president Santiago Bernabéu had once said about what made Castilians better—that they had bigger and more rounded cojones than other Spaniards. But del Bosque put it slightly differently. "I would say we are people with a sense of responsibility, somewhat august, cold, and quite serene, without great eccentricities." In other words, the Catalans did not have a monopoly on sense and sensibility, what they called in their language *seny*.

Del Bosque's humility belied an impressive track record during his time at Real Madrid. While never a great goal scorer—in fact, he scored only one goal in the eighteen games he played for the Spanish

national team—del Bosque was a hardworking player in a Real
Madrid that won five successive league titles between 1974 and 1980.
Later, in his four seasons as coach of Real Madrid, he presided over
one of its most successful periods in modern history. With him as
coach, the club won two UEFA Champions League titles, two domestic *La Liga* titles, a Spanish Super Cup, a UEFA Super Cup, and
an Intercontinental Cup.

I met del Bosque for the first time after he had been fired as Real
Madrid coach, having been judged not good enough a coach to handle superstars like Beckham. I had been warned that del Bosque was
a retiring kind of guy who distrusted the media and valued his privacy. But a friendship I had struck up with some of the Real Madrid
veterans provided me with a calling card. A visit to del Bosque's spa-
cious Madrid apartment, in a quiet residential block within a five-
minute drive of the Bernabéu, revealed a sitting room complete with
predictable totems of success—silverware and plaques, among them
one naming him the best soccer manager in the world. But it was also
taken up with simpler pursuits, like the computer course in basic English belonging to his beloved youngest son who has Down's syndrome
and surprising touches of humor, such as a cartoon effigy of Joan Gas-
part, one of the most disastrous presidents in the history of FC
Barcelona, smiling like a Goya witch.

Del Bosque was fired a day after winning his second league title as
coach of Real Madrid, to add to two Champion League trophies, and
a week after Beckham had been signed as part of club president Florentino Pérez's *galacticos* policy. He was fired because his low-key style
did not fit the image of the star-studded Madrid globetrotters. But
those who knew del Bosque better had long recognized a coach with
subtle skills of communication and bonding. "He is very psychologically refined," commented Real Madrid defender and Spanish international Sergio Ramos.

The wise man from Salamanca was, however, not a man without feelings. Del Bosque—a deeply committed family man who had devoted thirty-five years of his professional life to Real Madrid—never adapted to coaching in Turkey with Beşiktaş after leaving the Spanish capital, the deep hurt he had felt at being fired by Pérez replaced by the suffering of an exile. He lasted even less time in Turkey than Aragonés and returned to Madrid to be closer to the family that was the rock in his life.

With a personality that is rare in Spaniards who have reached high positions in public office, del Bosque never once complained in public or lobbied for position at other people's expense and unlike Aragonés retained enduring support among the decision makers of Spanish soccer and wide swaths of the media. Even before Aragonés was picked as national coach, del Bosque had been considered for the top job. When Aragonés decided to quit, he had become a natural choice to succeed the combustible old man from Hortaleza.

The Spanish players had, in jest but with an edge of seriousness, sung "We won't play without Luis" on their way back from Vienna two years earlier, having ended Spain's years of serial underachievement, and here they were being presented with someone who was the polar opposite in terms of personality. But del Bosque's stoic nature was a boon.

When he landed the top job, del Bosque had neither the need nor the inclination to change the club's soccer philosophy. To do that to La Roja in 2008 after Spain had finally achieved glory would have been heresy and drawn a torrent of criticism from the man he succeeded at Real, John Toshack, and from Aragonés. Yet del Bosque had more Catalans and Basques than Castilians on his squad—and Catalans claim to have within them not just *seny* (sense and sensibility) but also *rauxa* (an uncontrollable emotion, an outburst, any kind of irrational activity), while the Basques are the enduring torchbearers of *La Furia*, that fighting spirit on the field that Franco thought belonged to a quintessential Spanish trait of heroic conquest and crusade. Watching the Spanish squad in South Africa was to get a sense of all that, but in harmony.

As things turned out, the quiet-spoken, sincere, and conciliatory del Bosque turned out to be the perfect choice to strike a balance between the old and the new when he took over from the controversial and complex Luis Aragonés. Spain had just had its finest soccer hour, but a line was already forming full of young players ready to replace the internationals who had just been crowned European champions.

The Barcelona trio Pedro, Sergio Busquets, and Gerard Piqué all came in for the first time. The Real Madrid legend Raúl remained excluded. But del Bosque presided over evolution rather than revolution. There was no dramatic axing of a Beckham-type figure that marked Steve McClaren's appointment as English coach. Del Bosque even managed to keep the fiery Catalan Victor Valdés feeling valued as the third-choice goalkeeper. On form alone Valdés was an obvious choice, but many believed he would rock the boat if named to the squad but not picked to start. With del Bosque's calming influence on deck, no one rocked the boat, and Valdés was impeccably behaved, despite watching the tournament from the bench. In keeping Casillas as his captain, del Bosque managed to assure himself of someone who had the respect of the whole team, regardless of other players' club colors. A key axis linking the Real Madrid and Barca players was the long-term friendship and mutual professional respect between Casillas and Xavi, who had played together in representing Spain since they were teenagers.

Del Bosque understood his players, despite coming from a very different generation. He was born into a postwar Spanish generation that while still in childhood had begun to glimpse the beginning of a better future while destined to remain forever conscious of the memories of the Civil War. Did he remember how isolated from the rest of the world Spain seemed when he was growing up in the 1950s? Del Bosque told me, "Of course one felt it. I don't like to talk about this because it seems to identify one politically, but I remember my parents feeling very insecure about everything that was going on, speaking in whispers about certain subjects." Del Bosque then went on to tell me about his father:

> He was radical; he had progressive ideas. He was caught up in the Spanish Civil War, taken prisoner by the Franco forces, and served a sentence. You see, he was a pure-blooded Republican. He worked as a clerk for the national railways. He used to talk to me to convince me that nothing of what he lived through should ever be repeated. . . . I think we Spaniards of today are not sufficiently thankful to his generation. With every day that passes, the frontiers are disappearing. A lot of those who lived the drama of the Civil War have died—that has helped cure the wounds.

I asked him whether it was fair to go on typecasting Real Madrid as Franco's team. "Not especially. Anyway, Real Madrid was a soccer team. It was outside politics. It's a simplification to call it pro-Franco. . . . Real Madrid is pluralist; it's got a huge number of followers of all tendencies," he answered.

Del Bosque thought much the same of the Spanish squad he forged, despite the enduring rivalries at the club level. Bringing good soccer together—that was the hallmark of a Spanish team that had proved so successful in South Africa, with no sign of tension between the players of Barca and the players from Real Madrid.

In the run-up to the 2010 World Cup in South Africa, del Bosque strengthened the selection process that had taken shape under Aragonés and included a majority of Barca players in his first-choice squad, believing that this core of hugely talented players—because of the work ethos, team spirit, and style of play they had built up under Guardiola—would be pivotal in helping him build on the success of the 2008 Euro champions.

Canaries-born striker Pedro was selected for the first time, joining Cesc Fàbregas, another product of the Barca youth team who was Arsenal's star player and captain, and David Villa, who was on the move from Valencia to FC Barcelona. Barca's midfielders Iniesta and Xavi and Busquets were also brought in, along with defenders Pujol and Piqué, with Valdés, another Masia veteran, as one of the two reserve goalkeepers, along with Liverpool's genial extrovert Pepe Reina, La Roja's unofficial cheerleader who was much liked by all the players.

The Spanish squad, while more dependent on the manpower of FC Barcelona than at any stage in soccer history, and mirroring the club's style, nevertheless aspired to be truly representative of the nation's best. Thus, Real Madrid's brilliant and popular goalkeeper, the serene and widely respected Iker Casillas, was named captain and was joined on the squad by two of his most talented teammates, Sergio Ramos and Xabi Alonso. Other notable stars included in del Bosque's lineup were Liverpool's Torres—who was recovering from a knee injury—Valencia's Mata and Silva, Villarreal's Capdevila, Sevilla's Jesús Navas, and Athletic's Fernando Llorente, all part of a new generation of highly motivated and highly skilled players who together were capable of producing soccer that was both entertaining and effective.

Few of the protagonists in South Africa in 2010 defied celebrity status with the ease of Vicente del Bosque. A caricature of a pensionable Guardia Civil keeping a watchful eye from the dugout, the Spanish coach was overweight, balding, and mustachioed. His team may have set pulses racing on the field, but in a soccer scene where the cult of the manager had been built on virtuoso *La Liga* performances from Helenio Herrera and Johan Cruyff to Pep Guardiola at Barcelona and

Jorge Valdano via Fabio Capello to José Mourinho at Real Madrid, del Bosque had been respected rather than venerated, never generating a mass following. To fellow Spaniards he was a difficult man to get excited about—that is, until Spain's victory over Holland in the World Cup final turned him into a national hero.

Their status as European champions was underlined by a strong performance in the qualifying rounds—del Bosque's La Roja had suffered just one defeat in forty-nine games prior to the tournament—in another impressive year for Spanish club soccer (*La Liga* had long established itself together with the Premier League with a mass following among the global satellite television audience). Spain arrived in South Africa as the bookies' favorite. However, lingering doubts resurfaced about Spain on the eve of the first world championship to be held on African soil, part of the more apprehensive pretournament reporting along with the warnings of threatened race riots and the potential spread of AIDS brought in by HIV-positive prostitutes. The ghost of Quixote tilting at windmills lurked in the background.

One undeniable fact about the World Cup raised questions about del Bosque's ability to improve on Luis Aragonés's achievement of winning the European Championship. Only seven soccer nations had ever won it, and Spain was not on the list. Of the seven who were competing in South Africa, it was Argentina that was presented with the most tantalizing options. The presence of Argentine coach Diego Maradona divided commentators between those predicting the final debacle in world soccer's most enduring personal tragedy or, as Diego himself hoped, the realization of a dream.

Sectors of the English tabloid press were predictably jingoistic in thinking that Capello's squad could do well this time. More sober minds suggested that Germany was fielding a much-rejuvenated squad with attitude and style. And then there were Brazil, France, Italy, and Uruguay not at their historic best, but each capable of springing a surprise. If your prediction was based on heart as well as head, then Spain seemed the most obvious candidate to join the list of World Cup potential winners. Against tough European competition, the nation prone to bad luck and cursed with the label of underachievers had finally prevailed, and this was a team that played with verve, skill, and passion.

Yet the skeptics reared their heads during Spain's less than impressive first two weeks in the tournament. Del Bosque was given bad press after his team's shocking defeat by Switzerland. The old man from Hortaleza led the charge. Aragonés accused Spain of lacking the conviction to seize the game from the opening second, of lacking speed off the ball, of not looking for space well enough. He was particularly critical of del Bosque's decision to play both Xabi Alonso and Sergio Busquets in midfield, with both players often hanging back—especially Busquets, who is a defensive player. And he suggested that Casillas might have played better had he not been distracted by his ongoing love affair with Spanish television sports commentator Sara Carbonell. "The better team didn't win, just the better organized one," Aragonés concluded.

It was not an entirely unjustified judgment on a stuttering, nervous start by La Roja. Del Bosque's measured response simply made Aragonés's outburst sound less a betrayal than an irreverence. Refusing to share blame, del Bosque spoke in the kind of conciliatory language that had evaded Spain for much of its history. "Not one bad word will escape my mouth about him [Aragonés]," del Bosque said. "There is only one Spain—not one Del Bosque and another Aragonés one." Nor did del Bosque panic. He held a series of team meetings—none longer than twenty minutes—and he reinforced what he wanted from his squad, prompting defender Sergio Ramos to say how "psychologically refined" del Bosque was. Victory in the following matches allowed him to be judged more favorably. "He has been right all along," wrote *Marca*'s Emilio Contreras, "in his blind faith in Iker [Casillas, the

Spanish goalkeeper and captain], in his gamble on Xabi Alonso–Busquets partnership, in the freedom he has given Barca's Xavi, in his decision not to insist on starting with Torres, in his ability to make all the players feel partners of a team's success."

With La Roja, del Bosque, in the eyes of his fellow countrymen, sprung much more than a pleasant sporting surprise. For a while he forged a rare national consensus in a country that for most of its history has struggled to agree on what constitutes the common good. Del Bosque, a former Real Madrid player and coach, was happy to have a big Barca presence on his team, in a generous tribute to the extraordinary achievement of Guardiola in building a team ethos and a style that players understood and were happy with. And he achieved what no other Spanish coach had ever done before him without resorting to egotistical projection or tempestuous rages of an Aragonés or a Mourinho. He demonstrated that he was a master tactician as well as a quiet, soft-spoken manager who did not like hugging the limelight or indeed kissing his players in public.

Even in the presence of journalists and fans, away from the stadium, del Bosque's performance showed a very down-to-earth humanity. Accompanied by his wife, Mari Trini, and three children—two boys, Vicente and Alvaro, and a daughter, Gema—he conducted himself like an ordinary family man, taking souvenir snapshots of some of the players or getting his sons a signed shirt between meals and training sessions. Among the few disciplines he imposed on his players at the training camp in Potchefstroom was a restriction on their use of the Internet and cell phones as well as access to social networking to minimize their exposure to the pressures of twenty-four-hour news, excessive pursuit by fans, or the threat of hacking.

The university campus was billed by the World Cup hosts as a center of excellence where the South African cricketers prepared for their big tours. But the Spanish players and journalists were taken aback at first by its isolation. Such perceived austerity suited del Bosque—the man from Salamanca—and did no harm. "When we first arrived," recalled Spanish journalist Santiago Segurola, "I thought we had hit a scene out of The Last Picture Show. Coming from Spain, it struck me like a bleak Texas town going nowhere. But it was comfortable and there was soon a real spirit of cohesion in the camp, thanks largely to Del Bosque."

La Roja was pursued by hundreds of journalists throughout the tournament, but no story ever emerged of disunity or rebellion within the squad. If no complaints about del Bosque leaked from the locker room, it was because there weren't any, in striking contrast to the tension in other camps, not least France's and Argentina's. Del Bosque was not the controlling type, but he was hugely respected.

If del Bosque himself exhibited remarkable self-restraint in not showing favoritism to any one player, it was because he had seen all the players he picked increasingly doing what was expected of them, or "sweating the shirt," a phrase he grew up with as a young defender in Real Madrid. Only Torres had evidently underperformed compared to his stardom in Euro 2008, but del Bosque made a point of not holding this against him in public, blaming it instead on a struggle to return to full fitness after the previous season's injury and holding him to a cameo role in key games.

Del Bosque had seen what the *galactico* era had done to Real Madrid and was not impressed by celebrity or superegos or wasteful luxuries. At Real Madrid it had taken a José Mourinho to impose a semblance of coherence and team discipline in a club whose performance in recent years had been undermined by players with superegos, an interventionist president, and one of the biggest turnovers of managers known to top-flight club soccer. At FC Barcelona it had taken someone with the cultural and political roots of Guardiola to bring about one of FC Barcelona's most successful eras ever—a winning streak achieved with such style, solidarity, and dignity that it helped silence critics of the club's huge sponsorship deal with Qatar that the purists had claimed sullied Barca's identity. As it was, FC Barcelona put the deal to a democratic vote of its members, following a prolonged debate among fan clubs and in the media. Barca may have become a global brand, but it had yet to lose its cultural identity.

The 2010 World Cup showed del Bosque's ability to get players of extraordinary individual talent to work as a team. Del Bosque could afford a smile when Pujol's goal against the Germans in the semifinal provoked a genuinely heartfelt and shared celebration between FC Barcelona and Real Madrid.

The history of Spanish soccer is not short of magical moments, superstition, and divine intervention. But on this occasion, Spain's good fortune turned on enlightened teamwork in perfect harmony with their coach. Spain made history by repeating themselves, conquering Germany as they had done in the Euro 2008 final. The winning goal came in the seventy-third minute when Xavi found the advancing Pujol with a bending corner kick. The goal had been meticulously planned at halftime in a discussion between del Bosque and Pujol. The FC Barcelona captain had suggested that Germany's vulnerability lay in its static defense against the dead ball and that what was needed was a surprise attack involving a combination tried and tested at FC Barcelona between himself and Xavi.

The 1–0 result understated the significance of La Roja's achievement in beating a team that had come fresh from scoring eight times while knocking out Capello's England and Maradona's Argentina. Spain's play had proved itself to be both enjoyable and masterful. The victory over the hugely skilled and youthful German team—one of the resurgent powers of international soccer—proved critical. "The match against Germany was the turning point. I felt we had lost our fear and that we could win," del Bosque told me.

I had my second long meeting with del Bosque in late spring 2011, almost a year after his World Cup victory. This time he asked me to meet him not at his home, but in the bar of one of Madrid's tallest five-star hotels, one of several iconic skyscrapers on the northern route out of Madrid built during the boom years. In my childhood during the 1950s this was open countryside. Now it was part of the urban sprawl of modern Madrid. From the initial effusive greeting by a posse of doormen to the no less reverential refusal of the barman to charge for the bill, Don Vicente was treated as a VIP. Yet but for the choice of venue del Bosque came across as the same quiet Spaniard I had met back some eight years earlier. The same mustache, the same very ordinary suit, the same incisive way of talking about Spanish soccer and its challenges. Yet here was the man who had not only been given a noble title as a marquis by the king of Spain, but also topped the nation's popularity ratings in recognition of his World Cup achievement.

Del Bosque reflected with typical generosity toward others and was self-deprecating about his own role in making good things possible. He paid tribute to past managers such as Aragonés, to Guardiola's Barca, to Iker Casillas, "a great and natural captain," and all the other players. He identified two key points in the tournament. The first was when the squad had kept united and kept their faith after losing their first game against Switzerland. The second was when Spain conquered Germany in the semifinal. He did not have a harsh word to say about the Dutch team that Spain faced in the bruising final.

This was not the Dutch as conceived by Cruyff, but almost a caricature of *La Furia*, brutal, determined, but lacking grace or skill. Nine months before the World Cup an advertisement showed Dutch captain Giovanni van Bronckhorst (ex Barca) and star players Wesley Sneijder and Rafael van der Vaart (ex Real Madrid) and other players training with the intensity of soldiers preparing for war. "Tears of joy are made of sweat," ran a caption in the brilliant orange that had made

Dutch soccer so legendary in the past. But as David Winner, the historian of Dutch soccer, commented, "Individualism was dead, the collective was king, and results were all that mattered. And just in case we missed the message that lovable old Holland with its culture of charming soccer and losing had been kicked into the dustbin of history," the advertisement sneered, "a beautiful defeat is still a defeat."

Such a lead-up only fueled the intense interest in the final. If Holland was ditching the "beautiful soccer" of the Ajax glory days, it was facing La Roja, a Spanish team that owed its ethos, tactics, and style of play to the legacy of Rinus Michels and Johan Cruyff, the fathers of "total soccer" who carried it on at Barcelona. When Cruyff managed Barcelona he turned the Catalan giants into Europe's leading club and the standard-bearer for beautiful attacking soccer in a position regained under Guardiola and mirrored, at national level, first by Aragonés and then by del Bosque.

The final did not quite live up to expectations. The Dutch surpassed themselves in their aggression, and La Roja struggled to replicate the brilliance they had shown against the Germans. The ugliness of the Dutch game was epitomized by de Jong's surprisingly un-red-carded wild kick to Xabi Alonso's stomach earlier in the game. But Spain prevailed over a Holland team that was reduced to ten men when the English referee, Howard Webb, eventually dismissed the defender John Heitinga with a second caution in the 109th minute. Cesc Fàbregas, on as a substitute, fed Andrés Iniesta to score the winner seven minutes later.

As Iniesta celebrated before a television audience of more than 750 million, the Barca star removed his shirt to reveal the message *Dani Jarque siempre con nosotros* (Dani Jarque always with us). Jarque had suffered a fatal heart attack after a preseason game. Iniesta had never played club soccer with Jarque, who was a player with Espanyol, but both players had risen together through the Spanish national team ranks. The action earned Iniesta a bureaucratic yellow card, but his gesture proved a fitting act of human solidarity for La Roja at its moment of maximum glory. Up to that moment Spain had developed an exceptional, mesmerizing style of play with supreme artistry on and off the ball that demoralized and exhausted the opponent. If there was a potential flaw, it was that possession might turn into an end in itself. But Spain had scored, and conquered.

Epilogue

It takes just under four hours to travel by car or train across Spain's southern territory, from the mines of Rio Tinto to Alicante on the southeast coast. To travel the distance recently was to be reminded of the extraordinary transformation of Spanish soccer from its early roots to its modern achievement.

It has taken Spain just over a century to shake off the complex of its colonial past in sporting terms. Spaniards learned their first lessons about soccer from the group of British managers and engineers who came to exploit their mines. But the roles have long since reversed, with Spain looked up to not just by Britain but by other countries from which it learned the domineering force of modern soccer, with La Roja drawing on players from the two strongest and globally most popular national club leagues, the Spanish *La Liga* and England's Premier League. The success of La Roja's under-twenty-one and under-nineteen squads—both European champions in 2011—and of its less fortunate under-twenty side that showed themselves the best team of the category's World Cup despite losing on penalties to Brazil in the quarterfinals—suggests the depth of a generational shift toward excellence.

Just how much things had changed was underlined by the continuing brilliance of Vicente del Bosque's Spanish national squad in competitive games (nonfriendly) in the run-up to the 2012 European Nations Cup tournament. Spain topped the list of all the teams that qualified for the finals in every statistical category, from passing and keeping possession to shots and goals scored.

It was in Alicante in October 2011 that Spain demolished Scotland with a typical display of creative ball control and general menace in attack. The magic of La Roja's performance was epitomized by David Silva's perfect opening goal in a move that involved forty-two touches, ninety-four seconds, and all eleven Spanish players. Such is the quality of Spanish players that Silva had to fight hard for a place with the world and European champions, despite comfortably establishing himself as one of the undisputed stars of the Premier League in his first two seasons with Manchester City.

Silva belonged to a generation of Spanish players who brought fluidity and the rare element of surprise to the game so that soccer became an intricate piece of choreography rather than a north-to-south battlefield. This one-for-all-and all-for-one *tiqui-taca* soccer was what had led Spain to victory in the European championships in 2008 and in the World Cup in South Africa two years later. That this period also saw FC Barcelona laying claim to being the best club in the world over four seasons with a memorable victory over Manchester United in the Champions League in 2011 was not purely coincidental.

In Spain, Silva shared a "brotherhood" of style with Xavi, Cesc Fàbregas, and Andrés Iniesta—all three of them Barca players. Of that other Barca player, Lionel Messi, it is worth noting that his star shone brightest at FC Barcelona rather than with his native Argentina. It was not just that lesser club teammates fed off him. He has also fed off and flourished thanks to the team ethos and strategies of the rest of Guardiola's boys.

Barca players formed a majority of La Roja. But this did not make the World Cup of 2010 any less of a triumph for Spain, which had not won any major soccer tournament since its gold medal in the Olympics of 1992. That date symbolized the emergence of a sporting ambition that had over the previous decades been sacrificed to bad management and even worse politics, with some bad luck thrown in. And lest we forget, La Roja counted on players from other Spanish clubs, not least Real Madrid, although the intensified rivalry between it and FC Barcelona provoked by Mourinho's coaching of the men in white threatened the national consensus patiently built up by del Bosque.

The history of soccer is littered with stories of teams being destroyed by the politics of the locker room. Spanish clubs have not been immune to this, nor have Spanish national squads. But particularly during the Franco years it was the politics behind the locker room that gave Spanish soccer its particular dynamic, not always in a positive sense. At the club level, it fueled an intensive, competitive rivalry between two of the world's most powerful clubs, while failing to produce an agreed-upon pattern of play at the national level that could guarantee success.

It was the old mythologies of what constituted the true Spanish race that turned two earlier Spanish triumphs—the silver medal in the 1920 Olympics and victory over the Soviet Union in the European Nations Cup final of 1964—into legends of their time: trumpeted by the government and fans as examples of *La Furia Española,* the Spanish Fury. But this had nothing to do with style or technique, still less team management, and everything to do with the delusion of a nation capable of conquering any enemy on account of its superior spirit. Hence the figure of Don Quixote that has loomed large over much of our narrative.

So has the bullfighting analogy. There was perhaps more than a touch of irony in that La Roja's World Cup triumph should coincide within just over a year with the last bullfight ever to be fought in Barcelona, of all cities, as a result of a Catalan ban! But while Catalans, largely for political reasons, might have made up their minds about ending bullfights as a way of reaffirming an identity different from the rest of Spain, it is in the Catalan capital that in recent times one has seen the enduring similarities between the artistry of the greatest living torero and some of today's greatest soccer players.

That the torero in question, José Tomas, suffered a near-fatal goring weeks before the World Cup in 2010 only to choose Barcelona's last bullfight for his most defiant comeback appearance gives the analogy its poignancy. Tomas was no El Cordobes, the manic Beatles-haired bullfighter of the 1960s who entertained mass tourism with his crude mimicry of courage and style (his graceless stunts included jumping like a frog in front of the bull). Tomas was a throwback to the golden age of bullfighting in the first half of the twentieth century when bullfighters did not fool with bulls but genuinely risked their lives with them (indeed, some of them were killed in the process), while using their intricate technique to try to master and ultimately subdue the brute force of a bigger, weightier opponent, armed with horns sharpened like stilettos.

Similarities between bullfighting and Spanish soccer once belonged to the mythology of the Spanish character—of blood and guts and conquest as an end in itself, of death in the afternoon as the triumph of virility if not selfless sacrifice. But the spectacle of Tomas and La Roja took the analogy to another level. Both involved practitioners of relatively small stature who were able to use their skill, courage, and creativity to reduce a much greater physical force. These were poets in motion, as much as they were warriors.

It was during the 1950s that soccer as a mass sport overtook bullfighting as Spain's most popular entertainment, with fewer good toreros and a growing number of good soccer players. Traditionalists bemoaned the passing of true Spanish culture and the advent of the material world. In fact, national archetypes continued to straddle entertainment generally, with Spaniards rather than foreigners caught up in the bullfighting analogy. (There have been non-Spanish bullfighters, but none of them has been rated highly by the genuine bullfighting fans or aficionados.) In Spain it was the players of Real Madrid who have tended to indulge in bullfighting imagery, with Raúl as the last great totem, representing as he did the essence of *La Furia* in which the ideal player was both matador and *toro bravo*, fearless in his pursuit of the opposition, ruthless and uncompromising when it came to the kill. At FC Barcelona Gary Lineker was called El Matador because he knew when to take a goal opportunity when it presented itself near the penalty area, but he himself never claimed to want to be a bullfighter, unlike Raúl, who not only looked like one but also actually knew how to handle a cape like one and did so in packed soccer stadia, much to the delight of his fans.

The doctrines of *La Furia* led to successive Spanish national teams underperforming and underachieving. The adoption by La Roja of *tiqui-taca* was thus not merely a shift in tactics but a change of identity from bull to torero, with the sound of "Olé" often accompanying the passing movements performed by Spain's international player-stars as if it were poetry in motion.

The feel-good factor generated in most parts of the country by the World Cup victory of La Roja translated into a more enduring popular support for the Spanish national squad than at any time in its history, not just because of its success but also because of the quality of it—the talent of its players, the beauty of how they played, and the image of togetherness they and del Bosque conveyed, even if the old rivalries at the club level between FC Barcelona and Real Madrid in particular were fueled by the arrival in Spain, as Real Madrid's manager, of José Mourinho—soccer's agent provocateur. Politically, there was little to link the renewed sense of patriotism that La Roja's continued run of success in 2011 generated, with the ETA offering to lay down its arms in the Basque Country or the political resurgence of the center-right Madrid-headquartered Partido Popular. The wise, consensual, seemingly uncorrupted del Bosque continued to be one of the most popular figures in Spain, but remained strictly a soccer man, with no political ambition and in stark contrast to most of Spain's discredited politicians. Investment in youth training and the development—almost production line—of Spanish soccer players capable of commanding worldwide respect was one of the few good news stories that Spain had to offer amid the political and economic doldrums fueled by the euro crisis.

So how long can the success of Spanish soccer last? Just over a decade ago, it was France, one of only three teams (the others being West Germany and Spain) to hold both the World Cup and the European Championship, that was raising similar expectations with its Clairefontaine soccer academy and other training programs. France was eliminated from the 2002 World Cup in the group stage, and although there was a brief revival in the 2006 World Cup, when they were runners-up to Italy, it went downhill in subsequent years. Other countries such as Holland and Brazil that can claim to have created some of the best soccer of the postwar era also failed to keep up the momentum. Teams lose their hunger after too much success. Some players age or lose form quicker than others. Inspirational managers and players find their legacy diminished with the passage of time. Transitions from one generation to the next can be mismanaged, and all this can happen at the club as well as the national level. It's easier to quit than to succeed.

Much of the history of Spanish soccer is inevitably driven by the rivalry of FC Barcelona and Real Madrid—its politics, its players, its power, its stadia, its huge fan bases. Together in recent years they have been the beneficiaries of huge transfer investments, and the products of their youth academies (more so in the case of FC Barcelona) have evolved into a new generation of highly marketable stars. Looming large over the quality of La Roja is the brilliance of Spain's two biggest clubs that in recent years have surged past the rest of *La Liga*—and perhaps the world. Such a duopoly—dominating as it does television revenue, sponsorship, and the transfer market and with a debt burden softened by the deeply entrenched political, banking, and business support each club can rely on—risks turning *La Liga* into a duel between globetrotters.

But Spain has been happy for much of its history with having its two super sides thrash it out, with opinion polls showing that nearly 60 percent of Spaniards have Real Madrid or FC Barcelona as their favorite club, while a minority support one or the other when their team isn't playing. Undoubtedly, this has something to do with each club's quality of play and global projection. It may also reflect the fact that between them, the two clubs have come closest to accommodating a national mood.

I would like to believe that this journey through Spanish soccer is far from over and that the dynasty of La Roja could last a decade or more. Certainly, the success of Spain's youth teams and the strength in depth of its major clubs suggest the future could be as bright as the present. But then, could I be tilting at windmills?

ACKNOWLEDGMENTS

This book would not have come about without my late parents, Tom Burns and Mabel Marañón; the love of my immediate family, Kidge, Julia, and Miriam; and the enduring hospitality of my brother, Tom, and sister-in-law, Dolores.

Warms thanks too to all those quoted in the book and others who also helped in different ways: Jon Agiriano, Paco Arenosa, Chencho Arias, Patrick Buckley, Emilio Butragueño, José Manuel Delgado, Juan Blas Delgado, Juanjo Diaz, Anna Eizaguirre, Richard Foreman of Chalke Authors, K-tono Frade, Josep Fusté, Jorge Gallardo, Asis Garteiz Gandarias, Bruno Garteiz Gandarias, Regino Garcia-Badell, Rafael Garteiz Gandarias, Alfons Godall, Robert and Concha Graham, Iñigo Gurruchaga, Patrick Harverson, Andrew and Edwina Haynes, Jon Holmes, Graham Hunter, Pere Jansa, Jon Juaristi, Simon Kuper, Iñigo Lizarralde, Fidel Lopez Alvarez, Marjolijn van der Meer, Juan Milagro, Jose-Maria Minguella, Javi Navarro, Peter Nicholson, Carlos Oppe, Alice Owen, Philip Paddack, Chus Pereda, Sol Perez de Guzman, Frank Porral, Eduardo Prim, Luis Fernando Rojo, Jose Angel Sanchez, Ulises Sanchez Flor, Manolo Sanchis, Cuqui Sarrias, Santiago Segurola, Henk Spaan, Orfeo Suarez, Jose Miguel Tere, Carlos Tusquets, Carlos Uribe, Jorge Valdano, David White, Edwin Winkels, David Winner, and Paddy Woodworth. *Gracias tambien* to Annabel Merullo and team at PFD, Mike Jones and team at S&S, and Carl Bromley and team at Nation Books in the United States who made it all look better.

SELECTED BIBLIOGRAPHY

Alonso, José Manuel. *Athletic for Ever.* BBK, 1998.

Avery, David. *Not on Queen Victoria's Birthday.* Collins, 1974.

Ball, Phil. *Morbo.* WSC, 2003.

Barclay, Patrick. *Mourinho.* Orion, 2011.

Baren, Fritz, and Henk van Dorp. *Ajax, Barcelona, Cruyff.* Bloomsbury, 1998.

Benito, Carlos Moreno. *Una historia de una fabula.* Soubriet, 2003.

Bordegarai, Kepa. *Clemente.* Baroja, 1985.

Burns, Jimmy. *Barca: A People's Passion.* Updated ed. Bloomsbury, 2010.

———. *The Hand of God: The Life of Diego Maradona.* Updated ed. Bloomsbury, 2010.

———. *Spain: A Literary Companion.* John Murray, 1994.

———. *When Beckham Went to Spain.* Michael Joseph, 2004.

Burns, Tom. *La monarquia necesaria.* Planeta, 2007.

Cailoli, Lucia. *Messi.* Corinthian, 2010.

Carr, Raymond. *Spain.* Clarendon Press, 1966.

Collell, Jaume. *Pep Guardiola.* Peninsula, 2009.

Cubeiro, Juan Carlos, and Leonor Gallardo. *Mourinho vs. Guardiola.* Alienta, 2010.

Davies, Hunter. *Postcards from the Edge of Football.* Mainstream, 2010.

Diaz, Miguel Angel. *Los secretos de La Roja.* Cupula, 2010.

Di Stéfano, Alfredo. *Gracias, Vieja.* Aguilar, 2000.

Frade Hijo, K-tono. *Rincones del "Botxo."* BBK, 2010.

Galeano, Eduardo. *Football in Sun and Shadow.* Fourth Estate, 1997.

Gibson, Ian. *Fire in the Blood.* Faber, 1992.
Glanville, Brian. *The History of the World Cup.* Faber & Faber, 2010.
Goldblatt, David. *The Ball Is Round.* Penguin, 2007.
Gonzalez, Jose Miguel. *El futbol de Michel.* Pearson Educacion, 2003.
Gonzalez San Martin, Miguel. *Cronicas del Athletic.* BBK, 2008.
Graham, Robert. *Spain: Change of a Nation.* Michael Joseph, 1984.
Howse, Christopher. *Pilgrim in Spain.* Continuum, 2011.
Kamen, Henry. *Imagining Spain.* Yale, 2008.
Kuper, Simon. *Ajax, the Dutch, the War.* Orion, 2003.
———. *Football Against the Enemy.* Orion, 1994.
———. *The Football Men.* Simon & Schuster, 2011.
Levi, Carlos. *Atletico de Madrid.* Sile, 2003.
Marias, Javier. *Salvajes y sentimenates.* Aguilar, 2000.
Mason, Tony. *Passion of the People.* Verso, 1995.
Nash, Elizabeth. *Seville.* Signal Books, 2005.
Relaño, Alfredo. *El futbol contado con sencillez.* Maeva, 2001.
Robinson, John. *Soccer: The World Cup, 1930–1994.* Redwood Books, 1997.
San Martin, Miguel Gonzalez. *Los anos funámbulos.* BBK, 2008.
Santander, Carlos Fernandez. *El futbol durante la Guerra Civil y el Franquismo.* San Martin, 1990.
Suarez, Orfeo. *Hablamos de futbol.* Unicef, 2009.
Terrachet, Enrique. *Historia del Athletic de Bilbao.* Lagran, 1984.
Torres, Fernando. *My Story.* HarperSport, 2010.
Tremlett, Giles. *Ghosts of Spain.* Faber, 2007.
Valdano, Jorge. *Suenos de futbol.* ElPais/Aguilar, 1995.
Winkels, Edwin. *De methode Guardiola.* Hard Grass, 2010.
Winner, David. *Brilliant Orange.* Bloomsbury, 2001.
Woodworth, Paddy. *The Basque Country.* Signal Books, 2007.
Zambrano Vazquez, Francisco. *Don Jose Perez de Guzman y su fandango.* Diputacion Badajoz, 2008.

Media publications and websites: *Guardian, El Pais, El Mundo, Hard Gras, Times, New York Times,* Telegraph Newspapers, *Sun,* Mirror Newspapers, *Mundo Deportivo, Sport, As, Marca, La Vanguardia, Financial Times.*

INDEX

ABOUT THE AUTHOR

Jimmy Burns was born in Madrid. He is a prizewinning author, journalist, and blogger. His books include *The Land That Lost Its Heroes*, winner of the Somerset Maugham Prize; *The Hand of God: The Life of Diego Maradona*; *Barca: A People's Passion*; *When Beckham Went to Spain*; and *Papa Spy*. His website is www.jimmy-burns.com. He also has an author's site on Facebook.